The 68000:
Principles and
Programming

by

Leo J. Scanlon

Howard W. Sams & Co., Inc.
4300 WEST 62ND ST. INDIANAPOLIS, INDIANA 46268 USA

International Standard Book Number: 0-672-21853-4
Library of Congress Catalog Card Number: 81-51553

Edited by: *C. W. Moody*
Illustrated by: *D. B. Clemons*

Printed in the United States of America.

Preface

In the preceding decade we have witnessed an explosive growth in microprocessor technology. The earliest microprocessors were calculator-like 4-bit devices, which had limited processing capability, but made cost-effective controllers for industrial and commercial equipment. With improvements in design and fabrication techniques, the 4-bit microprocessors were followed by 8-bit devices, which offered increased processing power at prices that made them viable alternatives for applications at the low end of the traditional minicomputer market.

By the late 1970s, 4-bit microprocessors were in wide use in a variety of applications, including microwave ovens, hand-held games, calculators, scanner radios, and industrial scales. More sophisticated applications were left to 8-bit microprocessors. Indeed, these devices proved to be the foundation of today's booming personal computer market in which inexpensive table-top microcomputers are being used in the home to provide leisure time activities, balance the checkbook, and regulate energy usage. Microcomputers are also being used by small businesses for inventory control and accounting, and in a wide range of educational, medical, scientific, and other functions.

Despite the versatility of the 4- and 8-bit microprocessors, there are certain types of operations that these devices cannot do well, or cannot do at all. For instance, even the fastest 8-bit microprocessors are an order of magnitude slower than minicomputers in performing "number-crunching" operations on large numbers. This becomes crucial in time-critical applications, where a result may be required in several microseconds, rather than milliseconds. Speed is also a factor in many multiprocessing and multitasking operations, where control must be transferred from one processor or task to another in a very short amount of time. Further, the limited addressing range of 8-bit microprocessors (typically 64K bytes) makes them awkward for manipulating large data bases. If attempted at all with an 8-bit microprocessor, such applications are likely to require a lot of expensive hardware or (even more likely, and even more expensive) software. For these high-speed, sophisticated, and complex applications, the solution often lies in using a *16-bit microprocessor*, such as the 68000.

Although it was not the first 16-bit microprocessor on the market, the 68000 is significant for several reasons. Designed by Motorola, Inc., the 68000 is the first 16-bit microprocessor to have a 32-bit internal architecture, and the first to provide 16M-byte, nonsegmented direct memory addressing. This means that a user can access the entire 16M-byte memory map without segmentation or special address registers. Besides these "firsts," the Motorola designers have given the 68000 an impressive array of software and hardware features. In fact, as you shall see in this book, the 68000 is not "just another processor," but rather a *minicomputer on a chip*.

This book has nine chapters. Chapter 1 gives an overview of the 68000 microprocessor, including descriptions of the various registers contained within the integrated circuit. Also included is some background material on the design of the 68000, to give you an appreciation of *why* Motorola implemented this microprocessor as they did. Chapter 2 describes the Motorola 68000 Cross Macro Assembler, an assembler that many readers will use to develop assembly-language programs for the 68000.

Chapter 3 presents descriptions of the addressing modes and instruction set for the 68000. In this book, instructions are described in functional groups (add with subtract, multiply with divide, and so on), rather than alphabetically, to help you *understand* the instructions and how they "fit together." Chapter 3 contains a few short example programs, too, but more complex programming examples are saved for Chapters 4 and 5, where routines for math, list, and look-up table operations are given.

Chapter 6 presents descriptions of each of the pins on the 68000 integrated circuit (again, in functional groups), to give you some background in the hardware characteristics of this processor and to define signals which are mentioned in subsequent chapters. Chapter 7 describes the processing states, privilege states, and extensive "exception" structure of the 68000. Then, Chapter 8 presents a brief summary of the support circuits that can be interfaced to the 68000, as well as the fundamentals of programming I/O operations with attached peripheral devices. The final chapter, Chapter 9, surveys the system hardware and software support products that are currently available for the 68000. This chapter is followed by four appendixes, which provide reference information.

The arrangement of this book, starting with very fundamental material and gradually introducing more complex topics, is intended to increase your understanding of the 68000 microprocessor in an *orderly* manner. You are expected to have just a basic understanding of the rudiments of computer architecture (binary and hexadecimal numbering systems, Boolean logic, etc.) and familiarity with some type of assembly language.

The author is indebted to many dedicated people at Motorola, Inc., and Rockwell International Corporation for valuable assistance during the preparation of this book.

LEO J. SCANLON

Contents

CHAPTER 1

CHAPTER 2

CHAPTER 3

CHAPTER 9

APPENDIX A

APPENDIX B

APPENDIX C

APPENDIX D

List of Program Examples

CHAPTER 7

CHAPTER 8

CHAPTER 1

An Introduction to
The 68000 Microprocessor

This chapter presents an introduction to the features of the 68000 microprocessor. Before looking at any of these features in detail, let us take a brief survey of them in general.

OVERVIEW OF THE 68000

The 68000 has *17 general-purpose registers,* each 32 bits long, plus a 32-bit program counter and a 16-bit status register. Eight of the general-purpose registers are used as data registers for byte (8-bit), word (16-bit), and long-word (32-bit) operations. The other nine general-purpose registers are address registers, which can function as stack pointers and base address registers. All 17 general-purpose registers can serve as index registers.

Although the program counter is 32 bits long, only the low-order 24 bits are used in the chips currently being produced. These 24 bits provide the 68000 with an addressing range of 16M bytes (that is, 16,777,216 bytes)—the same range as an IBM System/370! This addressing range, when coupled with an auxiliary memory management unit, permits large, modular programs to be developed and executed without being bogged down with cumbersome (and time-consuming) software bookkeeping and paging.

Software Features

The software capabilities of the 68000 are impressive by any standard, and reflect the fact that this microprocessor has been designed by programmers, for programmers. As you will discover in Chapter 3, many of the instructions, when combined with the versatile addressing modes of the 68000, more closely resemble high-level language statements than the assembly-language instructions of traditional 4-bit and 8-bit microprocessors.

The 68000 can operate on five different types of data—bits, 4-bit binary-coded-decimal (BCD) digits, 8-bit bytes, 16-bit words, and 32-bit long words. Byte data may be addressed on even- or odd-address boundaries, whereas word and long-word data must only be addressed on even-address boundaries.

The instruction set contains a modest 56 basic instruction types, but 14 different addressing modes are available for accessing operands. The combination of the 56 instruction types, 14 addressing modes, and 5 data types means that there are more than *1000 instructions* that the 68000 can execute. And, if that's not enough, two of the 16 possible op-codes are currently unused, which makes them available for users who wish to add instructions of their own, such as floating-point math and string instructions.

The 68000 is offered in 4-, 6-, 8-, and 10-MHz versions, which have clock periods of 250, 167, 125, and 100 ns, respectively. The fastest instruction—for example, an instruction that copies the contents of one register into another—executes in four clock cycles, or 500 ns at 8 MHz. The slowest instruction—a 32-bit by 16-bit signed divide—can take up to 170 clock cycles, or 21.25 μs at 8 MHz, to execute.

Privilege States

To support multiuser and multitasking applications, the 68000 operates in two different states—a *user state* for normal functions and a *supervisor state* for system control. All instructions can be executed in the supervisor state, but a few "privileged" instructions (such as RESET and STOP) are unavailable in the user state. This feature provides a certain measure of system security by preventing one user or task from trespassing upon another's space or, worse yet, botching up the entire system through some inadvertent blunder.

Built-In Debugging Aids

Realizing that software generally takes more time to debug than to write, the designers of the 68000 built in a variety of debugging and error features. For example, illegal instructions, privilege violations, illegal addressing, traps (operating as system calls), divide by zero, and illegal memory accesses all cause the microprocessor to trap and switch to the supervisor state.

The 68000 also provides a *trace mode* for software debugging. In the trace mode, the 68000 "single-steps" through a program by trapping to a service routine after each instruction is executed.

Memory Allocation

Very few memory locations are dedicated to a specific task by the 68000. The lowest eight bytes of memory hold the reset vector and, therefore, must reside in read-only memory (ROM). Additional locations in the low 1024 bytes are allocated to interrupt vectors, error vectors, and vectors for various other types of "exceptions," but these locations can reside either in ROM or in read/write memory. The remainder of the 16M-byte memory map of the 68000 can be used any way the user wants.

Certainly, some memory addresses will need to be assigned to I/O devices in the system, because with the 68000 (as with all Motorola microprocessors) *input/output is memory mapped.* That is, the 68000 has no separate I/O instructions, but "sees" peripheral devices as memory locations in its 16M-byte memory map. In programming I/O operations, the instructions used to transfer data to and from peripheral devices are the same instructions that are used to move data in and out of memory.

Interrupt Structure

The interrupt structure of the 68000 is like that of most minicomputers. It provides seven levels of vectored interrupts, with a mask in the status register to lock out interrupts at or below the current priority level. When the 68000 receives an enabled interrupt request, it issues an acknowledge signal to all devices in the system. Upon receiving this acknowledge, the interrupting device must put a vector number on the data bus. This vector selects one of 192 interrupt service routines in memory.

Devices that cannot generate a vector number can interrupt the 68000 also. These devices cause the microprocessor to "autovector" to an interrupt service routine for the priority level of that device. Thus, the 68000 provides seven unique autovectors; earlier microprocessors provided only one.

Buses and Other Lines on the Chip

The 68000 microprocessor is housed in a 64-pin dual in-line package (DIP) roughly the size of a disposable cigarette lighter. Addresses for instructions and data come out of the package on 25 address lines—a *23-line address bus* (which selects a word in memory) and two byte-select lines (one to select the upper byte of the word, the other to select the lower byte). Data is transferred on a *16-bit data bus.* Like most 8-bit microprocessors (but unlike the 16-bit Intel 8086 and Zilog Z8000), the data bus and address bus occupy separate lines; they are not multiplexed. The Motorola designers realized that multiplexing these buses would have resulted in a smaller package, but would also have reduced performance by as much as 30%.[1]

The 68000 can be interfaced to both *asynchronous* peripheral devices and slower *synchronous* peripheral devices (such as those that are used with the 6800 and other 8-bit microprocessors), and has a separate set of control lines to support each type of device. The 68000 operates from a +5-volt power supply, and has two pins for power and two pins for ground. And since the processor needs a single-phase TTL-level clock, one more pin is used for the clock input.

Sources for the 68000

Introduced in 1979, the 68000 is now in full production. It is available from Motorola (as the *MC*68000) and from licensed alternate sources—Rockwell International (*R*68000), Hitachi (*HD*68000), Mostek (*MK*68000), and Signetics/Phillips (*SP*68000). In Europe, the 68000 is available from EFCIS, which is 65% owned by Thomson-CSF and 35% owned by the French Atomic Energy Commission. The addresses are:

Motorola Semiconductor, Inc.
3501 Ed Bluestein Boulevard
Austin, TX 78721

Signetics/Phillips
811 East Arques Avenue
Sunnyvale, CA 94086

Rockwell International
Electronic Devices Division
P.O. Box 3669, RC55
Anaheim, CA 92803

Mostek Corp.
1215 West Crosby Road
Carrollton, TX 75006

Hitachi America, Ltd.
1800 Bering Drive
San Jose, CA 95112

EFCIS
45 ave. de l'Europe
78140 Velizy-Villacoubaly
France

292 6404

INTERNAL REGISTERS

Since this book is primarily devoted to programming the 68000, the most logical place to begin is by discussing the internal registers that are available to programmers. Fig. 1-1 shows the 17 general-purpose registers, the 32-bit program counter, and the 16-bit status register of the 68000.

General-Purpose Registers

Eight of the general-purpose registers are data registers, seven are address registers, and two are stack pointers (one for user programs, the other for supervisor programs).

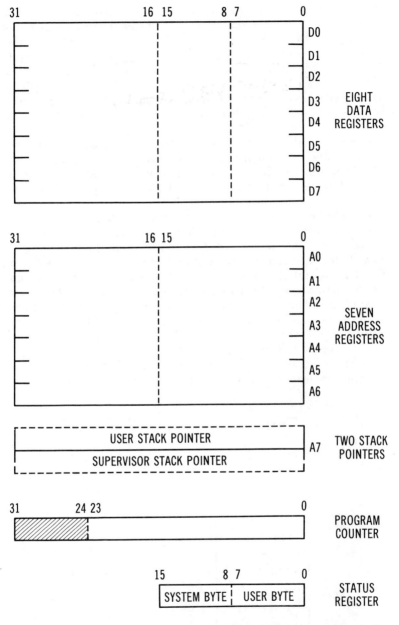

Courtesy Motorola, Inc.

Fig. 1-1. Programming model for the 68000.

The eight data registers (D0–D7) can be used to operate on byte (8-bit), word (16-bit), and long-word (32-bit) data; the applicable length is specified by a "data-size code" in the instruction. Byte operations are always performed on the low-order eight bits of a data register (bits 0 through 7), and word operations are always performed on the low-order 16 bits of a data register (bits 0 through 15), as indicated by the dashed lines in Fig. 1-1. When a byte or word operand is referenced in an instruction, only the low-order byte or word of the data register is used; the remaining information in the register is unaffected.

The seven address registers (A0–A6) can function as base address registers and software pointers to user-defined stacks in memory. They can also be used to hold temporary address values, so these addresses won't need to be recalculated elsewhere in the program.

The address registers can be used to access bytes, words, and long words in memory. As Fig. 1-2 shows, this data is stored in high-to-low order. Thus, byte 0, word 0 and long word 0 are most-significant. Bytes can have either even addresses (bytes 0, 2, and 4 in Fig. 1-2) or odd addresses (bytes 1, 3, and 5), but words and long words can have only even addresses. That is, *words and long words must always start at an even address.* Therefore, if a word is located at address n (n even), the next word is located at address $n+2$. Similarly, if a long word is located at address n (n even), the next long word is located at address $n+4$.

Referring again to Fig. 1-1, the dashed line between bits 15 and 16 indicates that information in an address register can be refer-

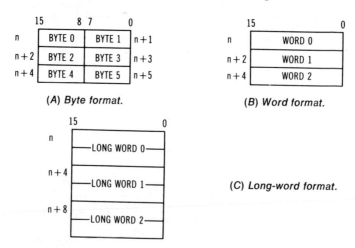

(A) Byte format.

(B) Word format.

(C) Long-word format.

Fig. 1-2. Byte, word, and long-word formats in memory.

enced as a 16-bit word (in bits 0 through 15) or a 32-bit long word. Many 68000 instructions refer to two operands—a source operand and a destination operand. When an address register is used as a source operand, either the low-order word or the entire long word is used, depending on the operation size. When an address register is used as a destination operand, the entire register is affected, regardless of the operation size.

Further, *operations on an address register do not affect the status register of the 68000.* This design feature allows your program to operate on data, change an address, then resume operating on the data without worrying about whether program status has changed.

The 68000 contains two stack pointers, but only one of them is active at any given time. The user stack pointer, which saves return addresses during subroutine calls, is active when the 68000 is in the user state. The supervisor stack pointer, which saves return addresses and status register contents during trap and interrupt routines, is active when the 68000 is in the supervisor state. Because the two stack pointers cannot be accessed simultaneously, they are depicted as "sharing" designator A7 in Fig. 1-1.

Any of the 17 general-purpose registers may be used as an index register. Indexing will be covered when we discuss the addressing modes of the 68000 in Chapter 3.

The Program Counter

Like all microprocessors, the 68000 executes programs by fetching an instruction from memory, executing it, and then fetching the next instruction. In the 68000, instructions can occupy from one to five words in memory, and the *program counter* determines which instruction word will be accessed next.

The program counter is 32 bits long, but only the low-order 24 bits are used in the chips currently being produced. Since instructions consist of words, rather than bytes, the program counter will always hold an *even* address. With 24 bits, the program counter can access memory addresses 0 through $FFFFFE (where the $ prefix indicates hexadecimal), a range of 8M words (or 8,388,608 words).

The Status Register

The 68000 status register is divided into a user byte and a system byte, as shown in Fig. 1-3. The contents of the entire status register can be read at any time, but the system byte can be modified only when the 68000 is in the supervisor state.

The user byte, often referred to as the *condition-code register,* contains five flag bits that provide information about the result of a previously executed instruction (in most cases, the preceding instruction). The five flags in the user byte are:

1. *Bit 0, Carry* (*C*)—This bit is set to 1 if an add operation produces a carry or a subtract operation produces a borrow; otherwise it is cleared to 0. Carry also holds the value of a bit that has been shifted or rotated out of a data register or memory location, and reflects the result of a compare operation.
2. *Bit 1, Overflow* (*V*)—This bit is meaningful only during operations on signed numbers. It is set to 1 if the addition of two like-signed numbers, or the subtraction of two opposite-signed numbers, has produced a result that exceeds the 2s-complement range of the operand; otherwise it is cleared to 0. Overflow is also set to 1 if the most-significant bit of the operand is changed at any time during an arithmetic shift operation; otherwise it is cleared to 0.
3. *Bit 2, Zero* (*Z*)—This bit is set to 1 if the result of an operation is 0; otherwise it is cleared to 0.
4. *Bit 3, Negative* (*N*)—This bit is meaningful only during operations on signed numbers. It is set to 1 if an arithmetic, logical, shift, or rotate operation produces a negative result; otherwise it is cleared to 0. In other words, the N flag follows the most-significant bit of an operand, regardless of whether the operand is 8, 16, or 32 bits long.
5. *Bit 4, Extend* (*X*)—This bit functions as a carry bit for multiple-precision operations. It is affected by add, subtract, negate, shift, and rotate operations, during which it receives the state of the carry (C) bit.

The 68000 has conditional branch instructions that test the state of the C, V, Z, and N flags, and cause program execution to continue in-line or at some other location in memory, based on the result of

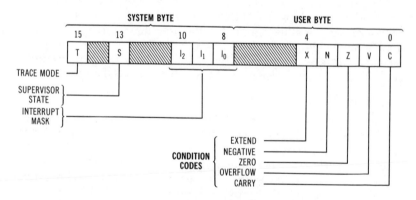

Courtesy Motorola, Inc.

Fig. 1-3. The 68000 status register.

this test. The condition-code flags are *always* affected by operations that alter the contents of a data register or memory, but (as mentioned earlier) are *never* affected by operations on an address register.

The system byte of the status register has three fields:

1. *Bits 8–10*—These bits hold an *interrupt mask* (I_0, I_1, and I_2) which determines the level of interrupt requests that will be serviced by the microprocessor. This 3-bit mask can be used to establish any of seven interrupt priority levels (the eighth level, all 0s, indicates "any priority accepted"), and causes all interrupt requests at or below that level to be ignored by the 68000.
2. *Bit 13, Supervisory* (S)—This bit indicates whether the 68000 is operating in the supervisor state (S = 1) or the user state (S = 0).
3. *Bit 15, Trace Mode* (T)—This bit controls the built-in debug circuitry in the 68000. When the T bit is set to a 1, the 68000 will "single-step" through a program. That is, after each instruction is executed the 68000 will enter the supervisor state (setting S = 1) and vector to a special, user-written trace service routine. The service routine can be used to examine the contents of selected memory locations and registers, look at status, or perform any number of other debugging tasks.

If the contents of the status register are ever read, all of its unused bits will be read as 0s.

BACKGROUND ON THE DESIGN OF THE 68000

At this point, you have a general understanding of the features of the 68000 microprocessor. The remaining chapters in this book will discuss these features, and others, in greater detail, and provide some information on how the 68000 can be used in a variety of applications. Before moving on to those topics, however, it is worthwhile to examine the rationale behind the design of the 68000, to see why Motorola implemented this microprocessor as they did.

The State of Microprocessor Technology

The powerful microprocessors and support chips of today are the outgrowth of the rapid evolution in integrated circuit (IC) technology in the recent past. Since the development of the metal-oxide semiconductor (MOS) transistor in the late 1950s, device complexity doubled every year through the 1970s. As a result, whereas early microprocessors contained from 5000 to 10,000 transistors on a chip, today's processors contain up to *110,000 transistors!* The primary contributing factors to this growth have been higher circuit density and advances in circuit design, which produced corresponding improvements in circuit speed and power dissipation. The rate of evolution has slowed somewhat because some technological limits are being approached, but the advances are still dramatic. Today, circuit densities and circuit speeds are doubling every *two* years, while at the same time, speed-power products are improving by a factor of four.[2] Further, yield enhancement techniques are driving production costs down and, hence, reducing product prices, thereby increasing demand and opening up new applications and new markets.

Motivations Behind the 68000

The advances just described make a complex microprocessor technically feasible, but several additional factors also motivated Motorola to develop the 68000. According to Edward Stritter and Tom Gunter,[3] the two principal architects of the 68000, one of these motivations arose from the *demand* for products to deal with the many new (and often sophisticated) applications for microprocessors. This demand is reflected in the overall market for microprocessors, which will have a compound growth rate of about 25% through the early 1980s, approaching an annual volume of 200 million units by 1983, with a market value approaching $500,000,000.[4] In fact, the microprocessor revolution is truly an *applications* revolution. It is estimated that by the year 2000, 5 to 10 billion microprocessors and microcomputers will be in service—about one for each living person on earth! In planning the 68000, the architects knew that their product must satisfy applications best suited to 16-bit microprocessors, such as those involving multiprocessing, multitasking, or high-speed complex calculations.

A second motivation for the 68000 came from the *high costs of developing software*. With programs currently costing $10.00 to $20.00 for each line of debugged code, it is not unusual for a single program to run up software development costs of $100,000 or more—which is clearly incompatible with hardware costs of a few hundred dollars. To help reduce these expenditures, Motorola made a strong commitment to support high-level languages and disciplined programming practices, and to make 68000 software easy to debug and self-testing in nature.

A third factor influencing the design of the 68000 was the high cost of designing and manufacturing a new microprocessor. The amount of money a manufacturer must spend for engineers, designers, scientists, and other personnel, as well as for design and fabrication equipment, is staggering and costs major manufacturers tens of millions of dollars each year. Obviously, designers must attack this problem in several ways. First, straightforward designs using "regular" structures are easier to implement, test, and manufacture.

thereby making them less expensive than exotic designs. (Of course, straightforward designs also tend to speed up the overall production cycle, giving the manufacturer an edge over his competition.) Second, each new architecture must be planned to last as long as possible, and must be easy to expand in the future.

Manufacturers can no longer afford to produce new architectures every year. Experience with trying to extend and improve earlier 8-bit microprocessor architectures demonstrates the need for planned expansion. Designers must have the least number of limitations in their designs, so that future enhancements of the chip can be made with the greatest possible ease. Among the common mistakes in the past have been limiting address size and failing to provide unused operation codes for additional, future instructions.

Design Implementation of the 68000

The designers of the 68000 had a sizeable task responding to the motivations we have just described. In order to fit all of the required functions onto the microprocessor chip, they adopted a fast, n-channel silicon process, called *HMOS* (high-density, short-channel MOS), which was originally developed by Intel Corporation. The HMOS process provides circuit densities twice those of standard NMOS, and a speed-power product four times better than standard NMOS. As a result, the current version of the 68000 has—perhaps coincidentally—about 68,000 transistors on the chip (Fig. 1-4).

To serve the potential applications market, the Motorola designers gave the 68000 a *general-purpose architecture*, rather than an architecture aimed at a specific class of applications. And because the 68000 (like other high-performance processors) will typically be used in large, memory intensive applications, the designers provided this microprocessor with a 16M-byte addressing capability, and complemented it with special features to support multiprocessing and multitasking, such as separate supervisor and user modes.

To address the high expense of software development, the designers made every effort to ensure that the 68000 would be easy to program. One way they did this was to give the software and hardware features found in the 68000 a high degree of *consistency*, or *orthogonality*. All data registers function identically, as do the address registers, and all data and address registers may serve as index registers. Further, most instructions can operate on bytes, words, or long words.

The number of mnemonics in the instruction set was intentionally kept to a minimum by grouping similar functions within a single mnemonic. This resulted in multipurpose instructions, such as MOVE, which can transfer data "from anywhere to anywhere,"

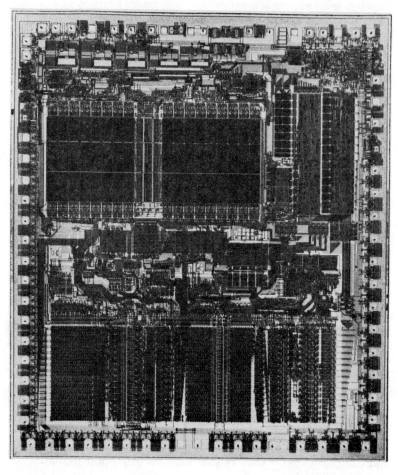

Fig. 1-4. Photomicrograph of the 68000 microprocessor chip.

rather than a large number of specialized load, store, and transfer instructions, á la the 6800 and other 8-bit microprocessors.

Furthermore, in developing the instruction set, the designers considered not only "statically frequent" instructions (those that appear most often in a program listing), but went a step further and looked for "dynamically frequent" instructions (those that get *executed* most often). With these statistics in mind, Motorola tried to create instructions that were as short as possible.

In support of *high-level languages*, Motorola provided instructions that perform operations which normally require several lines of code.

The most prominent examples are the link (LINK) and unlink (UNLK) instructions, which allocate and deallocate space on the stack for nested subroutine calls, and the check register against bounds (CHK) instruction, which allows the size of an array to be checked for an overflow condition. The instruction set was also designed so that most instructions could be used with all of the possible addressing modes, thereby allowing compilers to generate efficient code.

Finally, to minimize the costs of future design changes and enhancements, Motorola specified an architecture that would allow a number of different microprocessors to be produced. We alluded to this fact earlier in mentioning that although the 68000 is a 16-bit microprocessor, it is designed around a *32-bit internal architecture*. That is, within the chip, the data bus, address bus and all programmable registers (except the status register) are 32 bits wide. In 1982, Motorola announced three new microprocessors that use this same architecture. They are:

- The 68008, a hardware/software compatible version of the 68000 with an *8-bit external data bus*.
- The 68010, the first true "virtual machine" microprocessor. This device provides the ability for one super operating system to handle the supervisory chores for any number of subordinate operating systems.
- The 68020, which has all the features of the 68010, but operates on a *32-bit external data bus*.

Motorola's eye toward the future is also reflected in their decision to implement the 68000 with a *microprogrammed* architecture, rather than with random logic. Within the industry, the battle over microcode versus random logic is a never-ending controversy. Which is the better choice? Well, it depends on who you are asking. Some popular microprocessors use random logic (Motorola 6809, Intel 8089 I/O Processor, Zilog Z8000), some use microprogramming (Motorola 68000, DEC LSI-11, National Semiconductor 16032, TI 9900), and at least one (Intel 8086) uses a combination of the two approaches.[5]

It can be argued that random logic can cram more functions into the same area than a microcoded structure, and it is faster. Microcode, on the other hand, is easier (and therefore faster and cheaper) to design and to change. Microcode also produces a clean, symmetrical instruction set and a broad range of addressing modes, which can boost programming efficiency. In fact, the ability to combine the most memory-efficient addressing modes with the most time-efficient processor operations can reduce overall system cost substantially. Still, the time lost in internal decoding can negate the software gains that microprogramming has to offer, so compromise remains.

With these considerations in mind, Motorola chose the micro-programmed approach for several reasons:[2,6,7]

1. The regular structure of the decoding logic makes design, lay-out, detailed simulation, and testing easier. This results in considerable time savings and allows a more complex controller to be designed at a given design cost.
2. The processor architects can delay making some binding decisions. Once the basic overall chip design is determined, the circuit designers can go to work, even though actual microcode may not be written. This reduces the inherent sequentiality of the design process by allowing more overlap of the efforts of microcoders and circuit designers and, therefore, shortens design time.
3. Small "glitches" or programming problems that are inevitably found during the first silicon run can usually be corrected rapidly by changing the microcode, and without affecting other logic circuits on the chip. In contrast, changes to random logic designs could unintentionally cause many other problems, which would slow down the introduction of the processor.
4. Microcoding the processor makes future improvements and additions to the circuit easier to insert. New instructions that are programmed-in will probably work correctly the first time.

REFERENCES

1. Hartman, B. "16-Bit Microprocessor Camps on 32-Bit Frontier." *Electronics*, October 11, 1979, pp. 118–125.

2. Stritter, S. and Treddenick, N. "Microprogrammed Implementation of a Single Chip Microprocessor." *Proceedings of the 11th Annual Microcomputing Workshop*, November 1978, pp. 8–16.

3. Stritter, E. and Gunter, T. "A Microprocessor Architecture for a Changing World: The Motorola 68000." *Computer*, February 1979, pp. 20–29.

4. Russo, P. M. "VLSI Impact on Microprocessor Evolution, Usage, and System Design." *IEEE Transactions on Electron Devices*, August 1980, pp. 1332–1341. (This is an excellent and well-documented paper on the microprocessor market, and its future.)

5. Schindler, M. "System Performance Hinges on CPU Architecture." *Electronic Design*, May 10, 1980, pp. 115–122.

6. Bryce, H. "Microprogramming Makes the MC68000 a Processor Ready for the Future." *Electronic Design*, October 25, 1979, pp. 98–99.

7. Treddenick, N. "Implementation Decisions for the MC68000 Microprocessor." *Proceedings of the 3rd Rocky Mountain Symposium on Microcomputers*, Pingree Park, CO, August 1979, pp. 30–35.

BIBLIOGRAPHY

1. Dollhoff, T. *16-Bit Microprocessor Architecture*. Reston, VA: Reston Publishing Company, Inc., 1979. (Heavily oriented around the Texas Instruments 9900, but contains good background material and well-written overviews on other microprocessors.)

2. Grappel, R. and Hemenway, J. "The MC68000—A 32-Bit μP Masquerading as a 16-Bit Device." *EDN*, February 20, 1980, pp. 127–134.

3. Mhatre, G. "The CPU Evolution." *Electronic Engineering Times*, September 29, 1980, pp. 43–51.

4. Titus, C., *et al. 16-Bit Microprocessors*. Indianapolis: Howard W. Sams & Co., Inc., 1981.

5. Wakerly, J. F. *Microcomputer Architecture and Programming, Vol. 1*. New York: John Wiley & Sons, Inc., 1981.

6. Currently available microprocessors are surveyed in:
   (a) Bursky, D. "Microprocessors—4 to 32-Bit—Push Back Performance Limits." *Electronic Design*, November 22, 1980, pp. 109–115, 150–170.
   (b) Cushman, R. H. and Backler, J. "Seventh Annual μP/μC Chip Directory." *EDN*, November 5, 1980, pp. 94–210.

7. The following compare various 16-bit microprocessors:
   (a) Anon. "The 16-Bit Micro." *Electronic Engineering*, May 1980, pp. 149–159.
   (b) Flippin, A. "The 16-Bit Time Trials." *Microcomputing*, October 1980, pp. 182–190. (Compares seven 16-bit microprocessors, based on four benchmarks—table lookup, block move, jump table, and multiply.)
   (c) Grappel, R. "User's Viewpoint and Considerations for the Emerging 16-Bit Microprocessors." *Electro Preprints (1980)*, Session 19/1.
   (d) ———— and Hemenway, J. "A Tale of Four μPs: Benchmarks Quantify Performance." *EDN*, April 1, 1981, pp. 179–265. (This comprehensive study compares the LSI-11/23, 8086, 68000, and Z8000 using seven different benchmarks.)
   (e) ————. "Compare the Newest 16-Bit μPs to Evaluate Their Potential." *EDN*, September 5, 1980, pp. 197–201.
   (f) ————. "Evaluating the 16-Bit Chips." *Mini-Micro Systems*, December 1980, pp. 153–162.
   (g) Heering, J. "The Intel 8086, the Zilog Z8000, and the Motorola MC-68000 Microprocessors." *EUROMICRO Journal 6 (1980)*, pp. 135–143.
   (h) Moore, M. "The 16-Bit Super Processors Are Here." *Microcomputing*, August 1980, pp. 26–33.
   (i) Toong, H. D. and Gupta, A. "An Architectural Comparison of Contemporary 16-Bit Microprocessors," *IEEE Micro*, May 1981, pp. 26-37.

CHAPTER 2

Cross Macro Assembler

Readers of this book can be expected to use any of a variety of computers to develop programs for their 68000-based applications. Some will develop those programs on computers from Motorola, such as an EXORciser® or EXORmacs® development system, others will use a minicomputer, mainframe computer, or "universal" development system. Regardless of the base system, however, we will assume that *all* readers will write their programs in assembly language, rather than machine language. Therefore, some kind of *assembler* will be required to translate an assembly-language user program, or *source* program, into a machine-language program, or *object* program, which the 68000 can execute.

There are two basic types of assemblers. A *cross assembler* is an assembler that runs on a computer other than the one for which it assembles object programs. The computer on which the cross assembler runs is typically one with extensive software support and fast peripherals, such as an IBM System/360 or System/370, or a Digital Equipment Corp. PDP-11. A *resident assembler* is an assembler that runs on the computer for which it assembles programs. The Motorola EXORmacs® development system has a resident assembler for the 68000.

Rather than attempting to describe all of the various assemblers that readers may use for the 68000, this chapter will concentrate on the features of just one assembler, Motorola's Cross Macro Assembler. The Cross Macro Assembler is a cross assembler than can run on an M6800- or M6809-based EXORciser® development system, or

---

® EXORciser and EXORmacs are trademarks of Motorola, Inc.

on an IBM System/370 or a DEC PDP-11. It is also a *macro assembler,* because it allows the programmer to define sequences of instructions as "macros." Macros are discussed in more detail later in this chapter.

This chapter is not intended to be an exhaustive description of the Cross Macro Assembler (hereafter referred to as *assembler*), but rather just a summary of its features for easy reference. For the full details on this program, see the Motorola *MC68000 Cross Macro Assembler Reference Manual.*[1]

ASSEMBLER STATEMENTS

A source program is a logical sequence of source *statements* designed to perform a specific task. A source statement may be either an assembly-language instruction, a comment, or an assembler directive.

ASSEMBLY-LANGUAGE INSTRUCTIONS

Assembly-language instructions are comprised of up to five *fields,* as follows:

Line Number [Label] Mnemonic [Operand] [Comment]

The line number is an editor- or assembler-generated source line identifier of up to four decimal digits. The other four fields are user-generated. Of these, only the mnemonic field is *always* required in an instruction. The label and comment fields are always optional (and are so identified by showing them enclosed in brackets) and may be used at the discretion of the programmer. The operand field is only used with instructions that require an operand; otherwise it must be omitted.

The 68000 assembler uses a *free format* in which the fields may appear anywhere on a line. However, each field must be separated from the preceding field by at least one blank space.

The Label Field

The label field is the first user-generated field in a line. Any assembly-language instruction can be labeled, but labels are most often used in conjunction with jump, jump to subroutine, and branch instructions. These instructions place a new value in the program counter, and thereby alter the sequential execution of a program. The label identifies the instruction to which program control is to be transferred.

If present, a label will be a string of from 1 to 30 alphanumeric characters in which the first character must be alphabetic (A–Z).

All 30 characters are significant, but only the first 8 characters will be listed on the symbol table printout. The symbols, A0 through A7, D0 through D7, CCR, SR, SP, and USP are register designators used by the assembler and must not be used as a label.

If a label starts in the first column, it must be terminated with at least one blank space. If the label starts in any other column, it must be terminated with a colon (:).

The Mnemonic Field

The mnemonic field holds the three-, four-, or five-letter acronym for the assembly-language instruction. The assembler uses an internal look-up table to translate this acronym, called a *mnemonic*, into its binary equivalent.

Some instructions for the 68000 require one operand, others require two operands, and still others require no operands. The mnemonic "tells" the assembler how many operands, and which types of operands, should be obtained from the operand field. We will not list the legal mnemonics here, but they are listed and described in Chapter 3.

As mentioned in Chapter 1, the 68000 can operate on byte, word, and long-word data. Some instructions can operate on just one size of data, others can operate on two sizes of data, and still others can operate on all three sizes of data. For instructions that can operate on more than one size, the 68000 must be "told" which size of data is being operated on. This is done by appending a special assembler suffix, called a *data size code*, to the mnemonic. For example, an instruction that adds a value in data register D0 to a value in data register D1 will have the form

ADD.X   D0,D1

where the suffix, .X, specifies the length of data being added, and may be .B (for byte), .W (for word), or .L (for long word).

If the data size code is omitted, the assembler assumes that word-size data is being processed. Therefore, our add instruction can have any of four variations:

ADD.B   D0,D1—Adds the low-order byte of D0 to the low-order byte of D1.
ADD.W   D0,D1—Adds the low-order word of D0 to the low-order word of D1.
ADD   D0,D1—Also adds the low-order word of D0 to the low-order word of D1.
ADD.L   D0,D1—Adds the entire 32-bit long-word contents of D0 to the entire 32-bit long-word contents of D1.

The Operand Field

The operand field may or may not be omitted, depending on the instruction. If present, the operand field will contain either one or two operands, separated from the mnemonic field by at least one blank space. If two operands are required, they must be separated by a comma. For these instruction types, the first operand is the *source operand* and the second operand is the *destination operand*. The source operand references the value that will be added to, subtracted from, compared to, or stored into the destination operand. For this reason, the source operand is never altered by the operation, whereas the destination operand is almost always altered by the operation. In Chapter 3, we will discuss the addressing characteristics of operands for each of the instructions in the instruction set for the 68000.

The Comment Field

The optional comment field is used as a personal convenience by the programmer to make the program easier to follow. The comment field is ignored by the assembler, but is included in the listing. If used, comments must be separated from the preceding field by at least one blank space.

STAND-ALONE COMMENTS

In addition to providing brief explanations for individual lines in a program, comments are also used by themselves to introduce a program or a portion of code, to list the registers and memory locations affected, or for a variety of other documentation tasks. To include stand-alone comments in a source program, enter an asterisk (*) into column 1; at assembly time, the assembler will recognize the asterisk as the beginning of a comment line and will ignore that line.

ASSEMBLER DIRECTIVES

Assembler directives, or "pseudo-operations," provide directions to the assembler. They assign the object program to certain areas in memory, define symbols, allocate memory locations for temporary storage, control the format of the printout, and perform a variety of minor housekeeping functions. With the exception of the define constant (DC) directive, directives are not translated into object code.

Like assembly-language instructions, assembler directives are comprised of up to five fields, as follows:

Line Number   [Label]   Directive   [Operand]   [Comment]

As previously mentioned for assembly-language instructions, the line number is an editor- or assembler-generated source line identifier of up to four decimal digits. The other four fields are user-generated. Of these, only the directive field is always required. Note that the label, operand, and comment fields are enclosed in brackets, which designates them as "optional" fields. This needs some clarification, however. The comment field is the *only* field that is always optional; it may be used or omitted at your discretion. Labels and operands are a different story. Labels can be used with only five directives, and operands are used only with directives that *require* an operand. Table 2-1 summarizes the assembler directives and shows their valid formats.

As with assembly-language instructions, assembler directive statements can be entered with a free format in which the fields may appear anywhere on a line. However, each field must be separated from the preceding field by at least one blank space.

Assembly Control Directives

The assembler's two "origin" directives, absolute origin (ORG) and relative origin (RORG), allow the programmer to locate programs, subroutines, or data anywhere in memory. Programs and data may be located in different areas of memory depending on the memory configuration of the system. Startup routines, interrupt service routines, and other required programs may also have to be scattered throughout memory to meet system requirements.

The assembler maintains a *location counter* (comparable to the internal program counter of the 68000 microprocessor) which "points to" the memory location that is to receive the object code for the next instruction or data item. Both ORG and RORG cause the assembler to place a new, specified address in the location counter, and then use that value to assign the memory locations of subsequent statements. However, ORG causes the subsequent statements to be assigned to *absolute* memory locations, whereas RORG causes these statements to be assigned to *relative* memory locations.

The ORG directive is used when you want to select the starting address at which programs or data are to be stored. The two available forms of this directive, ORG and ORG.L, affect how instructions that make forward references in the program are assembled. If ORG is used, instructions that make forward references are assembled in a short, quick-executing form, but all forward references must be to locations in the address range 0 to hexadecimal location 7FFF. If ORG.L is used, instructions that make forward references are assembled in a longer, slower-executing form, but the forward references can be to anywhere in memory.

The RORG directive is useful for a variety of applications, including the following:

- Mixing assembly-language programs with high-level language programs, in which you don't care where the object code is stored.

Table 2-1. Assembler Directives

DIRECTIVE	FUNCTION	FORMAT	
Assembly Control			
ORG	Absolute origin.	ORG	Expression
		ORG.L	Expression
RORG	Relative origin.	RORG	Expression
END	End of source program.	END	
Symbol Definition			
EQU	Equate symbol value (permanent).	Label EQU	Expression
SET	Set symbol value (temporary).	Label SET	Expression
Memory Allocation			
DC	Define constant.	[Label] DC.B	Operand(s)
		[Label] DC[.W]	Operand(s)
		[Label] DC.L	Operand(s)
DS	Define storage.	[Label] DS.B	Operand
		[Label] DS[.W]	Operand
		[Label] DS.L	Operand
Listing Control			
PAGE	Advance paper to top of next page.	PAGE	
LIST	List the assembly.	LIST	
NOLIST	Do not list the assembly.	NOLIST	
		NOL	
SPC n	Skip *n* lines on assembly listing.	SPC	n
NOPAGE	Do not number pages on source output.	NOPAGE	
LLEN m	Set line length to *m* columns.	LLEN	m
TTL	Print title at top of each page.	TTL	Title string
NOOBJ	Do not generate object code.	NOOBJ	
FAIL	Print error message.	FAIL	Expression
G	Output generated code from DC strings.	G	
Conditional Assembly			
IFEQ	Assemble if equal to zero.	IFEQ	Expression
IFNE	Assemble if not equal to zero.	IFNE	Expression
ENDC	End of conditional assembly.	ENDC	
Macro Directives			
MACRO	Define a macro.	Label MACRO	
ENDM	End of macro definition.	ENDM	
MEXIT	Skip to end of macro definition (ENDM).	MEXIT	

- Developing *relocatable* subroutines, which can be executed from anywhere in memory.
- Constructing program components, which will later be combined into one large program.

The remaining assembly control directive, end of source program (END), tells the assembler that it has reached the end of the source program.

Symbol Definition Directives

These two directives, equate symbol value (EQU) and set symbol value (SET), are used to assign numeric values to symbols in the program. In both cases, the assembler evaluates the expression in the operand field and assigns the result to the symbol in the label field. However, symbols assigned with a SET directive may be redefined later in the program, whereas symbols assigned with an EQU directive cannot be redefined.

Expressions and symbols are fully described later in this chapter, but briefly, an *expression* is a combination of symbols, constants, algebraic operators, and parentheses (comparable to the right side of an algebra equation), while a *symbol* is a string of alphanumeric characters, like a label. For the EQU and SET directives, the result of the expression must be an integer that will be used to represent an address or a data value.

Since EQU-generated assignments are permanent, this directive is often used to define subroutine addresses, device addresses, often-used constants, and the like. Here are some examples:

```
SUBR    EQU    $2000
CONST   EQU    5634
PIA2    EQU    $FEFF00
```

You can also define one symbol in terms of another. For example:

```
LAST    EQU    FINAL
STRT3   EQU    START+3
```

The symbol in the operand field must, of course, have been previously defined.

Since SET-generated assignments can be temporary, this directive is used to define variable data, such as masking patterns or conversion factors. For example, the following SET directives may appear in the same program:

```
MASK1   SET    $FFFE
MASK1   SET    $FFFD
```

In this example, as the program is assembled, any reference to MASK1 will be replaced with the value $FFFE until the second

SET directive is encountered. At that time, any reference to MASK1 will cause the value $FFFD to be used.

Memory Allocation Directives

The define constant (DC) and define storage (DS) directives are used to allocate one or more consecutive locations in read/write memory. The referenced locations can be either *initialized* with some specified set of values (with a DC directive) or simply *reserved* for later use by the program (with a DS directive). Note from Table 2-1 that like some assembly-language instruction mnemonics, the DC and DS directives require data-size codes to specify whether bytes (.B), words (.W), or long words (.L) are being allocated.

The DC directive can be used to set up data tables, ASCII message tables, indirect addresses, and the like. To do this, the assembler will evaluate each expression in the operand field as a numeric value, and place that value in the associated location in memory. Multiple operands must be separated by commas. Here are a few examples:

> TABLE DC.W 10,5,7,2—Word locations starting at TABLE receive the binary equivalents of the decimal values 10, 5, 7, and 2, respectively.
> ALBL   DC LABEL+1—Word location ALBL receives the *address* of LABEL plus 1, in a word-size operand.
> TABL1 DC.L 10,5,7,2—Long words starting at TABL1 receive the binary equivalents of the decimal values 10, 5, 7, and 2, right-justified.

Characters in an ASCII string need not be separated with commas, but simply enclosed within single quotes ('). For example, the directive

> ATBLE DC.B 'A2EF'

will store the ASCII values for the characters A, 2, E, and F into the four byte locations that start at label ATBLE.

If you enter an odd number of byte operands, either ASCII or non-ASCII, the assembler will attempt to eliminate a possible address misalignment by filling the remaining odd byte with zeros. For example:

> STRNG DC.B 'ABCDE'—Memory receives ASCII codes for the characters A through E in five contiguous bytes. The sixth byte will be 0 unless the next source statement is another DC.B.
> CONST DC.B 43—Location CONST receives decimal 43. The odd byte will receive 0 unless the next source statement is another DC.B.

If you enter an odd number of ASCII operands with a DC.W or DC.L directive, the assembler will fill unallocated bytes on the right with zeros. For example:

NUMBR DC.L '12345'—Memory will have '1234' and '5'000 in eight contiguous bytes.

N1   DC 'X'—Memory will have 'X' and 0 in two contiguous bytes.

The DS directive allows you to assign a name to a memory area and declare the number of locations to be allocated, without initializing those locations in any way. Consider these examples:

TEMP0 DS.B 10—Allocate 10 contiguous bytes.
TEMP1 DS.W 10—Allocate 10 contiguous words.

Unlike the DC directive, the DS directive has no built-in protection against address misalignment. If you wish to force alignment on a word boundary, follow a DS.B directive with DS 0.

The listing control directives will not be described here because they are mostly self-explanatory, and because they are fully described in the Motorola *MC68000 Cross Macro Assembler Reference Manual*.[1] However, before continuing on it is worthwhile to discuss the characteristics of expressions that can appear in the operand field of an assembly-language instruction or an assembler directive.

EXPRESSIONS IN THE OPERAND FIELD

An *expression* is a combination of symbols, constants, algebraic operators, and parentheses that is evaluated (by the assembler) as an integer-valued data or address operand.

Symbols

Like labels, symbols are strings of from 1 to 30 alphanumeric characters that begin with a letter (A–Z). All 30 characters are significant, but only the first 8 characters will be listed when the symbol table is printed. The symbols A0 through A7, D0 through D7, CCR, SR, SP, and USP are special register names used by the assembler that can appear in the operand field, but not in the label field.

A symbol can have an absolute value or a relative value. A symbol will have an *absolute* value if (1) it is assigned an absolute value by an EQU or SET directive or (2) if an ORG statement has preceded the definition of the symbol. A symbol will have a *relative* value if (1) it is assigned a relative value by an EQU or SET directive or (2) if an RORG directive has preceded the definition of the symbol or (3) if neither an ORG nor an RORG has preceded the definition of the symbol (which defaults to RORG 0).

Constants

The assembler will accept both numeric constants and ASCII literals. A string of decimal digits (e.g., 12345) is interpreted as a decimal number, and a string of hexadecimal digits preceded by a dollar sign (e.g., $ABCD) is interpreted as a hexadecimal number. An ASCII literal is a string of up to four ASCII characters enclosed within single quotes (e.g., 'ABCD').

Algebraic Operators

The assembler allows you to combine terms of an expression with the use of four arithmetic operators, four logical operators, and one special operator. The *arithmetic operators* are: + (add), − (subtract), * (multiply), and / (divide). For example, the equate sequence

```
START     EQU   $2000
STARTP6   EQU   START+6
STARTM1   EQU   START−1
```

assigns symbols STARTP6 and STARTM1 with the addresses $2006 and $1FFF, respectively. The *logical operators* have the following definitions:

- Logical AND (&) causes each bit in the left expression to be logically ANDed with the corresponding bit in the right expression.
- Logical OR (!) causes each bit in the left expression to be ORed with the corresponding bit in the right expression.
- Shift left (<<) causes the left expression to be left-shifted by the number of bit positions specified in the right expression. The left expression is filled with zeros from the right.
- Shift right (>>) causes the left expression to be right-shifted by the number of bit positions specified in the right expression. The left expression is filled with zeros from the left.

The *special operator,* unary minus (−), causes a term in the expression to be negated, or subtracted from zero. This operator can only occur at the beginning of an expression or immediately before a left parenthesis.

How Expressions Are Evaluated

As mentioned at the beginning of this section, expressions are a combination of symbols, constants, algebraic operators, and parentheses. At assembly time, the assembler evaluates parenthetical expressions first, and processes the innermost parentheses before the outer ones. Next, the operators are processed in this order: unary minus, shift, AND and OR, multiply and divide, add and subtract.

Operators of the same precedence (for example, "*" and "/") are evaluated from left to right. All intermediate values are truncated to a 32-bit integer value. The result of an expression is also a 32-bit integer.

CONDITIONAL ASSEMBLY

The conditional assembly feature of the assembler allows you to include or exclude portions of the source program, depending on conditions existing at assembly time. Typical uses of conditional assembly are:

1. To include or exclude certain variables.
2. To place diagnostics or special conditions in test runs.
3. To create specialized versions of a multiuse program.

In the 68000 assembler, the portion of the source program to be included or excluded must be preceded by either of two directives, IFEQ or IFNE, and terminated by an ENDC directive. When preceded by an IFEQ directive, the portion is assembled only if the expression in the operand field is *equal to zero*. When preceded by an IFNE directive, the portion is assembled only if the expression is *not equal to zero*.

For example, using conditional assembly it is possible to write a program whose I/O section varies, depending on whether the program is used in a disk environment or in a paper-tape environment. To do this, you might assign a flag called DORT as a disk I/O or tape I/O indicator. If DORT is zero, the program will be assembled for a disk environment; if DORT is nonzero, the program will be assembled for a paper-tape environment. Fig. 2-1 shows the structure of this program's I/O section.

MACROS

You will often find the need to perform a particular task several times within a program. Rather than writing out the sequence of instructions for this task each time it is needed, you can write out the sequence just once in one of two ways: as a *subroutine* or as a *macro*. As most readers already know, a subroutine is a sequence of instructions that appears just once in a program. Each time the subroutine is "called," program control is transferred to the subroutine. When the subroutine has completed its task, a return instruction (RTS, in the 68000) transfers control back to the calling program. Subroutines are discussed in detail in Chapter 3.

Like a subroutine, macros allow you to assign a name to an instruction sequence. Each time you use that name in an operand field of your source program, the assembler will replace the macro name with the associated sequence of instructions. Therein lies the difference between a subroutine and a macro. The instructions in a subroutine are invoked when the program is *executed;* the instructions in a macro are inserted into the program when the source pro-

```
                              IFEQ   DORT    DISK I/O STATEMENTS
                    DISKIO  •
                            •
                            •
                            ENDC
                            IFNE   DORT    TAPE I/O STATEMENTS
                    TAPEIO  •
                            •
                            •
                            ENDC
```

Fig. 2-1. Conditional assembly chooses between disk I/O and tape I/O.

gram is *assembled.* You will not see a stand-alone macro sequence in an object program, as you will a subroutine. Macros have the following advantages:

1. Shorter source programs.
2. Better program documentation.
3. Use of debugged instruction sequences. Once the macro has been debugged, you are assured of an error-free instruction sequence every time you use the macro.
4. Easy to change. Change the macro definition and the assembler will make the changes for you every time the macro is used.
5. Macros can be used to establish *macro libraries* which one programmer or a group of programmers can use in generating programs.
6. Quicker execution. The microprocessor is not delayed by call and return instructions, as it is for subroutines.

The disadvantages of macros are:

1. Repetition of the same instruction sequences, since the macro is expanded every time it is used.
2. A single macro may create a lot of instructions.
3. Lack of standardization.
4. Possible effects on registers and status flags that may not be clearly described.

Defining a Macro

Every macro definition consists of three parts:

1. *Macro Header*—The MACRO directive, with the macro name in the label field.
2. *Macro Body*—The statements that constitute the macro code.
3. *Macro Terminator*—The ENDM directive, which marks the end of the macro definition.

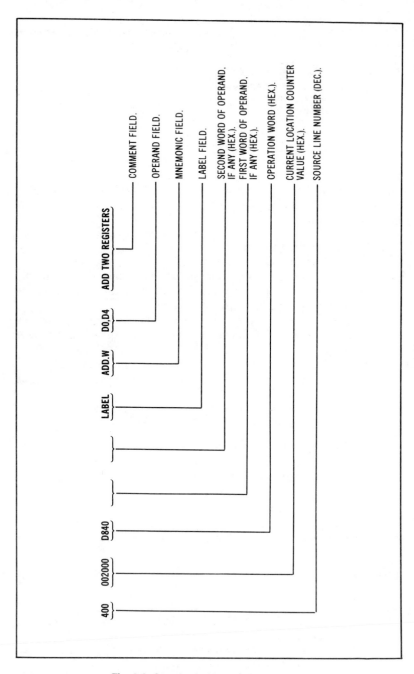

Fig. 2-2. Standard object listing format.

40

The assembler allows you to pass up to nine parameters to the macro by placing these parameters in the operand field of the macro call. The assembler also allows you to define a macro that includes instructions with variable data-size codes!

One more macro-related directive that has not yet been mentioned is MEXIT. This directive is used with conditional assembly statements to cause all remaining statements in a macro to be skipped. The Motorola *MC68000 Cross Macro Assembler Reference Manual*[1] includes the full details on the use of macros with the 68000, so readers who plan to use macros should refer to this document. Additional information on macros can be found in Campbell-Kelly's book.[2]

LINE LISTING FORMAT

Fig. 2-2 shows the line format for object listings that will be printed out by the assembler. The listing for each page may also have a page header, comment lines, expansion lines, and error lines. The final page of the listing will have a "total errors" line and the symbol table.

REFERENCES

1. *MC68000 Cross Macro Assembler Reference Manual.* Phoenix, AZ: Motorola Semiconductor Products, Inc., 1979.

2. Campbell-Kelly, M. "An Introduction to Macros." *American Elsevier,* 1973. (A complete monograph on macros.)

CHAPTER 3

The 68000 Instruction Set

This chapter gives a detailed description of the 68000 instruction set and its 14 addressing modes. Many books treat the instructions individually, discussing them one by one in alphabetical order. Although that approach has definite merit in a reference manual, it tends to leave the reader somewhat bewildered (and probably bored) after the fifth or sixth instruction. Here, instructions are grouped by function, with similar instructions together. That is, add instructions are grouped with subtract instructions, shift instructions are grouped with rotate instructions, and so on. This approach is intended to help you *understand* the instruction set, and how individual instructions "fit together," rather than simply learning them as disjointed entities.

Later on, after you have run a few programs, you will only have to use the information in this chapter occasionally, to look up details about specific instructions. Once you feel comfortable with the instruction set, most questions can be resolved by referring to Appendix D, where the instructions are summarized alphabetically.

INSTRUCTION FORMAT IN MEMORY

Instructions can occupy from one to five words in memory, as shown in Fig. 3-1. The first word is an operation-code word, which the manufacturers' literature refers to as an *op-word*. The op-word contains the binary bit pattern that the 68000 decodes to determine the instruction type, the operand addressing mode(s), and the length of the instruction. Additional *extension words* are required for operand addressing modes that use constants (immediate values), absolute addresses, or displacement offsets. Therefore, the longest instruction would consist of an op-word followed by two pairs of extension words—one pair for the source operand and the other for the destination operand.

Two-word immediate operands and two-word (or "long") absolute addresses in an instruction will be assembled into *high-word/*

15   0

OPERATION WORD (FIRST WORD SPECIFIES OPERATION AND MODES)
IMMEDIATE OPERAND (IF ANY, ONE OR TWO WORDS)
SOURCE EFFECTIVE ADDRESS EXTENSION (IF ANY, ONE OR TWO WORDS)
DESTINATION EFFECTIVE ADDRESS EXTENSION (IF ANY, ONE OR TWO WORDS)

Courtesy Motorola, Inc.

Fig. 3-1. Instruction format in memory.

low-word order in memory. That is, if the high-order word of the operand is stored at ADDR, the low-order word will be stored at ADDR+2. This is the standard convention in the 68000, so any long-word data or address operand referenced by your programs must also be stored in high-word/low-word order in memory.

ADDRESSING MODES

The 68000 has 14 operand addressing modes, seven more addressing modes than the Intel 8086 and four more than the Zilog Z8000, giving it perhaps the most flexible addressing capability of any 16-bit microprocessor on the market. As Table 3-1 shows, these 14 modes fall into six basic addressing groups—register direct, address register indirect, absolute, program counter relative, immediate, and implied. Table 3-1 also presents the formula by which the *effective address* (the actual address of an operand) is calculated, the assembler format for each operand that employs that mode, and the number of extension words (if any) the mode adds to an instruction. If you wish to know how a particular addressing mode affects the execution time of an instruction, refer to Table B-1 in Appendix B.

If an operand in memory is being addressed (as it will if you use any of the address register indirect, absolute, or program counter relative modes), you must ensure that the effective address does not violate the addressing rules of the 68000. These rules are as follows:

1. *Byte operands can be accessed from either an odd or even address.*
2. *Word and long-word operands must be accessed from an even address.*

Table 3-1. The Addressing Modes of the 68000

Mode	Generation	Assembler Syntax	Extension Words
Register Direct Addressing			
Data register direct.	EA = Dn	Dn	–
Address register direct.	EA = An	An	–
Address Register Indirect Addressing			
Register indirect.	EA = (An)	(An)	–
Register indirect with postincrement.	EA = (An), An←An + N	(An)+	–
Register indirect with predecrement.	An←An – N, EA = (An)	–(An)	–
Register indirect with displacement.	EA = (An) + d_{16}	d(An)	1
Register indirect with index. $+\ =$	EA = (An) + (Ri) + d_8	d(An,Ri)	1
Absolute Data Addressing			
Absolute short.	EA = (Next Word)	xxxx	1
Absolute long.	EA = (Next Two Words)	xxxxxxxx	2
Program Counter Relative Addressing			
Relative with displacement.	EA = (PC) + d_{16}	d	1
Relative with index.	EA = (PC) + (Ri) + d_8	d(Ri)	1
Immediate Data Addressing			
Immediate.	DATA = Next Word(s)	#xxxx	1 or 2
Quick immediate.	DATA Is in Op-Word	#xx	–
Implied Addressing			
Implied register.	EA = SR, USP, SP, PC		–

Notes: EA = Effective Address
An = Address Register
Dn = Data Register
Ri = Address or Data Register
    Used as Index Register

SR = Status Register
PC = Program Counter
SP = Active System Stack Pointer
USP = User Stack Pointer
d_8 = 8-Bit Offset (Displacement)

d_{16} = 16-Bit Offset (Displacement)
N = 1 for Byte, 2 for Words, and
    4 for Long Words
( ) = Contents of
← = Replaces

If you attempt to access a word or long-word operand using an odd address, the 68000 will generate an address error exception (see Chapter 7). These address boundary considerations are something that programmers of 4-bit and 8-bit microprocessors never had to contend with.

Most of the addressing mode descriptions in this chapter include an example of the usage of the mode with the move instruction of the 68000. The move instruction has the general format

MOVE.X   (EA$_{source}$),(EA$_{destination}$)

where the suffix ".X" represents the data size code (.B, .W, or .L, per Chapter 2) for the data being moved. Note that the move instruction always has two operands—one operand addresses the memory location or register that contains the data to be moved (the *source*), the other addresses the memory location or register that the data is to be moved to (the *destination*).

The move instruction is one of the most impressive in the repertoire of the 68000. It can move anything, from anywhere to anywhere. Depending on which modes are used for source and destination addressing, the move instruction can move data between two registers, from register to memory, from memory to register, or directly from one memory location to another (without affecting any register). It can also move an immediate value into a register or memory location.

Register Direct Addressing

Register direct addressing fetches a data operand from (or loads it into) either a data register or address register. For example, the instruction

MOVE.L   A0,D1

copies the 32-bit contents of address register A0 into data register D1, without affecting the contents of A0. Note that register direct addressing is used here to both fetch the source operand from A0 and to load it into destination register D1.

Address Register Indirect Addressing

In these modes, the contents of an address register "points to" the operand. That is, the specified address register holds a base address which the 68000 will use to calculate the effective address of the operand. (The operand will be a data value unless the instruction is a jump or jump to subroutine, in which case the operand will be an address.) The relationship between the base address and the effective address depends on which of five addressing modes is being employed.

For the simplest of these five modes, called *address register indirect addressing*, the address register holds the effective address itself. For example, the instruction

MOVE.W   (A0),D1

will load the low-order 16 bits of data register D1 with the word whose memory address is in address register A0. Fig. 3-2 shows how this instruction operates if A0 points to location $53F00, and location $53F00 contains the value $1C9A.

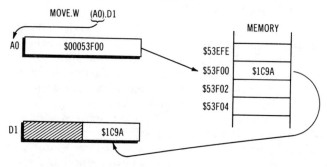

Fig. 3-2. Address register indirect addressing.

Indirect Addressing With Postincrement and Predecrement

Many applications involve operating on a block of contiguous data in memory, such as a data table or a string. With most microprocessors, this involves accessing an operand and then incrementing or decrementing the address pointer (depending on whether the next operand lies higher or lower in memory). The 68000 frees the programmer from the increment/decrement task, by providing postincrement and predecrement modes with address register indirect addressing.

The first of these modes, *address register indirect with postincrement,* uses the operand, then adds 1, 2, or 4 to the address register. The value that is added to the address—1, 2, or 4—depends on whether a byte (1), word (2), or long word (4) is being operated on. For example, if the source block is being pointed to by A0 and the destination block is being pointed to by A1, the instruction

MOVE.W   (A0)+,(A1)+

will copy one data word from the source block to the destination block, then automatically increment each pointer by 2 (to point to the next source and destination word locations). Of course, this move instruction can be used in a loop to transfer any number of data words from one part of memory to another, in order of increasing

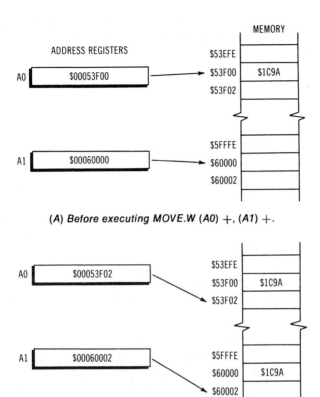

(A) Before executing MOVE.W (A0) +, (A1) +.

(B) After executing MOVE.W (A0) +, (A1) +.

Fig. 3-3. Postincrementing an address register.

addresses. Fig. 3-3 shows how instruction MOVE.W (A0)+,(A1)+ operates if A0 and A1 initially point to locations $53F00 and $60000, respectively, and source location $53F00 contains the value $1C9A.

A similar mode, *address register indirect with predecrement*, subtracts 1, 2, or 4 from an address register *before* the register is used. Therefore, this mode is also useful for moving blocks of data from one area of memory to another, but the move is performed in order of decreasing addresses. For example, the instruction

    MOVE.W   −(A0),−(A1)

will copy one data word from the source block to the destination block, but decrement each pointer by 2 (to point to the next source and destination word locations) before doing so.

As mentioned in Chapter 1, all eight address registers of the 68000 are available for use as *stack pointers*. One of these registers, A7,

47

acts as the system stack pointer (SP), which leaves the other seven address registers (A0 through A6) free for configuring user stacks in memory. Therefore, *the 68000 can maintain up to eight separate user stacks in memory!* From the preceding paragraphs you can see that the postincrement and predecrement modes are useful for manipulating these stacks.

Since stacks "build" in the direction of address 0, the predecrement mode is used to push a value onto the stack and the postincrement mode is used to pull a value off of the stack. If address register A0, for instance, is being employed as a user stack pointer, the instruction

MOVE.L   D0,−(A0)

causes the 32-bit contents of D0 to be pushed onto the stack, and the instruction

MOVE.L   (A0)+,D0

restores the 32-bit contents of D0 from the stack. Incidentally, a variation of the move instruction, called *move multiple registers* (*MOVEM*), is available for moving a group of registers to and from a stack.

Indirect Addressing With Displacements and Indexes

At this point, we have described three of the five address register indirect addressing modes. The remaining two modes support data tables by permitting displacements and indexes to be added to the address pointer.

One of these modes, *address register indirect with displacement*, adds a 16-bit signed integer to the contents of an address register, then uses the result to address an operand in memory. This mode is especially useful for accessing a selected element in a list or table. For these applications, the address register holds the starting address of the table, and the displacement in the instruction specifies the relative position of the element in the table.

The displacement is given in bytes, so for tables comprised of byte data the displacement is simply the element number (0, 1, 2, etc.). For tables comprised of word or long-word data, the displacement must be an even-numbered integer that represents the element number multiplied by 2 or 4. For example, if address register A0 holds the starting address of a word-based table in memory, the instruction

MOVE.W   14(A0),D1

will load the value of the eighth element (Element 7) into the low word of data register D1. Fig. 3-4 shows how this instruction operates for a table that starts at location $53F00. Adding the displace-

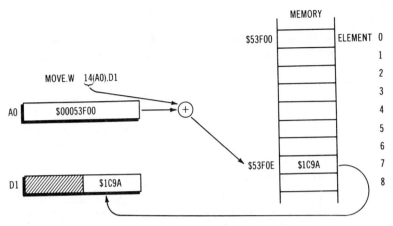

Fig. 3-4. Applying a displacement to an address register.

ment, decimal 14 (hex $E), to the starting address in A0 yields an effective address of $53F0E, which is assumed to contain the value $1C9A.

Note that because the displacement is a 16-bit signed integer, the address register indirect with displacement mode can span up to 32,767 bytes higher in memory, or up to 32,768 bytes lower in memory, than the address in the address register. If you are operating on word or long-word data, these displacement limits translate to 16,383 words or 8191 long words forward, and to 16,384 words or 8192 long words backward.

The final addressing mode of this group, *address register indirect with index,* derives the effective address of the operand by adding an 8-bit signed integer and the contents of an index register (a data register or an address register) to an address register. Therefore, the effective address equation looks like this:

$$EA = (An) + (Ri) + d_8$$

The assembler gives you the choice of applying the entire 32-bit contents of the index register or just its low-order word, by appending either an ".L" or a ".W" data size code to the index register symbol. Either way, the size of the index register does not affect the execution time of the instruction.

Because it offers two separate offsets, this particular addressing mode is useful for accessing two-dimensional arrays. For such applications, an address register usually holds the starting address of the array, and the displacement and index register provide row and column offsets (or column and row offsets, depending on how the array is structured). Normally, a data register holds the index (in *bytes*) and a symbol is used to specify the displacement (also in *bytes*).

For example, suppose you have a 68000-based system that monitors six different pressure valves in a chemical processing plant. This system takes a reading of each valve once every half-hour, and records these readings in memory. In one week's time, these readings will form an array that has 336 blocks (48 readings/day for seven days) of six elements each, for a total of 2016 data values. If the starting address of the array is held in A0, the block displacement (reading number times twelve) in D0 and the valve number in the symbol VALVE, the instruction   *6 valves × 2 bytes per reading?*

    MOVE.W   VALVE(A0,D0.W),D1

can be used to enter any selected pressure-valve reading into the low word of data register D1. In Fig. 3-5, this instruction is used to extract the value of the third reading (Reading 2) of Valve 4 from an array that starts at location $53F00.

Absolute Data Addressing

In absolute data addressing, the effective address itself is specified as the operand. The 68000 has two absolute addressing modes—*absolute short addressing*, in which the operand is a 16-bit address (sign-extended to 32 bits), and *absolute long addressing*, in which the operand is a full 32-bit address.

The absolute short-addressing mode allows you to access only the lowest 32K bytes in memory (addresses 0 through $7FFF) or the highest 32K bytes in memory (addresses $FF8000 through $FFFFFF), whereas the absolute long-addressing mode allows you to access any location in the 16M-byte addressing range of the 68000. However, absolute short-addressed instructions occupy one less word in memory, and execute in four less cycles, than absolute long-addressed instructions. With two separate absolute addressing modes, the 68000 supports applications that need a very large addressing space without penalizing the efficiency of applications that need only a small addressing space. Of course, the large-address applications will make use of absolute short addressing, too, to access frequently used data and temporary data that is stored in the extreme 32K bytes of memory.

For example, to load the word in location $3F00 into the low-order half of data register D1, we can use the instruction

    MOVE.W $3F00,D1

which is the absolute short-addressed (2-word, 12-cycle) equivalent of the absolute long-addressed (3-word, 16-cycle) instruction

    MOVE.W $03F00,D1

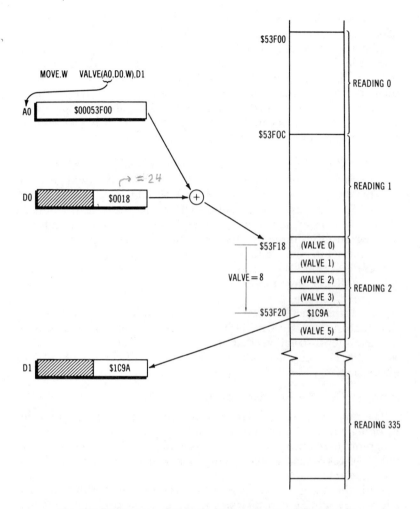

Fig. 3-5. Extracting a data value from a two-dimensional array.

Note that the data size code (.W, in this case) refers to the size of the *data* being moved, rather than the length of the absolute address.

Quite often, the absolute address operand is specified as a label rather than a hexadecimal number, as in the instruction

    MOVE.L   TABLE,A0

This instruction will load the contents of the long word starting at TABLE into address register A0. (To load the *address* of TABLE into A0, you must use either the immediate data addressing mode

51

—the description is upcoming—with the move instruction, or the 68000 load effective address instruction, LEA.)

Will the preceding move instruction translate address TABLE into an absolute short address or an absolute long address? That is, will the object code for the move instruction occupy two words in memory and take 12 cycles to execute, or occupy three words in memory and take 16 cycles to execute? The answer depends on whether TABLE is located at a lower address or a higher address than the move instruction. The rules are as follows:

- If TABLE has a lower address than the move instruction (a *backward reference* is being made), the assembler will generate the appropriate absolute short or long address.
- If TABLE has a higher address than the move instruction (a *forward reference* is being made), and the instruction falls under an ORG directive, the assembler will attempt to generate an absolute short address. You can force the assembler to generate absolute long addresses for forward references by using an ORG.L directive.

Note that the assembler generates absolute addresses for instructions that are origined with an ORG directive. It will generate *relative* addresses for instructions that are origined with an RORG directive. With this fact in mind, let us move on to a discussion of relative addressing.

Program Counter Relative Addressing

The program counter relative addressing modes are useful for developing position-independent, or "relocatable," programs. These are programs that once written and assembled can be executed anywhere in the memory space. Programs sold in ROM, for instance, are often relocatable.

With this form of addressing, the 68000 calculates the effective address by adding a displacement value to the address contained in the program counter. What address does the program counter contain? It contains the address of one of the words in the instruction—an extension word that holds a signed displacement. Therefore, program counter relative addressing is used to access operands that are situated some number of bytes higher or lower in memory than the current instruction.

The 68000 has two program counter relative addressing modes—relative with displacement and relative with index. In the simpler mode, *relative with displacement,* the effective address is the sum of the address in the program counter and a sign-extended 16-bit displacement in the extension word of the instruction. That is,

$$EA = (PC) + d_{16}$$

Fortunately, with an assembler you need not specify the displacement directly; the assembler will calculate it for you. For example, the instruction

```
MOVE.W   LABEL,D1
```

will cause the assembler to calculate the displacement (in bytes) between the extension word of the move instruction and location LABEL, and store this displacement in the extension word. At execution time, the 68000 microprocessor will load the contents of location LABEL into the low-order 16 bits of data register D1. You will note that because the displacement is a 16-bit signed integer, LABEL must be no more than 16,383 words higher in memory, or no more than 16,384 words lower in memory, than the extension word of the instruction.

Incidentally, note that the preceding move instruction gives no indication as to whether the assembler will use program counter relative addressing or absolute addressing to calculate the effective address of LABEL. The answer is, quite simply, that *labels preceded by an RORG directive will cause the assembler to generate program counter relative addressing, whereas labels preceded by an ORG directive will cause the assembler to generate absolute addressing.*

The assembler does not restrict you to labels in order to specify a relative address. You may, if you wish, specify the address in relation to the *location counter* of the assembler (see the Assembler Directives section of Chapter 2). The location counter is referenced by using an asterisk (*) character in the operand field. For example, the instruction

```
JMP   *+10
```

causes program control to be transferred to the instruction that lies 10 bytes (five words) past the extension word of this jump instruction. However, if at all possible, references to the location counter should be avoided and labeled references should be used instead.

With the more complex form of program counter relative addressing, *relative with index*, the effective address is the sum of three terms—the address of the extension word in the program counter, a sign-extended 8-bit displacement integer in the extension word, and the contents of an index register (either a data register or an address register). That is,

$$EA = (PC) + (Ri) + d_8$$

This mode is particularly useful for reading values from a list or data table. For such applications, the sum of the program counter

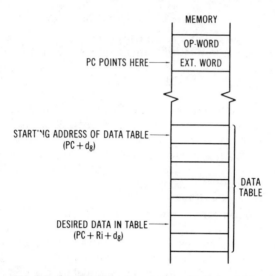

Fig. 3-6. Program counter relative with index addressing.

and 8-bit displacement addresses the beginning of the table, and the index register provides the offset to the desired data element. This is illustrated in Fig. 3-6.

You can use either the low word of the index register or its entire 32-bit contents by appending a .W or .L data size code to the register symbol in the instruction. (As usual, omitting the data size code defaults to word size.) As an example, if a data table starts at location TABLE, the instruction

   MOVE.W   TABLE(D0.L),D1

will cause the assembler to calculate the displacement between the extension word of the instruction and location TABLE, and use this displacement to form the extension word. At execution time, the 68000 microprocessor will add the 32-bit contents of data register D0 to the calculated starting address of the data table, then load the 16-bit contents of the memory location addressed by the result into the low-order 16 bits of data register D1. Because the displacement is an 8-bit signed integer, TABLE must be no more than 63 words higher in memory, or 64 words lower in memory, than the extension word of the instruction.

Immediate Data Addressing

Immediate data addressing is used to specify a constant value as a source operand. This value will be contained in the instruction, rather than in a register or a memory location. There are two im-

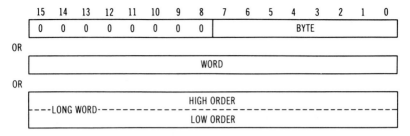

Fig. 3-7. Extension word formats for immediate data.

mediate data addressing modes, called *immediate* and *quick immediate*.

The *immediate mode* allows you to specify a byte, word, or long-word constant. If the constant is a byte or a word value, it will reside in an extension word that follows the operation word. If the constant is a long-word value, it will reside in two extension words that follow the operation word. The formats of these words are shown in Fig. 3-7.

Further, the data will be sign-extended if the destination is an address register, but will not be sign-extended if the destination is a data register. For example, the instruction

```
MOVE.W   #$834E,D0
```

loads the value $834E into the low word of data register D0, without affecting the high word. However, the similar instruction

```
MOVE.W   #$834E,A0
```

loads the value $FFFF834E into address register A0, affecting all 32 bits.

The *quick immediate mode* can be used with only three instructions—add quick (ADDQ), subtract quick (SUBQ), and move quick (MOVEQ). The ADDQ and SUBQ instructions allow an unsigned integer value between 1 and 8 to be added to or subtracted from a register or memory location. These are the increment and decrement instructions of the 68000. The MOVEQ instruction allows a signed, byte-length value (−128 to +127) to be loaded into a data register; the data is sign-extended, so all 32 bits of the register are affected. For example, the instruction

```
MOVEQ   #−2,D0
```

causes the value $FFFFFFFE (the 2s-complement representation of −2, sign-extended to a long word) to be loaded into data register D0. These three instructions are characterized as "quick" because they occupy only one word in memory (the immediate data is em-

55

bedded in the operation word) and, therefore, execute much faster than their immediate mode equivalents.

Implied Addressing

Some instructions use a certain internal register to perform an operation, without identifying that register in the operand field. That is, the addressing of these registers is *implied*. For example, the jump (JMP) instruction always loads an address into the program counter, although the program counter is not explicitly identified as a destination register in the instruction. Besides the program counter (PC), the system stack pointer (SP), the user stack pointer (USP), supervisor stack pointer (SSP), and status register (SR) are also used as implied registers. Table 3-2 lists the instructions that use implied addressing, and the registers implied.

Addressing Modes That Sign-Extend Addresses or Data

Although the data registers and address registers of the 68000 are general-purpose in nature, the data registers are primarily used to hold data and the address registers are primarily used to hold 32-bit memory addresses. For this reason, *the addressing modes do not sign-extend information loaded into data registers, but always sign-extend information loaded into address registers.* Table 3-3 summarizes the addressing modes that cause information to be sign-extended. Later in this chapter we will discuss the instructions that cause information to be sign-extended.

EFFECTIVE ADDRESSING MODE CATEGORIES

As you have seen in the preceding portion of this chapter, each of the 14 addressing modes of the 68000 is designed to perform a particular addressing function. Some modes can be used to access an operand in a register, others can be used to access an operand at a known memory address, or at a given displacement from a known memory address, and so on. Further, some modes can be used to refer to any of several information types (e.g., the address register indirect modes can access either data or addresses in memory), whereas other modes have more restricted usage (e.g., the address register direct mode can refer to an address operand, but not to a data operand). For this reason, the individual addressing modes can be characterized in terms of four different addressing categories, as follows:

1. *Data*—If an effective addressing mode can be used to refer to data operands, it is considered a data addressing mode.
2. *Memory*—If an effective address mode can be used to refer to memory operands, it is considered a memory addressing mode.

Table 3-2. Implicit Instructions

Instruction	Implied Register(s)
Branch Conditional (Bcc), Branch Always (BRA)	PC
Branch to Subroutine (BSR)	PC, SP
Check Register Against Bounds (CHK)	SSP, SR
Test Condition, Decrement and Branch (DBcc)	PC
Signed Divide (DIVS)	SSP, SR
Unsigned Divide (DIVU)	SSP, SR
Jump (JMP)	PC
Jump to Subroutine (JSR)	PC, SP
Link and Allocate (LINK)	SP
Move Condition Codes (MOVE CCR)	SR
Move Status Register (MOVE SR)	SR
Move User Stack Pointer (MOVE USP)	USP
Push Effective Address (PEA)	SP
Return From Exception (RTE)	PC, SP, SR
Return and Restore Condition Codes (RTR)	PC, SP, SR
Return From Subroutine (RTS)	PC, SP
Trap (TRAP)	SSP, SR
Trap on Overflow (TRAPV)	SSP, SR
Unlink (UNLK)	SP

Courtesy Motorola, Inc.

3. *Control*—If an effective addressing mode can be used to refer to memory operands without an associated size, it is considered a control addressing mode.

4. *Alterable*—If an effective addressing mode can be used to refer to alterable (writable) operands, it is considered an alterable addressing mode.

Table 3-4 lists the effective addressing mode categories for each of the addressing modes of the 68000. This table will be important to you as a 68000 programmer, because many of the instructions restrict operands to certain categories, or combinations of categories. For example, the add quick instruction has the general form

```
ADDQ   #<data>,<ea>
```

in which only alterable addressing modes are allowed in the effective address field. This means that any addressing mode except program counter relative and immediate can be used in the effective

Table 3-3.
Addressing Modes That Sign-Extend Addresses or Data

Addressing Modes	Type of Sign-Extension
Address register direct (as a destination).	Word address extended to long word.
Address register indirect with displacement.	Word displacement extended to long word.
Address register indirect with index.	1. Byte displacement extended to long word. 2. Word index extended to long word.
Absolute short address.	Word address extended to long word.
Program counter relative with displacement.	Word displacement extended to long word.
Program counter relative with index.	1. Byte displacement extended to long word. 2. Word index extended to long word.

address field. Therefore, ADDQ #2,A0 is a legal instruction, but ADDQ #2,#2 is not legal (for obvious reasons, in this case).

An instruction that can use a combination of categories in an operand field is the move instruction, which has the general form

```
MOVE    <ea>,<ea>
```

For this instruction, all addressing modes are allowed for the source field, unless the operation size is byte (in which case the address register direct addressing mode is not allowed). For the destination field, only "data alterable" addressing modes are allowed. This means that for the destination field, the allowable addressing modes are those which are categorized as *both* a data addressing mode and an alterable addressing mode. So the *data alterable* addressing modes include data register direct, the address register indirects, and the absolute modes. Conversely, the address register direct, program counter relative, and immediate modes are excluded from the set of data alterable modes.

Since address register direct is not a data alterable addressing mode, may we presume that nothing can be moved into an address register? Of course not; there must be *some* way to initialize these registers! The answer is that nothing can be moved into an address register using a *MOVE* instruction, but the 68000 has another instruction, called *move address* (*MOVEA*), that can be used for this purpose. Incidentally, although the manufacturers' 68000 users' manuals define MOVE and MOVEA as two distinct instructions, most 68000 assemblers (including those from Motorola) permit an ad-

Table 3-4. Effective Addressing Mode Categories

Addressing Mode	Addressing Categories				Assembler Syntax
	Data	Memory	Control	Alterable	
Data register direct.	X			X	Dn
Address register direct.				X	An
Register indirect.	X	X	X	X	(An)
Register indirect with postincrement.	X	X		X	(An)+
Register indirect with predecrement.	X	X		X	-(An)
Register indirect with displacement.	X	X	X	X	d(An)
Register indirect with index.	X	X	X	X	d(An,Ri)
Absolute short.	X	X	X	X	xxxx
Absolute long.	X	X	X		xxxxxxxx
PC relative with displacement.	X	X	X		d
PC relative with index.	X	X	X		d(Ri)
Immediate.	X	X			#xxxx

Table 3-5. The 68000 Instruction Set

Mnemonic	Description	Mnemonic	Description
ABCD	Add Decimal With Extend	MOVEM	Move Multiple Registers
ADD	Add	MOVEP	Move Peripheral Data
AND	Logical AND	MULS	Signed Multiply
ASL	Arithmetic Shift Left	MULU	Unsigned Multiply
ASR	Arithmetic Shift Right		
		NBCD	Negate Decimal With Extend
Bcc	Branch Conditionally	NEG	Negate
BCHG	Bit Test and Change	NOP	No Operation
BCLR	Bit Test and Clear	NOT	One's Complement
BRA	Branch Always		
BSET	Bit Test and Set	OR	Logical OR
BSR	Branch to Subroutine		
BTST	Bit Test	PEA	Push Effective Address
CHK	Check Register Against Bounds	RESET	Reset External Devices
CLR	Clear Operand	ROL	Rotate Left Without Extend
CMP	Compare	ROR	Rotate Right Without Extend
DBcc	Test Condition, Decrement and Branch	ROXL	Rotate Left With Extend
DIVS	Signed Divide	ROXR	Rotate Right With Extend
DIVU	Unsigned Divide	RTE	Return From Exception
EOR	Exclusive-OR	RTR	Return and Restore
EXG	Exchange Registers	RTS	Return From Subroutine
EXT	Sign Extend		
		SBCD	Subtract Decimal With Extend
JMP	Jump	Scc	Set Conditional
JSR	Jump to Subroutine	STOP	Stop
		SUB	Subtract
		SWAP	Swap Data Register Halves
LEA	Load Effective Address		
LINK	Link Stack	TAS	Test and Set Operand
LSL	Logical Shift Left	TRAP	Trap
LSR	Logical Shift Right	TRAPV	Trap on Overflow
		TST	Test
MOVE	Move	UNLK	Unlink

Courtesy Motorola, Inc.

dress register to be specified in the destination field of a MOVE instruction. These assemblers will simply interpret your MOVE instruction as a MOVEA, and generate the object code accordingly.

INSTRUCTION TYPES

As mentioned previously, the 68000 has 56 basic instruction types. The assembler mnemonics and the description of these instructions are summarized in Table 3-5. Further, eight of these instructions have variations to perform special operations; the variations are summarized in Table 3-6.

Table 3-6. Variations of Instruction Types

Instruction Type	Variation	Description
ADD	ADD	Add
	ADDA	Add Address
	ADDQ	Add Quick
	ADDI	Add Immediate
	ADDX	Add With Extend
AND	AND	Logical AND
	ANDI	AND Immediate
CMP	CMP	Compare
	CMPA	Compare Address
	CMPM	Compare Memory
	CMPI	Compare Immediate
EOR	EOR	Exclusive-OR
	EORI	Exclusive-OR Immediate
MOVE	MOVE	Move
	MOVEA	Move Address
	MOVEQ	Move Quick
	MOVE from SR	Move From Status Register
	MOVE to SR	Move to Status Register
	MOVE to CCR	Move to Condition Codes
	MOVE USP	Move User Stack Pointer
NEG	NEG	Negate
	NEGX	Negate With Extend
OR	OR	Logical OR
	ORI	OR Immediate
SUB	SUB	Subtract
	SUBA	Subtract Address
	SUBI	Subtract Immediate
	SUBQ	Subtract Quick
	SUBX	Subtract With Extend

Courtesy Motorola, Inc.

The instruction set can be divided into eight functional groups. Here is a listing of the groups, and a general description of what functions they perform:

1. *Data movement instructions* move information between memory locations, I/O devices, and general-purpose registers, in any combination.
2. *Integer arithmetic instructions* perform single-precision and multiple-precision arithmetic operations on binary numbers.
3. *Logical instructions* perform logical AND, OR and Exclusive-OR operations on memory locations and registers.
4. *Shift and rotate instructions* shift and rotate the contents of memory locations and registers.
5. *Bit manipulation instructions* test the state of individual bits, and perform some operation based on the result of that test.
6. *Binary-coded-decimal (BCD) instructions* add and subtract BCD digits.
7. *Program control instructions* perform branches, jumps, and subroutine calls, to control the sequence of program execution.
8. *System control instructions* include privileged instructions, trap-generating instructions, and instructions that use or modify the status register.

In this chapter, we will describe the 68000 instruction set by groups, in the order just presented. Let us begin by describing the data movement instructions, which include the now-familiar MOVE instruction.

DATA MOVEMENT INSTRUCTIONS

The data movement instructions (Table 3-7) are used to transfer information between memory and the data and address registers. This group actually includes two additional instructions, link (LINK) and unlink (UNLK), but these are primarily used with subroutines, so they will be described separately, following the discussion of the program control instructions.

Move Instruction

The fundamental instruction in this group is the *move* (*MOVE*) instruction, which can be used to transfer byte, word, or long-word data between two memory locations, between a memory location and a data register, or between two data registers.

With the 68000 in the user state, the move instruction allows you to update the condition code register (MOVE <ea>,CCR) or read the entire status register (MOVE SR,<ea>). In the supervisor state, the move instruction allows you to update the status register

Table 3-7. Data Movement Instructions

Mnemonic	Assembler Syntax	Operand Size	Allowable Addressing Modes — Source	Allowable Addressing Modes — Destination	Condition Codes X N Z V C
EXG	EXG Rx,Ry	32	Dn or An	Dn or An	– – – – –
LEA	LEA <ea>,An	32	Control	An	– – – – –
MOVE	MOVE <ea>,<ea>	8, 16, 32	All (1)	Data Alterable	– * * 0 0
	MOVE <ea>,CCR	16	Data	CCR	* * * * *
	MOVE <ea>,SR (2)	16	Data	SR	* * * * *
	MOVE SR,<ea>	16	SR	Data Alterable	– – – – –
	MOVE USP,An (2)	32	USP	An	– – – – –
	MOVE An,USP (2)	32	An	USP	– – – – –
MOVEA	MOVEA <ea>,An	16, 32	All	An	– – – – –
MOVEM	MOVEM <list>,<ea>	16, 32	Control or (An)+	Control Alterable or –(An)	– – – – –
	MOVEM <ea>,<list>	16, 32			– – – – –
MOVEP	MOVEP Dx,d(Ay)	16, 32	Dn	d(An)	– – – – –
	MOVEP d(Ay),Dx	16, 32	d(An)	Dn	– – – – –
MOVEQ	MOVEQ #d,Dn	32	#d (3)	Dn	– * * 0 0
NOP	NOP		PC + 2 → PC		– – – – –
PEA	PEA <ea>	32	Control		– – – – –
SWAP	SWAP Dn	16	Dn	Dn	– – – – –

Notes: (1) If the operation size is byte, the address register direct addressing mode is not allowed.
(2) This operation is privileged.
(3) Eight bits of immediate data, which are sign-extended to a long operand.

(MOVE <ea>,SR), read the user stack pointer (MOVE USP,An), or write to the user stack pointer (MOVE An,USP). In the preceding effective address fields (those labeled as <ea>), an address register may not be used as a source or destination.

Using Move With Stacks

The move instruction can also be used to transfer data to and from stacks in memory. These include the system stacks (the supervisor stack and the user stack) and user-defined stacks. Since stacks build toward memory location 0, the address register indirect with predecrement mode is employed to *push* data onto the stack. For example, the instruction

```
MOVE   D0,—(SP)
```

pushes the low word of D0 onto the active system stack. Conversely, the address register indirect with postincrement mode is employed to *pull* data from the stack, so the instruction

```
MOVE   (SP)+,D0
```

retrieves the next word from the active system stack, and loads it into the low word of D0.

Move Multiple Registers (MOVEM) Instruction

Quite often you will want to move the contents of more than one register. The most common example of this is saving a number of general-purpose registers on the stack while a subroutine is being executed, to make that subroutine *reentrant*. A subroutine is reentrant if it can be interrupted and reentered by the interrupting program.

The move multiple registers (MOVEM) instruction can be used to transfer up to 16 registers (data registers D0–D7 and address registers A0–A7) to or from memory. Register-to-memory transfers have the format

```
MOVEM   <list>,<ea>
```

and memory-to-register transfers have the format

```
MOVEM   <ea>,<list>
```

In both cases, <list> represents the list of registers to be moved. The assembler allows registers to be listed in two ways. One way is to list individual register names, separated by slash (/) characters. For example, the instruction

```
MOVEM   D3/D4/D5/A1,$53F00
```

moves the low words of D3, D4, D5, and A1 into the four consecutive words that start at location $53F00. (In this case, the registers will be stored in the order they are listed in the instruction, but that won't always be true; we will discuss this point shortly.)

If the register list includes consecutive data or address registers, the assembler permits you to list just the first and last registers, separated by a hyphen (-). Therefore, the preceding example could also be written as

MOVEM   D3–D5/A1,$53F00

The MOVEM instruction always transfers register contents to and from memory in a predetermined sequence, regardless of the order used to specify them in the register list. *For address register indirect with predecrement addressing, registers are transferred in the order A7 through A0, then D7 through D0. However, for all control modes, and for address register indirect with postincrement addressing, registers are transferred in the reverse order—D0 through D7, then A0 through A7.* These differences allow you to build stacks and lists in one direction and access them in the opposite direction. Fig. 3-8 shows some examples.

Address-Moving Instructions (MOVEA, LEA, PEA)

The 68000 has three instructions that are specifically designed to transfer addresses, rather than data. Two of these instructions, *move address (MOVEA)* and *load effective address (LEA)*, are similar and can be easily confused by programmers. Both cause an address to be loaded into an address register, but whereas LEA loads the *effective address* of the referenced operand (a memory location), MOVEA loads the *contents* of the referenced operand (a memory location, a register, or an immediate value), and assumes that it constitutes an address. Further, LEA always obtains a 32-bit address, while MOVEA can access either a 16-bit word address (loaded sign-extended to 32 bits) or a 32-bit long address. Fig. 3-9 shows two examples of the LEA instruction.

As you can see, LEA and MOVEA are extremely useful instructions. If your program requires a certain calculated address in several different instructions, you can use LEA to calculate the address just once, and place that address in an address register. Thereafter, each reference to the addressed operand can be made with address register indirect addressing. This will not only save programming time, but will also generate programs that occupy less space in memory and execute faster. How is that so? Because address register indirect addressing adds no extension words to an instruction, which will conserve memory space. It also executes four to eight cycles faster than the address register indirect with displacement or offset, absolute or program counter relative mode used to precalculate the address.

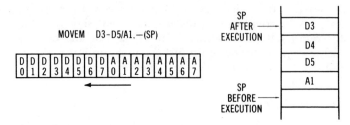

(A) Stacking register contents, with predecrement addressing.

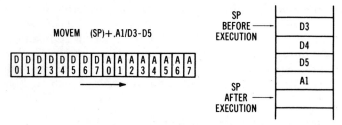

(B) Unstacking register contents, with postincrement addressing.

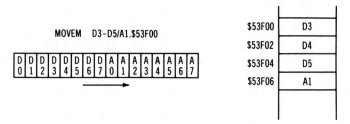

(C) Storing register contents, with absolute addressing.

Fig. 3-8. Examples of the MOVEM instruction.

MOVEA is useful for accessing addresses that are stored in memory. For example, if you have a linked list in memory in which each node begins with a pointer to the next node, the address of the second node could be obtained with the instruction

    MOVEA.L   LIST,A0

and the address of the third and successive nodes could be obtained with the instruction

    MOVEA.L   (A0),A0

Note, incidentally, that a MOVEA instruction whose source operand is an *immediate* label is equivalent to an LEA instruction.

That is, MOVEA.L #LABEL,A0 and LEA LABEL,A0 are equivalent instructions. Although both instructions will take the same amount of time to execute (12 cycles), LEA is preferred for this application because it is more readily understandable.

The last of these three address-moving instructions, *push effective address* (*PEA*), is similar to LEA, insofar as it moves a computed effective address, rather than the contents of the addressed location. With PEA, however, the address is pushed onto the active system

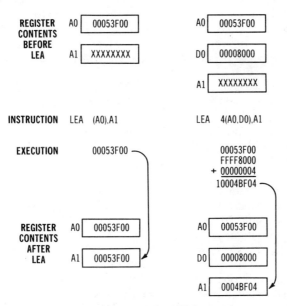

Fig. 3-9. Examples of the LEA instruction.

stack (user stack or supervisor stack). The PEA instruction is handy for passing parameters to a subroutine, by pushing the address of a parameter—or the starting address of several consecutively stored parameters—onto the stack. For example, the push-then-call operations may be performed with this instruction sequence:

```
PEA   PARAM
JSR   SUBR
```

Because the JSR pushes a 4-byte return address onto the stack *after* the PEA has pushed its 4-byte address onto the stack, the parameter address must be accessed by skipping over the return address, as in this instruction:

```
MOVEA.L   4(SP),A0
```

With the parameter address removed from the stack, the subroutine should "clean up" the stack, by moving the return address one long word higher in memory and then updating the stack pointer. Both of these tasks can be performed with one instruction,

MOVE.L   (SP)+,(SP)

Communicating With 8-Bit Peripherals, Using MOVEP

As was mentioned in Chapter 1, the 68000 can be interfaced to older 8-bit synchronous devices as well as to new 16-bit asynchronous devices, and has separate control lines for each type of device. Readers who have programmed 8-bit systems know that the attached peripheral devices usually have registers which "occupy" a number of consecutive bytes in memory.

The *move peripheral data* (*MOVEP*) instruction is designed to transfer information between a 68000 data register and an attached 8-bit peripheral device, in "bursts" of two or four bytes. In the 68000 system, 8-bit peripherals must be connected to either the high eight bits of the data bus (lines D8–D15) or the low eight bits of the data bus (lines D0–D7). The MOVEP instruction communicates with peripherals on the high half of the bus by issuing even-numbered addresses, and communicates with peripherals on the low half of the bus by issuing odd-numbered addresses. In a memory map, these peripherals would "occupy" alternate bytes in memory—consecutive even bytes or consecutive odd bytes.

Two-byte transfers are made by specifying a word operand (MOVEP or MOVEP.W) and 4-byte transfers are made by specifying a long-word operand (MOVEP.L). Peripherals must be addressed using the address register indirect with displacement mode. Fig. 3-10 shows two examples of the MOVEP instruction—a long transfer with an even address and a word transfer with an odd address. Note, incidentally, that MOVEP is the only 68000 instruction that permits you to use an odd address with a word or long-word operand!

The *execution time of the MOVEP instruction* depends on whether data is being transferred to/from an asynchronous device or a synchronous device. Transfers to and from asynchronous devices will take 16 CLK cycles for a two-byte transfer or 24 cycles for a four-byte transfer. These values are taken from Table B-12 in Appendix B. Transfers to or from synchronous devices will take quite a bit longer, because the 68000 must synchronize with a clock that is running at one-tenth the speed of CLK. Chapters 6 and 8 provide more information on this subject.

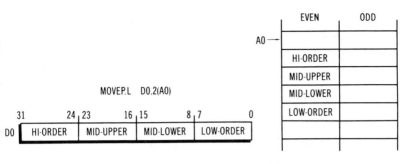

(A) Long transfer with an even address.

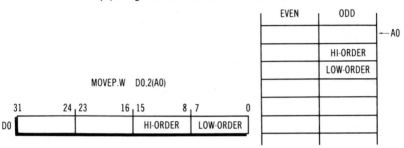

(B) Word transfer with an odd address.

Fig. 3-10. Byte transfers with MOVEP.

Move Quick (MOVEQ), a Handy Move-Immediate

Because programmers often need to operate with a small constant, the designers of the 68000 provided three "quick" instructions—move quick, add quick, and subtract quick—that allow you to specify such a constant in the op-word. The first of these instructions, *move quick* (*MOVEQ*), causes a specified byte-length value to be sign-extended to 32 bits and loaded into a data register. Because the constant is eight bits long, any integer value between −128 and +127 can be moved into a data register.

The MOVEQ instruction occupies only one word in memory and executes in four cycles. By contrast, its move-immediate counterpart (MOVE.L #d_8,Dn) occupies two words in memory and executes in 20 cycles. Most assemblers, including those from Motorola, take advantage of these savings by actually interpreting a properly configured move-immediate instruction as a MOVEQ, and generating the object code accordingly.

Register Swap (SWAP) and Exchange (EXG) Instructions

These two similar instructions have very different uses. The *swap register halves* (*SWAP*) instruction exchanges the high-order and low-order 16 bits of a 32-bit data register. This instruction provides access to the contents of the upper word of a register, and is necessary because (as you will recall) word operations are *always* performed on the lower word. Similarly, SWAP can be used to access the upper two bytes of a data register. SWAP alone will set up access to the mid-upper byte; a SWAP plus a rotate will set up access to the high-order byte.

The *exchange registers* (*EXG*) instruction exchanges the entire 32 bits of two registers. It can have three formats:

1. To exchange two data registers, use EXG Dx,Dy.
2. To exchange two address registers, use EXG Ax,Ay.
3. To exchange a data register and an address register, use EXG Dx,Ay.

The No-Operation (NOP) Instruction

The *no-operation* (*NOP*) instruction is a simple one-word implied addressing instruction that is generally used only during program development. The NOP instruction performs no operation—it does not alter any status flags, registers (other than the program counter), or memory locations, but it does perform the very useful function of reserving space in memory.

Programmers often code NOPs into a source program being developed, to leave room for instructions that may have to be added later. Since each NOP instruction occupies only one word in memory, at least two NOPs (preferably three NOPs) should be inserted at the spot where space is to be reserved.

NOP instructions may also be inserted into object programs, to replace instructions that have been *deleted,* so that the program does not have to be reassembled. In this case, you should replace each word of the deleted instruction with $4E71, the hexadecimal value that represents a NOP instruction.

INTEGER ARITHMETIC INSTRUCTIONS

The 68000 can add, subtract, multiply, divide, and compare two binary operands. It can also clear, test, sign-extend, and negate (2s-complement) a single, specified operand. The instructions that perform these tasks are summarized in Table 3-8.

Add Instructions

There are five instructions that can be used to add binary numbers. The first of these, *add binary* (*ADD*), adds two byte, word, or long-word data operands. Because the operands are assumed to be *data* values, one must be in a data register; the other may be in a memory location, an address register (unless byte operands are being added), or another data register. The ADD instruction can affect all five condition codes, as follows:

1. Carry (C) is set if the result cannot be contained in the destination operand; otherwise C is cleared.
2. Overflow (V) is set if two like-signed numbers (both positive or both negative) are added and the result exceeds the operand's 2s-complement range of numbers, which causes the sign bit to be changed; otherwise V is cleared.
3. Zero (Z) is set if the result is zero; otherwise Z is cleared.
4. Negative (N) is set if the sign bit of the result is a logic 1; otherwise N is cleared.
5. Extend (X) is set to the same state as the carry (C) bit.

For add operations, the status of the V and N flags is pertinent only if signed numbers are being added. Incidentally, if the destination operand is an address register, the condition codes are *not* affected. In fact, the assembler recognizes this form of the add instruction as a variation, called *add address (ADDA)*.

The ADD instruction is useful for adding two byte, word, or long-word operands, if at least one of the operands lies in a data register. However, many applications involve adding multiple-precision operands, or operands that are both contained in memory. For these applications, the 68000 has an instruction, *add extended (ADDX)*, that adds the contents of two data registers or two memory locations. The ADDX instruction affects the C, V, N, and X flags in the same way the ADD instruction does. However, with ADDX, *zero (Z) is cleared if the result is nonzero; otherwise Z is unaffected!* This feature is very handy in multiprecision operations, because it causes Z to reflect the zero/nonzero status of an *entire* add operation, rather than the status of just the high-order term.

If the operands are in data registers, the ADDX instruction is normally preceded by an ADD instruction. For example, the following sequence adds a 64-bit integer in D0 and D1 to another 64-bit integer in D2 and D3:

```
ADD.L    D0,D2        Add low 32 bits.
ADDX.L   D1,D3        Add high 32 bits.
```

If the operands are in memory, you must clear X and set Z before adding them (remember, Z will remain set if each subsequent add produces a zero result). Memory-to-memory adds always use predecrement addressing, so the address registers must initially point one byte, word, or long-word higher in memory than the low-order operands. For example, if A0 and A1 point to two 64-bit operands in memory, these operands could be added with this sequence:

Table 3-8. Integer Arithmetic Instructions

Mnemonic	Assembler Syntax	Operand Size	Allowable Addressing Modes Source	Allowable Addressing Modes Destination	Condition Codes X N Z V C
ADD	ADD <ea>,Dn ADD Dn,<ea>	8, 16, 32 8, 16, 32	All (1) Dn	Dn Alterable	* * * * * * * * * *
ADDA	ADDA <ea>,An	16, 32	All	An	– – – – –
ADDI	ADDI #d,<ea>	8, 16, 32	#d	Data Alterable	* * * * *
ADDQ	ADDQ #d,<ea>	8, 16, 32	#d (2)	Alterable (1)	* * * * *
ADDX	ADDX Dy,Dx ADDX –(Ay),–(Ax)	8, 16, 32 8, 16, 32	Dn –(An)	Dn –(An)	* * * * * * * * * *
CLR	CLR <ea>	8, 16, 32	Data Alterable		– 0 1 0 0
CMP	CMP <ea>,Dn	8, 16, 32	All (1)	Dn	– * * * *
CMPA	CMPA <ea>,An	16, 32.	All	An	– * * * *
CMPI	CMPI #d,<ea>	8, 16, 32	#d	Data Alterable	– * * * *
CMPM	CMPM (Ay)+,(Ax)+	8, 16, 32	(An)+	(An)+	– * * * *
DIVS	DIVS <ea>,Dn	16	Data	Dn	– * * * 0
DIVU	DIVU <ea>,Dn	16	Data	Dn	– * * * 0
EXT	EXT Dn	16, 32	Dn		– * * 0 0
MULS	MULS <ea>,Dn	16	Data	Dn	– * * 0 0

Table 3-8. (cont)

			Data	Dn					
MULU	MULU <ea>,Dn	16	Data	Dn	–	*	*	0	C
NEG	NEG <ea>	8, 16, 32	Data Alterable		*	*	*	*	*
NEGX	NEGX <ea>	8, 16, 32	Data Alterable		*	*	*	*	*
SUB	SUB <ea>,Dn SUB Dn,<ea>	8, 16, 32 8, 16, 32	All (1) Dn	Dn Alterable	* *	* *	* *	* *	* *
SUBA	SUBA <ea>,An	16, 32	All	An	–	–	–	–	–
SUBI	SUBI #d,<ea>	8, 16, 32	#d	Data Alterable	*	*	*	*	*
SUBQ	SUBQ #d,<ea>	8, 16, 32	#d (2)	Alterable (1)	*	*	*	*	*
SUBX	SUBX Dy,Dx SUBX –(Ay),–(Ax)	8, 16, 32 8, 16, 32	Dn –(An)	Dn –(An)	* *	* *	* *	* *	* *
TAS	TAS <ea>	8	Data Alterable		–	*	*	0	0
TST	TST <ea>	8, 16, 32	Data Alterable		–	*	*	0	0

Notes: (1) If the operation size is byte, the address register direct addressing mode is not allowed.
(2) Immediate operand, with a value from 1 to 8.

MOVE	#4,CCR	Make Z = 1, all other bits = 0.
ADDX.L	—(A0),—(A1)	Add low 32 bits.
ADDX.L	—(A0),—(A1)	Add high 32 bits.

Fig. 3-11 shows the arrangement of the operands in memory, and how the pointers are affected by the addition operation.

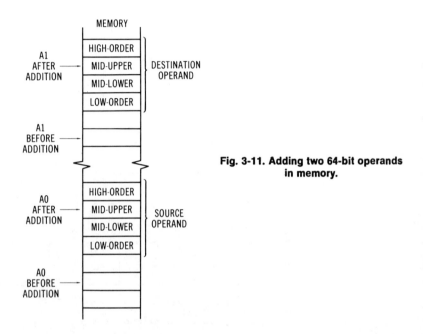

Fig. 3-11. Adding two 64-bit operands in memory.

The last two add instructions, *add immediate* (*ADDI*) and *add quick* (*ADDQ*), are used to add a constant value to an addressed operand. With ADDI, the constant can be a byte, word, or long-word value, and the instruction occupies from two to five words in memory. With ADDQ, the constant can only have a value between 1 and 8, but the instruction occupies only one to three words in memory. Further, ADDQ can be used to add a value to an address register, whereas ADDI cannot. Note that ADDQ replaces the increment instruction found in 8-bit microprocessors.

Subtract Instructions

The 68000 has a subtract equivalent of each of the five add instructions. Three of these instructions, *subtract binary* (*SUB*), *subtract immediate* (*SUBI*), and *subtract quick* (*SUBQ*), affect the condition codes in the same way. Specifically,

1. Carry (C) is set if the subtraction generates a *borrow*, which

indicates that the result cannot be contained in the destination operand; otherwise C is cleared.

2. Overflow (V) is set if two unlike-signed numbers (one positive, the other negative) are subtracted and the result exceeds the operand's 2s-complement range of numbers; otherwise V is cleared.
3. Zero (Z) is set if the result is zero; otherwise Z is cleared.
4. Negative (N) is set if the sign bit of the result is a logic 1; otherwise N is cleared.
5. Extend (X) is set the same as the carry (C) bit.

The multiprecision subtract instruction, *subtract extended* (*SUBX*), affects C, V, N, and X in the same way, but clears Z only if the result is nonzero; otherwise Z is unaffected. The fifth subtract instruction, *subtract address* (*SUBA*), affects no flags.

Negate Instructions

Two subtract-like instructions allow you to 2s-complement a byte, word, or long-word operand in memory or in a data register. These instructions, *negate* (*NEG*) and *negate extended* (*NEGX*), take the 2s-complement by subtracting the operand from zero.

The NEG instruction affects the condition codes in the same way as the SUB instruction, but since one operand is zero here we can be more explicit about the conditions that set the individual flags. Therefore, for NEG:

1. Carry (C) and negative (N) are set if the addressed operand is a nonzero positive number; otherwise C and N are cleared.
2. Overflow (V) is set if the addressed operand has the value $80 (byte), $8000 (word), or $80000000 (long word); otherwise V is cleared.
3. Zero (Z) is set if the addressed operand is zero; otherwise Z is cleared.
4. Extend (X) is set the same as the carry (C) bit.

The NEGX instruction has the same affect on the C, V, N, and X flags, but clears Z only if the result is nonzero; Z is *unaffected* if the result is zero. As was explained with ADDX, this feature causes Z to reflect the zero/nonzero status of an entire multiprecision operation, rather than the status of just the high-order term.

Multiply and Divide Instructions

The 68000 has two multiply instructions—*signed multiply* (*MULS*) and *unsigned multiply* (*MULU*). These instructions multiply two word operands, and return the 32-bit product in a data register. Numbers longer than 16 bits can also be multiplied using MULS and MULU. We will see examples of this in Chapter 4, where a 32-bit by 32-bit multiply routine is given for both signed and unsigned numbers.

The 68000 also has two divide instructions—*signed divide* (*DIVS*) and *unsigned divide* (*DIVU*). These instructions divide a 32-bit dividend (in a data register) by a 16-bit divisor (in memory or a data register), and return the 16-bit quotient and 16-bit remainder in the lower half and upper half of the data register, respectively.

If you attempt to divide by zero, the 68000 will generate a trap (described in Chapter 7). Otherwise, a division—signed or unsigned —will have the following effect on the condition codes:

1. Carry (C) is always cleared.
2. Overflow (V) is set if division overflow is detected; otherwise V is cleared.
3. Zero (Z) is set if the quotient is zero; otherwise Z is cleared. The state of Z is undefined if overflow occurs.
4. Negative (N) is set if the quotient is negative (for DIVS) or the most-significant bit of the quotient is set (for DIVU); otherwise N is cleared. The state of N is undefined if overflow occurs.
5. Extend (X) is not affected.

If overflow occurs, the 68000 sets the V flag and terminates the operation, without affecting the divisor or dividend. Overflow occurs when the dividend is so much larger than the divisor that the quotient cannot be contained in 16 bits.

For an unsigned divide, the dividend must be at least 65,536 times larger than the divisor for overflow to occur. For a signed divide, the quotient must exceed +32,767 or −32,768 for overflow to occur. It is possible to write a program that will *always* return a valid quotient and remainder, regardless of whether or not overflow occurred. Such a program is given in Chapter 4.

Sign Extend (EXT)

The 68000 makes it possible to operate on mixed-size data, with an instruction called *sign extend* (*EXT*). This instruction extends the sign bit (the most-significant bit) of a number in a data register from a byte to a word, or from a word to a long word, as shown in Fig. 3-12. Thus, the EXT instruction makes it possible to perform such operations as adding a byte to a word or multiplying a word by a byte.

Clear Instruction (CLR)

Another "housekeeping" instruction in this group, *clear* (*CLR*), resets the addressed byte, word, or long word to zero. It can be used

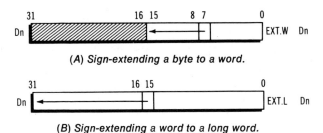

(A) Sign-extending a byte to a word.

(B) Sign-extending a word to a long word.

Fig. 3-12. How the EXT instruction sign-extends data.

to clear a data register or a memory location, but not an address register. (There are not too many instances in which you will want to clear an address register but, for those cases, instruction SUBA.L An,An is the most effective way to do the job.)

Readers with time-critical applications should be aware that CLR is only faster than the equivalent MOVE #0,<ea> instruction when the low byte or low word of a data register is being cleared! Clearing all 32 bits of a data register is two cycles faster with MOVEQ #0,Dn than with CLR.L Dn and, in most cases, clearing a memory location with MOVE.x #0,<ea> (where x = B, W, or L) takes the same amount of time as clearing it with CLR.x <ea>. In fact, if you are using the address register indirect with predecrement mode to address memory, instruction MOVE.x #0,−(An) will clear the memory location two cycles *faster* than CLR.x −(An).

The Compare Instructions

Most programs do not execute all instructions consecutively, as they are stored in memory, but include jumps, branches, loops, subroutine calls, and other factors that cause program execution to be transferred from one place to another in memory. The instructions that actually cause this transfer to occur will be described later in this chapter when we discuss the program control instructions for the 68000. At this point we will discuss the compare instructions, which are commonly used to configure the condition codes upon which program control instructions make their transfer/no-transfer "decisions."

The four compare instructions for the 68000 perform very much like subtract instructions. That is, each of these instructions subtracts a source operand from a destination operand, and sets or clears the condition code flags based on the result (see Table 3-9). However, unlike subtract instructions, *the compare instructions do not save the result of the subtraction.* Their sole purpose is to configure the condition codes for transfer/no-transfer decision-making by subsequent program control instructions.

Table 3-9. Compare Instruction Results

Condition	X	N*	Z	V*	C
Source < Destination	–	0	0	0/1	0
Source = Destination	–	0	1	0	0
Source > Destination	–	1	0	0/1	1

*Pertinent only when comparing 2s-complement numbers.

The *compare* (*CMP*) instruction compares a source operand with a byte, word, or long-word operand in a data register. Word or long-word addresses can be compared to an address register using a variation of CMP, called *compare address* (*CMPA*). The *compare immediate* (*CMPI*) instruction compares a byte, word, or long-word immediate value with a destination operand. The *compare memory* (*CMPM*) instruction compares two operands in memory, using address register indirect with postincrement addressing. This particular instruction, CMPM, is especially useful for comparing strings; an example is upcoming later in this chapter (Example 3-3).

A Compare-With-Zero Instruction, TST

You will recall that the negate instructions, NEG and NEGX, are actually subtract instructions that perform a specialized task—they subtract an operand from zero. Similarly, the 68000 has a specialized compare instruction, *test an operand* (*TST*), that compares an operand with zero. Like the compare instructions, TST subtracts the operand from zero, and sets or clears the condition code flags based on the result, but does not save that result. Here is how the TST instruction affects the condition code bits:

1. Carry (C) and overflow (V) are always cleared.
2. Zero (Z) is set if the addressed operand is zero; otherwise Z is cleared.
3. Negative (N) is set if the addressed operand is a negative number; otherwise N is cleared.
4. Extend (X) is not affected.

Test and Set an Operand (TAS)

The *test and set an operand* (*TAS*) instruction performs the same basic operation as the test an operand (TST) instruction—it compares the operand with zero and sets or clears the condition codes based on the result—but TAS also unconditionally sets the most-significant bit of the operand. Further, TAS can only operate on byte operands, so it will set bit 7 of the byte.

Despite their operational similarities, TST and TAS have very

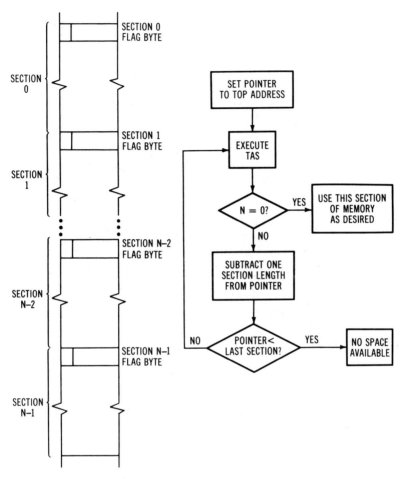

Fig. 3-13. Using TAS to allocate memory.

dissimilar functions. As we saw in the preceding section, TST is used to find out whether an operand has a value of zero. However, TAS is primarily used to test the state of a flag in memory, then set that flag. This is particularly useful in multitasking applications, to allocate memory space to the various tasks. It is also useful in multiprocessing applications, to prevent one processor from accessing a portion of memory that is currently being used by another processor.

Fig. 3-13 illustrates the use of TAS in a *multitasking* application. This illustration shows a portion of memory that has been divided into N sections, and also gives a simple flowchart of an algorithm that could be used to locate the next available section. This algorithm requires two address registers—one to hold a pointer to the section being tested and another to hold a pointer to the last section (Section 0). The program for this algorithm will include several instructions that have already been described—MOVEA or LEA (to initialize the test pointer), SUBA (to decrement the test pointer), and CMPA (to compare the two pointers). It will also include some conditional branch instructions, which will be described with the program control instructions.

In a *multiprocessing* application, TAS allows a processor to interrogate a test byte (via the condition codes) and then place a 1 into the most-significant bit of the byte. If the memory is busy, the program can keep checking until it is free. The following routine performs this task:

MFREE	TAS	TEST	Test and set the byte, TEST.
	BNE	MFREE	If TEST not = 0, test again.
	.		
	.		(Processor program instructions.)
	.		
	CLR.B	TEST	Clear TAS byte.

It is important to note that TAS is the only 68000 instruction that performs an *indivisible read-modify-write cycle*. This prohibits another processor from interfering with the TAS operation once it has been initiated.

LOGICAL INSTRUCTIONS

There are seven logical instructions, shown in Table 3-10. The basic instructions in this group are AND *logical* (AND), *Exclusive*-OR *logical* (EOR), and *Inclusive*-OR *logical* (OR). These three instructions can operate on byte, word, and long-word operands, one of which must be in a data register. The second operand can be in memory, a data register, or an address register for the AND and OR instructions, or in memory or a data register for the EOR instruction. EOR cannot operate on an address register.

Another instruction, *logical complement* (NOT), can be used to 1s-complement a data register or memory location. Thus, you can employ NOT to complement unsigned operands, and NEG or NEGX to complement signed operands.

Variations of the AND, OR, and EOR instructions permit a constant to be used as the source data. These variations, AND *immediate* (ANDI), *Exclusive*-OR *immediate* (EORI), and *Inclusive*-OR *immediate* (ORI), can operate on a memory or data register operand of any length. These instructions can also be used to operate on the status register or condition codes. Operations on the status register (SR) are privileged.

Table 3-10. Logical Instructions

Mnemonic	Assembler Syntax	Operand Size	Allowable Addressing Modes		Condition Codes				
			Source	Destination	X	N	Z	V	C
AND	AND <ea>,Dn	8, 16, 32	Data	Dn	–	*	*	0	0
	AND Dn,<ea>	8, 16, 32	Dn	Alterable	–	*	*	0	0
ANDI	ANDI #d,<ea>	8, 16, 32	#d	Data Alterable	–	*	*	0	0
	ANDI #d,SR (1)	8, 16	#d	SR	*	*	*	*	*
EOR	EOR Dn,<ea>	8, 16, 32	Dn	Data Alterable	–	*	*	0	0
EORI	EORI #d,<ea>	8, 16, 32	#d	Data Alterable	–	*	*	0	0
	EORI #d,SR (1)	8, 16	#d	SR	*	*	*	*	*
NOT	NOT <ea>	8, 16, 32		Data Alterable	–	*	*	0	0
OR	OR <ea>, Dn	8, 16, 32	Data	Dn	–	*	*	0	0
	OR Dn,<ea>	8, 16, 32	Dn	Alterable	–	*	*	0	0
ORI	ORI #d,<ea>	8, 16, 32	#d	Data Alterable	–	*	*	0	0
	ORI #d,SR (1)	8, 16	#d	SR	*	*	*	*	*

Note: (1) If the operand size is *byte*, only the lower eight bits of the status register are affected. If the operand size is *word*, all 16 bits of the status register are affected and the instruction is *privileged*.

SHIFT AND ROTATE INSTRUCTIONS

The 68000 has four shift instructions and four rotate instructions. Table 3-11 summarizes these instructions and Fig. 3-14 shows how they operate. As Table 3-11 shows, each instruction has three vari-

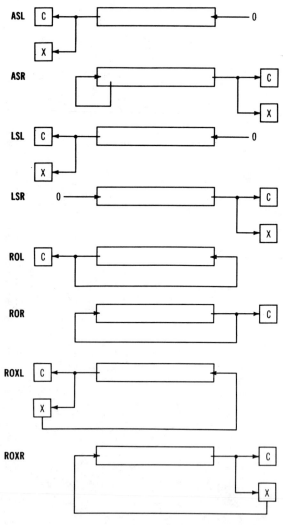

Fig. 3-14. How the shift and rotate instructions operate.

Table 3-11. Shift and Rotate Instructions

Mnemonic	Assembler Syntax	Operand Size	Source	Destination	X	N	Z	V	C
ASL	ASL Dx,Dy ASL #d,Dn ASL \<ea>	8, 16, 32 8, 16, 32 16	Dn (1) #d (2) 	Dn Dn Memory Alterable	*	*	*	*	*
ASR	ASR Dx,Dy ASR #d,Dn ASR \<ea>	8, 16, 32 8, 16, 32 16	Dn (1) #d (2) 	Dn Dn Memory Alterable	*	*	*	*	*
LSL	LSL Dx,Dy LSL #d,Dn LSL \<ea>	8, 16, 32 8, 16, 32 16	Dn (1) #d (2) 	Dn Dn Memory Alterable	*	*	*	0	*
LSR	LSR Dx,Dy LSR #d,Dn LSR \<ea>	8, 16, 32 8, 16, 32 16	Dn (1) #d (2) 	Dn Dn Memory Alterable	*	0	*	0	*
ROL	ROL Dx,Dy ROL #d,Dn ROL \<ea>	8, 16, 32 8, 16, 32 16	Dn (1) #d (2) 	Dn Dn Memory Alterable	—	*	*	0	*
ROR	ROR Dx,Dy ROR #d,Dn ROR \<ea>	8, 16, 32 8, 16, 32 16	Dn (1) #d (2) 	Dn Dn Memory Alterable	—	*	*	0	*
ROXL	ROXL Dx,Dy ROXL #d,Dn ROXL \<ea>	8, 16, 32 8, 16, 32 16	Dn (1) #d (2) 	Dn Dn Memory Alterable	*	*	*	0	*
ROXR	ROXR Dx,Dy ROXR #d,Dn ROXR \<ea>	8, 16, 32 8, 16, 32 16	Dn (1) #d (2) 	Dn Dn Memory Alterable	*	*	*	0	*

Notes: (1) Source data register contains the shift count. Count = 0 to 63, where 0 produces a count of 64.
(2) The data is the shift count, 1 to 8.

ations—two that operate on a data register (byte, word, or long word) and one that operates on memory (word only).

If the operation is being performed on a data register, the shift or rotate count may be specified as the contents of another data register (count = 0 to 63, where 0 produces a count of 64) or as an immediate value between 1 and 8. A word operand in memory may be shifted or rotated by only one bit position.

Shift Instructions

Signed numbers can be shifted using the *arithmetic shift left* (*ASL*) and *arithmetic shift right* (*ASR*) instructions. ASR preserves the sign of the operand, by replicating the sign bit throughout the shift operation. For ASL, the sign bit is not preserved, but overflow (V) is set if the sign bit is ever changed.

Unsigned numbers can be shifted using the *logical shift left* (*LSL*) and *logical shift right* (*LSR*) instructions. For all four instructions, bits shifted out of the operand are entered into the carry (C) and extend (X) condition code flags. In addition to their value in general data manipulation, the shift instructions can also be used as fast-executing multiply and divide instructions, because *each left shift multiplies an operand by two, and each right shift divides an operand by two!*

Rotate Instructions

In all four of the rotate instructions, bits displaced out of the operand are entered into carry (C). However, for the *rotate left* (*ROL*) and *rotate right* (*ROR*) instructions, the bit displaced out of one end of the operand is entered into the opposite end of the operand. With the *rotate with extend left* (*ROXL*) and *rotate with extend right* (*ROXR*) instructions, the bit displaced out of one end of the operand is entered into the extend (X) flag, as well as carry (C), and the previous value of X is entered into the opposite end of the operand.

The rotate with extend instructions provide a capability we have not had until now—the capability of accessing the three high-order bytes in a data register. You will recall that all byte operations take place on the low-order byte of a data register. How can you operate on the *second* byte (the "mid-lower" byte) of the register? You can do so by bringing that byte into the low-order position, using instruction ROL #8,Dn or ROR #8,Dn. In fact, the mid-upper and high-order bytes of a data register can be accessed, too; the mid-upper with a SWAP instruction, the high-order with an ROL.L #8, Dn instruction. The upper three bytes can be accessed *consecutively*, as in string operations, by executing three ROR.L #8,Dn instructions.

Speeding Up Shifts and Rotates on Memory

Since words in memory can be shifted or rotated only one bit position at a time, an n-bit shift or rotate will take at least "n" times as long as a 1-bit shift or rotate to execute. Table B-7 (in Appendix B) shows that shifting or rotating a word in memory takes 8+ cycles, where "+" represents the time required to calculate the effective address (see Table B-1). Therefore, a 2-bit shift will take $(2 \times 8+)$ cycles, a 3-bit shift will take $(3 \times 8+)$ cycles, and so on.

Referring to Table B-7 once again, you will note that shifting or rotating a *data register* by "n" bit positions takes only $(6 + 2n)$ cycles. Thus, a 1-bit shift will take 8 cycles, a 2-bit shift will take 10 cycles, and a 3-bit shift will take 12 cycles. Clearly, for some values of "n" you can save a considerable amount of execution time by reading a memory operand into a data register, shifting (or rotating) the register, then writing the result back into memory. This will require three instructions. Using Tables B-2 and B-7, we can calculate their total execution time as:

Instruction	Execution Time
MOVE <ea>,Dn	4+
ASL #n,Dn	$6 + 2n$
MOVE Dn,<ea>	4+
	Total time $= (14+) + 2n$

In summary, then, an n-bit shaft or rotate takes $(n \times 9+)$ cycles in memory and $[(14+) + 2n]$ cycles in a data register. At what point does it become advantageous to perform the operation in a data register? Well, a 1-bit shift should be performed in memory (8+ cycles in memory vs. 16+ cycles in a register), as should a 2-bit shift (16+ cycles in memory vs. 18+ cycles in a register). However, a 3-bit shift takes 24+ cycles in memory, but only 20+ cycles in a data register! The conclusion is this: *If you need to shift or rotate memory by three or more bit positions, the operation should be performed in a data register.*

BIT MANIPULATION INSTRUCTIONS

There are four instructions that test the state of a specified bit in a data register or a byte in memory. These instructions, summarized in Table 3-12, record the state of the specified bit in the zero (Z) condition code flag. If the bit $= 0$, then $Z = 1$; if the bit $= 1$, then $Z = 0$.

Three of the bit manipulation instructions also change the bit unconditionally, following the test, as follows:

Table 3-12. Bit Manipulation Instructions

| Mnemonic | Assembler Syntax | Operand Size | Allowable Addressing Modes | | Condition Codes |
			Source	Destination	X N Z V C
BTST	BTST Dn,<ea> BTST #d,<ea>	8, 32 8, 32	Dn #d	Data, Except Immediate Data, Except Immediate	– – * – – – – * – –
BSET	BSET Dn,<ea> BSET #d,<ea>	8, 32 8, 32	Dn #d	Data Alterable Data Alterable	– – * – – – – * – –
BCLR	BCLR Dn,<ea> BCLR #d,<ea>	8, 32 8, 32	Dn #d	Data Alterable Data Alterable	– – * – – – – * – –
BCHG	BCHG Dn,<ea> BCHG #d,<ea>	8, 32 8, 32	Dn #d	Data Alterable Data Alterable	– – * – – – – * – –

Instruction	Operation Performed on Bit
Bit test (*BTST*)	Bit is not affected.
Bit test and set (*BSET*)	Bit is set to logic 1.
Bit test and clear (*BCLR*)	Bit is cleared to logic 0.
Bit test and change (*BCHG*)	State of bit is reversed.

The bit number may be specified as the contents of a data register or as an immediate value. Either way, if a bit in a data register is being tested, the bit number may range from 0 to 31; if a bit in memory is being tested, the bit number may range from 0 to 7.

BINARY-CODED-DECIMAL (BCD) INSTRUCTIONS

Besides the binary arithmetic instructions we discussed earlier, the 68000 has three instructions that can be used to operate on binary-coded-decimal (BCD) values. All three of these BCD instructions (Table 3-13) operate only on byte-length data, where each byte contains two 4-bit BCD digits. Further, like the "extended" binary arithmetic instructions, the BCD instructions include the X bit in the operation and only change the Z bit if a nonzero result is generated. For this reason, you must remember to *initialize X = 0 and Z = 1 before the first BCD operation;* this can be most easily done with the instruction, MOVE #4,CCR.

Add BCD (ABCD) and Subtract BCD (SBCD) Instructions

The *add decimal with extend* (*ABCD*) and *subtract decimal with extend* (*SBCD*) instructions can perform a decimal add or decimal subtract on the low bytes of two data registers or on two bytes in memory. The ABCD and SBCD instructions can affect all five condition codes, as follows:

1. Carry (C) is set if ABCD generates a carry or SBCD generates a borrow; otherwise C is cleared.
2. Overflow (V) and negative (N) are *undefined* for both instructions.
3. Zero (Z) is cleared if the result is nonzero; otherwise Z is *unchanged.* For multibyte adds and subtracts, Z will thereby reflect the status of the entire operation, rather than just the status of the operation on the last bytes.
4. Extend (X) is set to the same state as the carry (C) bit.

Although the BCD instructions have certain similarities to the "extended" binary arithmetic instructions, the fact that the BCD instructions are restricted to *byte* operations means that programming BCD operations will be somewhat different than programming binary operations. For example, it will obviously take more instruc-

Table 3-13. Binary-Coded-Decimal (BCD) Instructions

Mnemonic	Assembler Syntax	Operand Size	Allowable Addressing Modes		Condition Codes
			Source	Destination	X N Z V C
ABCD	ABCD Dy,Dx ABCD −(Ay),−(Ax)	8 8	Dn −(An)	Dn −(An)	* U * U * * U * U *
SBCD	SBCD Dy,Dx SBCD −(Ay),−(Ax)	8 8	Dn −(An)	Dn −(An)	* U * U * * U * U *
NBCD	NBCD <ea>	8		Data Alterable	* U * U *

tions to add or subtract a multibyte BCD number than a multibyte binary number, because multibyte binary numbers can be added using combinations of the word or long-word forms.

Less evident is the fact that *data registers are, for the most part, limited to adding or subtracting single-byte (two-digit) BCD values!* It is difficult to add or subtract multibyte BCD values in a data register because to access the mid-order byte of a data register, that byte must be rotated into the low-order byte position. However, the rotate instructions (ROR, ROL, ROXR, and ROXL) always affect the Z bit, which *destroys* the intermediate zero status of your BCD operation. So unless you are prepared to save the CCR before and after rotate operations, you should conduct multibyte BCD operations in memory, rather than in data registers.

If you are adding or subtracting multibyte BCD operands in *memory*, these operands must be stored in high-to-low order, just like multibyte binary operands (refer back to Fig. 1-2). This ordering is self-evident when you consider that the ABCD and SBCD instructions can only use predecrement addressing to operate on memory. For example, the instruction sequence

```
MOVE   #4,CCR
ABCD   —(A0),—(A1)
ABCD   —(A0),—(A1)
ABCD   —(A0),—(A1)
ABCD   —(A0),—(A1)
```

will add two 8-digit BCD numbers (four bytes) in memory. Fig. 3-15 shows how these numbers are stored in memory, and how source

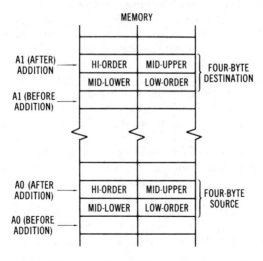

Fig. 3-15. Adding two 4-byte BCD numbers in memory.

pointer A0 and destination pointer A1 are altered by the addition sequence.

Negate BCD (NBCD) Instruction

The *negate decimal with extend* (*NBCD*) instruction subtracts the addressed byte operand (contents of a data register or memory) and the extend (X) bit from zero. If X is clear, it generates the 10s complement; if X is set, it generates the 9s complement.

PROGRAM CONTROL INSTRUCTIONS

As mentioned in our discussion of the compare instructions, program instructions are stored consecutively in memory, but programs rarely execute in exactly that order. All but the simplest programs include branches, jumps, and subroutine calls that alter the sequence in which the microprocessor executes the program. The program control instructions (Table 3-14) are the 68000 instructions that can transfer program execution from one part of memory to another. This group of instructions can be subdivided into three categories—conditional instructions, unconditional instructions, and return instructions.

Conditional Instructions

The first three entries in Table 3-14 represent the conditional instructions for the 68000. Their mode of operation differs depending on the state of one or more flags in the condition code register. Unlike the previous instruction tables in this chapter, Table 3-14 does not list the actual mnemonics for these instruction types, but instead presents their symbolic forms—Bcc, DBcc, and Scc—in which the "cc" suffix represents the condition being tested. The "cc" suffixes are summarized in Table 3-15. The Bcc instructions will not accept the always true (T) and always false (F) conditions, but all 16 of the conditions are testable by the DBcc and Scc instructions.

The 14 *branch conditionally* (*Bcc*) instructions are the same as those implemented on the Motorola 6800 microprocessor. With these instructions, if the selected test condition is met, program control is transferred to the instruction at location (PC) + displacement, otherwise execution continues with the next instruction in the program. The value in the PC is the Bcc instruction location plus two. Displacement is a 2s-complement integer count of the number of bytes between the PC value and the location of the label. If your operand is a label (as it normally is), the assembler will calculate the displacement. If the instruction is of the form

BNE   *+10

Table 3-14. Program Control Instructions

Mnemonic	Assembler Syntax	Operand Size	Allowable Addressing Modes Source	Destination	Condition Codes X N Z V C
Conditional Instructions					
Bcc	Bcc <label>	8, 16	If cc, then PC + d → PC		– – – – –
DBcc	DBcc Dn,<label>	16	If cc, then Dn – 1 → Dn; if Dn ≠ –1, then PC + d → PC		– – – – –
Scc	Scc <ea>	8	If cc, then 1s → (ea); otherwise 0s → (ea)	Data Alterable	– – – – –
Unconditional Instructions					
BRA	BRA <label>	8, 16	PC + d → PC		– – – – –
BSR	BSR <label>	8, 16	PC → –(SP); PC + d → PC		– – – – –
JMP	JMP <ea>		<ea> → PC	Control	– – – – –
JSR	JSR <ea>		PC → –(SP); <ea> → PC	Control	– – – – –
Return Instructions					
RTR	RTR		(SP) + → CCR; (SP) + → PC		* * * * *
RTS	RTS		(SP) + → PC		– – – – –

Table 3-15. Conditional Tests

Suffix "cc"	Condition	True if
EQ	Equal to.	$Z = 1$
NE	Not equal to.	$Z = 0$
MI	Minus.	$N = 1$
PL	Plus.	$N = 0$
*GT	Greater than.	$Z \wedge (N \veebar V) = 0$
*LT	Less than.	$N \veebar V = 1$
*GE	Greater than or equal to.	$N \veebar V = 0$
*LE	Less than or equal to.	$Z \vee (N \veebar V) = 1$
HI	Higher than.	$C \wedge Z = 0$
LS	Lower than or same as.	$C \vee Z = 1$
CS	Carry set.	$C = 1$
CC	Carry clear.	$C = 0$
*VS	Overflow.	$V = 1$
*VC	No overflow.	$V = 0$
T	Always true.	
F	Always false.	

*Two's-complement arithmetic.

Symbols: $\wedge$ = Logical AND
$\vee$ = Logical Inclusive-OR
$\veebar$ = Logical Exclusive-OR

your operand specifies the displacement value (decimal 10, in this case), in bytes.

The Bcc instructions can be one or two words long. If you use the form, *Bcc.S,* the assembler will produce a one-word instruction with an 8-bit, signed relative displacement embedded in the op-word. With this form, the branch "target" instruction can be up to 126 bytes higher in memory, or 128 bytes lower in memory, than the Bcc op-word plus two. If you omit the .S suffix, the assembler will produce a two-word instruction with a 16-bit signed, relative displacement in the second word. With this form, the branch target can be up to 32,766 bytes higher in memory, or 32,768 bytes lower in memory, than the Bcc op-word plus two (the displacement word). Thus, *if your Bcc instruction starts at location N, the form Bcc.S provides branch limits of N + $80 and N − $7E, whereas the form Bcc provides branch limits of N + $8000 and N − $7FFE.*

Here are some examples of conditional branch instructions:

1. The sequence

```
ADD   D0,D1
BCS   TOOBIG
```

branches to label TOOBIG if the add operation produces a carry out of the low word of D1.

2. The sequence

```
SUB   D0,D1
BEQ   ZERO
```

branches to label ZERO if the subtract operation produces a zero result in the low word of D1.

3. To merely *check* whether the low words of D0 and D1 are identical, without affecting either register, you could use a compare instruction, rather than a subtract instruction. The sequence

```
CMP   D0,D1
BEQ   ZERO
```

branches to label ZERO if the low words in D0 and D1 are the same.

4. Some tests require you to choose between two different Bcc instructions, based on whether you are testing the result of an operation on unsigned numbers or signed numbers. To illustrate this, suppose you want to branch to label D1MORE if the low word in D1 is higher-valued than the low word in D0. The sequence

```
CMP   D0,D1
BHI   D1MORE
```

would be used if the contents of D0 and D1 are *unsigned,* whereas

```
CMP   D0,D1
BGT   D1MORE
```

would be used if the contents of D0 and D1 are *signed.*

The conditional branch instructions are often used as the last instruction in a *loop,* to terminate the loop when a certain "cc" condition has occurred. Example 3-1 illustrates this usage with a program that searches a selected portion of memory for a specified word value. The starting and ending addresses in memory are in A0 and A1, respectively, and the search value is in the low word of D0.

This program enters a loop in which it compares the value pointed to by A0 with the value in D0. If the search value is found, BEQ.S DONE branches the 68000 to DONE, where A0 is decremented. (This is necessary because A0 was postincremented, and ends up pointing one word *past* the compare location.) If no match occurs, CMPA.L A0,A1 tests for out-of-range, and returns to LOOP if A0 is less than or equal to A1 (true if $C = 0$, thus we use the instruction BCC.S as the terminator).

Example 3-1. Searching for a Word Value in Memory

```
*  THIS PROGRAM CHECKS WHETHER A SELECTED PORTION OF
*  MEMORY CONTAINS A SPECIFIED WORD VALUE. UPON ENTRY,
*  A0 AND A1 MUST HOLD THE STARTING AND ENDING ADDRESSES
*  TO BE SEARCHED, AND THE LOW WORD OF D0 MUST HOLD THE
*  VALUE BEING TESTED.
*  UPON COMPLETION, IF THE VALUE IS FOUND, Z = 1 AND A0 HOLDS
*  THE ADDRESS OF THE MATCHING WORD LOCATION.
*  IF THE VALUE IS NOT FOUND, Z = 0 AND A0 = A1.
           ORG      $2000
LOOP       CMP      (A0)+,D0        VALUE FOUND?
           BEQ.S    DONE              YES.    EXIT.
           CMPA.L   A0,A1           END OF MEMORY?
           BCC.S    LOOP              NO.    KEEP CHECKING
DONE       SUBA.L   #2,A0           DONE.    ADJUST A0.
```

Readers who have programmed any of the popular 8-bit micro-processors are well aware that repetitive loops are commonly governed by some kind of decrementing counter, usually a register. After each execution of the loop, the counter is decremented by one, and the loop is terminated when the count reaches zero, or underflows through zero. This process has always required at least two instructions—a decrement instruction and a conditional branch instruction. You will be pleased to know that with the 68000 these tasks are combined in a set of *test, decrement, and branch* (*DBcc*) instructions.

When a DBcc instruction is executed, the 68000 interrogates the condition codes to find out whether the specified condition (any of the 16 conditions in Table 3-15) has been met. If the condition is met, program execution "falls through" to the next instruction. If the condition is not met, however, the 68000 decrements the low word of a specified data register by one; if the data register has been decremented to -1, program execution "falls through" to the next instruction, otherwise the 68000 branches to the labeled location in memory. Do you understand that? Even if you *think* you do, read this paragraph again to be sure, then study Fig. 3-16 to embed it in your mind.

At this point, you should realize that a single DBcc instruction, such as

```
    DBNE   D0,LOOP
```

performs exactly the same function as a three-instruction sequence, such as

```
    BNE.S   NEXT
    SUBQ    #1,D0
    BPL     LOOP
```

And, besides eliminating two lines of source code, a DBcc instruction occupies two less words in memory than its equivalent three-instruction sequence (two words for DBcc vs. four words for the

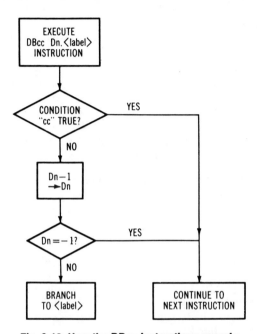

Fig. 3-16. How the DBcc instructions operate.

sequence). Also, a DBcc instruction will usually execute about twice as fast as the three-instruction sequence. A DBcc instruction executes in 10 cycles if the branch is taken, and executes in 12 cycles if the branch is not taken. In contrast, the three-instruction sequence executes in 22 cycles if the branch is taken, and executes in either 10 cycles or 24 cycles if the branch is not taken (depending on whether the "cc" condition is met or the counter decrements to −1).

Do not make the mistake of assuming that the DBcc instructions are just fancy Bcc-with-counter instructions, however. There are several important differences between the DBcc instructions and the Bcc instructions, and you should keep them in mind. These differences are:

1. The DBcc instructions work in reverse of the Bcc instructions. That is, the Bcc instructions are branch-on-condition instruc-

tions, whereas the DBcc instructions are *don't-branch-on-con-dition* instructions. With the DBcc instructions, execution falls through if the condition is *true*, rather than false.

2. With the DBcc instructions, there are two paths out of the loop. These instructions not only fall through if the condition is true, but also fall through if the counter reaches −1. Therefore, the DBcc instructions can also be characterized as *do-until-equal* (to −1) instructions.

3. The Bcc instructions may branch forward or backward in a program, but the DBcc instructions may only branch backward, to a lower address in memory. The branch label must be no more than 32,766 bytes ($7FFE) lower in memory than the DBcc instruction.

4. The Bcc instructions can be one- or two-word instructions, but the DBcc instructions are always two-word instructions. Therefore, because the DBcc instructions have no "short" variant, the suffixed form, DBcc.S, is illegal.

As mentioned earlier, the DBcc instructions can be used with all 16 "cc" suffixes, including the suffixes T (always true) and F (never true). The T suffix provides the instruction form

```
DBT   Dn,<label>
```

which *always* fails (always falls through to the next instruction); it is nothing more than a two-word no-op instruction. The more-useful F suffix allows you to omit the condition test and base the branch/no-branch decision solely on the state of the counter. Example 3-2 shows how the DBF instruction can be used to move a block of data in memory. Note that because the counter must decrement to −1, rather than zero, counter D0 must be initialized with the long word count *minus one*. If eight long words are to be moved, D0 must initially contain the value $0007.

Example 3-2. A Block Move Program

```
*   THIS PROGRAM COPIES A BLOCK OF DATA FROM ONE PART OF
*   MEMORY TO ANOTHER. D0 CONTAINS THE NUMBER OF LONG
*   WORDS, MINUS 1, TO BE MOVED. A0 POINTS TO THE SOURCE AND
*   A1 POINTS TO THE DESTINATION.
*
          ORG     $2000
BLKMOV    MOVE.L  (A0)+,(A1)+      MOVE A LONG WORD.
          DBF     D0,BLKMOV        LOOP UNTIL D0 + 1 BLOCKS
                                   ARE MOVED.
          END
```

Incidentally, this program should impress programmers who have programmed a block move on an 8-bit microprocessor, because it involves only two instructions and occupies only three words in memory. It is fast, too. The MOVE.L instruction executes in 20 cycles and the DBF instruction executes in either 10 cycles (if the branch is taken) or 14 cycles (if the branch is not taken). Therefore, moving N long words takes $(30N + 4)$ cycles. Using this relationship, moving 100 long words will take just 3004 cycles, or 375.5 μs at 8 MHz!

The only conditional instructions that have not yet been discussed are the *set according to condition* (*Scc*) instructions. These instructions test the specified "cc" condition (any of those in Table 3-15), and set the addressed byte to all 1s if the condition is met and to all 0s if it is not met. Since these instructions affect no condition code flags, they are intended to establish indicators that can be tested later, rather than tested immediately.

An ASCII String Search Subroutine

Before moving on, it might be instructive to discuss a more ambitious programming example, one that has a good mix of the instructions we have discussed so far. Example 3-3 shows the program we will look at here, a subroutine that checks for the first occurrence of a string of ASCII characters (called the "test string") in another ASCII string (the "main string") in memory. This task is not only of academic interest; it is quite common in text processing applications.

In Example 3-3, we have assigned address register A0 to point to the main string (the string to be searched) and A1 to point to the test string (the string for which we are searching). In a text processing application, the text string is very likely to be a word, a phrase, a name, a telephone number, or some other item that we wish to access for a subsequent operation. The only other parameter that needs to be specified is the length of the test string; this count, in bytes, is entered in the low word of data register D0.

The result of the search is returned in address register A2. If the test string is in the main string, A2 will contain its starting address. If the test string is not in the main string, A2 will contain zero.

The ASEARCH subroutine in Example 3-3 begins by moving two data registers and two address registers onto the system stack, so that they will be intact upon return from the subroutine. The remainder of the subroutine is comprised of two parts. In the first part, the 68000 reads the first character of the test string into data register D3, and then enters a loop (CHKEND) in which this character is compared to each byte in the main string. The character in D3 is also compared to the asterisk terminator, to detect a nonmatch if the entire main string has been searched.

If the first character of the test string is encountered somewhere

Example 3-3. An ASCII String Search Subroutine

```
*   THIS SUBROUTINE SEARCHES AN ASCII STRING IN MEMORY (CALLED
*   THE "MAIN STRING") FOR THE PRESENCE OF ANOTHER ASCII
*   STRING (CALLED THE "TEST STRING"). THE MAIN STRING IS
*   TERMINATED BY AN ASCII ASTERISK (*) CHARACTER.
*   UPON CALLING THE SUBROUTINE, THE STARTING ADDRESSES OF
*   THE MAIN AND TEST STRINGS MUST BE IN ADDRESS REGISTERS A0
*   AND A1, RESPECTIVELY, AND THE LENGTH OF THE TEST STRING,
*   IN BYTES, MUST BE IN DATA REGISTER D0.
*   THE RESULT OF THE SEARCH IS RETURNED IN ADDRESS REGISTER
*   A2. IF THE TEST STRING IS FOUND, A2 WILL HOLD ITS STARTING
*   ADDRESS WITHIN THE MAIN STRING. IF THE TEST STRING IS NOT
*   FOUND, A2 WILL BE ZERO. A2 IS THE ONLY REGISTER AFFECTED.
*
                ORG       $1000
ASEARCH MOVEM     D1/D3,−(SP)     SAVE DATA REGS AND
                MOVEM.L   A0/A3,−(SP)     ADDRESS REGS ON STACK.
*
*   SEARCH FOR FIRST CHARACTER OF TEST STRING.
*
                MOVE.B    (A1),D3         READ FIRST TEST CHAR INTO
                                          D3.
FIRST   SUBA.L    A2,A2           MAKE A2 = 0 TO START.
CHKEND  CMPI.B    #'*',(A0)       END OF MAIN STRING?
                BEQ.S     RETRN           YES.    GO EXIT.
                CMP.B     (A0)+,D3        MAIN CHAR = TEST CHAR?
                BNE.S     CHKEND          NO.     KEEP SEARCHING.
*
*   FIRST TEST CHAR FOUND, COMPARE REMAINDER OF TEST STRING.
*
                MOVE      D0,D1           MOVE TEST STRING COUNT
                                          INTO D1.
                SUBQ      #2,D1           D1 = COUNT − 2.
                MOVEA.L   A1,A3           MOVE TEST STRING ADDR
                                          INTO A3.
                ADDQ.L    #1,A3           A3 POINTS TO SECOND TEST
                                          CHAR.
                MOVEA.L   A0,A2           A2 = CURRENT MAIN STRING
                                          ADDR.
                SUBQ.L    #1,A2
LOOP    CMPI.B    #'*',(A2)       END OF MAIN STRING?
                BEQ.S     RETRN           IF SO, RETURN.
                CMPM.B    (A3)+,(A2)+     MAIN CHAR = TEST CHAR?
                BNE.S     FIRST           NO.     RESUME THE SEARCH.
                DBF       D1,LOOP         YES.    CONTINUE
                                          COMPARISON.
                SUBQ.L    #A1,A0          TEST STRING FOUND
                MOVEA,L   A0,A2           PUT START ADDR. IN A2
RETRN   MOVEM.L   (SP)+,A0/A3     RESTORE REGISTERS.
                MOVEM     (SP)+,D1/D3
                RTS
                END
```

in the main string, the 68000 drops down to the lower part of the subroutine, in which the remaining test string characters are compared with the main string. To make this comparison, we take the byte count of the test string and put it into D1, then subtract *two*, because the DBF instruction checks for −1, rather than 0, and because we are processing the *second* byte of the test string, rather than the first byte. At this point, the potential main string matching address is recorded in A2. The LOOP portion of this part of the subroutine compares the rest of the test string, and branches back to FIRST if the *entire* test string has not been located. The subroutine ends with two MOVEM instructions, to retrieve the saved registers from the stack, and an RTS instruction, which fetches the return address and thereby transfers control back to the calling program.

Unconditional (Jump and Branch) and Return Instructions

As with the earlier, 8-bit 6800 microprocessor, Motorola has provided the 68000 with jump and subroutine call instructions in both a long form and a short form. The jump instructions are called *jump* (*JMP*) and *branch always* (*BRA*). The subroutine call instructions are called *jump to subroutine* (*JSR*) and *branch to subroutine* (*BSR*).

The long forms of these instructions, JMP and JSR, can be used to transfer program control anywhere in the 16M-byte memory map, whereas the short forms, BRA and BSR, are limited to some displacement relative to the branch instruction. Like the conditional branch (Bcc) instructions, BRA and BSR can be used with either an 8-bit displacement or a 16-bit displacement, where the shorter, 8-bit displacement is selected by appending a .S suffix to the instruction mnemonic (BRA.S or BSR.S).

All four of these instructions cause program control to be transferred by loading a new address into the program counter. However, the subroutine call instructions, JSR and BSR, also provide a way for the 68000 to return to the instruction following JSR or BSR, by pushing the address of this instruction onto the stack. Unlike all other stack operations, the JSR and BSR instructions push the high word of the address onto the stack first, causing the return address to be stored in low-word/high-word order.

The *return from subroutine* (*RTS*) instruction retrieves the return address from the system stack, and loads it into the program counter. Therefore, RTS must be the last instruction to be executed in any subroutine.

To illustrate the subroutine call and return operations, suppose a program contains these two instructions:

Program Counter	Instruction	Comment
$A2000	JSR $4EFE	Subroutine call.
$A2004	MOVE D0,D1	Next in-line instruction.

Fig. 3-17 shows the program counter and system stack at three points in the program—before the JSR instruction is executed (3-17A), after the JSR instruction is executed (3-17B), and after the RTS instruction in the subroutine is executed (3-17C).

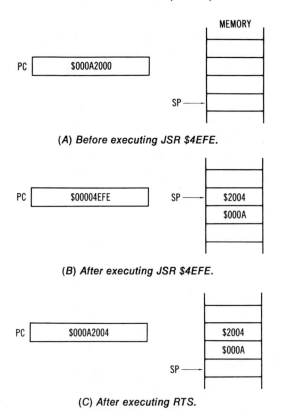

(A) Before executing JSR $4EFE.

(B) After executing JSR $4EFE.

(C) After executing RTS.

Fig. 3-17. Subroutine call and return operations.

In our earlier discussion of the data movement instructions, we noted that the instruction form

MOVEM   <list>, −(SP)

is useful for saving selected registers on the stack while a subroutine is being executed in order to make that subroutine *reentrant* (that is, interruptible). There are many applications in which the condition codes must also be saved, so that the *context* of the program is preserved during execution of a subroutine. This too is possible, with another previously discussed instruction:

```
MOVE   SR,-(SP)
```

Of course, before returning from the subroutine, the saved values must be pulled off of the stack. This can be done with the instruction sequence

```
MOVEM  (SP)+,<list>
MOVE   (SP)+,CCR
```

However, the 68000 includes a special version of the RTS instruction, called *return and restore condition codes* (*RTR*), which pulls the condition code register as well as a return address from the stack. Thus, RTR eliminates the need for a pull-into-CCR instruction at the end of a subroutine. Example 3-4 shows how the condition codes and certain working registers can be preserved during a subroutine, and uses RTR (rather than RTS) to initiate the return.

Example 3-4. Preserving Condition Codes and Registers During a Subroutine

```
      JSR      SUBR              CALL SUBROUTINE.
      MOVE     D0,D1             NEXT IN-LINE INSTRUCTION.
      .
      .
      .
SUBR  MOVE     SR,-(SP)          SAVE STATUS REGISTER ON
                                 STACK.
      MOVEM.L  D3-D5/A1,-(SP)    SAVE REGISTERS ON STACK.
      .                          ⎱(Other subroutine
      .                          ⎰ instructions.)
      .
      MOVEM.L  (SP)+,A1/D3-D5    RESTORE REGISTERS.
      RTR                        RETURN AND RESTORE
                                 CONDITION CODES.
```

THE LINK AND UNLINK INSTRUCTIONS

The *link* (*LINK*) and *unlink* (*UNLK*) instructions (Table 3-16) are used to allocate and deallocate data areas on the system stack for nested subroutines, linked lists, and other procedures. Following a procedure call (e.g., a call to a nested subroutine), LINK sets up an address register pointer to the data area and moves the stack pointer down in memory, just past the data area. Upon completion of the subroutine, UNLK reverses this sequence, thereby restoring the stack pointer and address registers to their original, pre-LINK values.

The LINK instruction has two operands, an address register, and a 16-bit signed displacement. While the nested subroutine is being

Table 3-16. Link and Unlink Instructions

| Mnemonic | Assembler Syntax | Operand Size | Allowable Addressing Modes | | Condition Codes |
			Source	Destination	X N Z V C
LINK	LINK An,#d	Unsized	An		– – – – –
UNLK	UNLK An	Unsized		An	– – – – –

executed, the address register holds the starting address of that subroutine's stack data area; this address register is referred to as the *frame pointer* (*FP*). The displacement value specifies the amount of stack space, in bytes, to be allocated to the data area. When LINK is executed, the 68000 pushes the 32-bit contents of the FP onto the stack, decrements the stack pointer (SP) by four, loads that stack pointer value into the FP, then adds the displacement value to the stack pointer. Note that the displacement value has two characteristics—(1) because the stack pointer value must always be even, the displacement value must be an even number, and (2) because the displacement value is *added* to the stack pointer, it should be negative for most applications.

After LINK has been executed, the address register holds the starting address of the data area, and the stack pointer points to the location that follows the data area. At this point, the subroutine can easily use the data area, by accessing it with the address register indirect with displacement (or index) addressing mode. Figs. 3-18A and 3-18B show the system stack after a subroutine call and after LINK, respectively.

Fig. 3-18C shows the stack pointer addressing an even lower memory location, due to some subroutine push operations. This illustration is included to demonstrate that the UNLK instruction will affect an orderly return (shown in Fig. 3-18D), *regardless* of how the stack pointer has been altered in the interim. The UNLK instruction, which is normally executed just before returning from the subroutine, simply loads the stack pointer from the FP register, then reinitializes the FP by pulling its original value from the top of the stack. Following UNLK, both the FP and the SP contain the values they held prior to LINK.

SYSTEM CONTROL INSTRUCTIONS

Table 3-17 summarizes the instructions that the manufacturers' literature identifies as system control instructions. Note that there are three types of system control instructions—privileged instructions, trap-generating instructions, and status register instructions. All of the status register instructions, and most of the privileged instructions, have been discussed previously in this chapter, so we will not repeat their descriptions here.

Privileged Instructions

As you know, privileged instructions are instructions that can be executed only when the 68000 is in the supervisor state. Any attempt to execute one of the privileged instructions from the user state will cause an exception to occur (discussed in Chapter 7).

The *reset external devices* (*RESET*) instruction causes the $\overline{\text{RESET}}$ pin of the 68000 MPU chip to be asserted for 124 clock cycles. This line is usually wired to all external devices in the system, and will cause those devices to be reset, without affecting the processor. The RESET instruction can be used to recover from catastrophic system failures.

As we shall learn in Chapter 7, interrupts and other exceptions cause the 16-bit status register and the 32-bit program counter to be pushed onto the supervisor stack, to preserve the state of the program when the exception occurred. The *return from exception* (*RTE*) instruction pulls these values from the stack upon completion of the exception service routine. Thus, RTE is to exception service routines what RTS (and even more so, RTR) is to subroutines!

Stop program execution (*STOP*) loads an immediate value into the status register, and then causes the 68000 microprocessor to stop

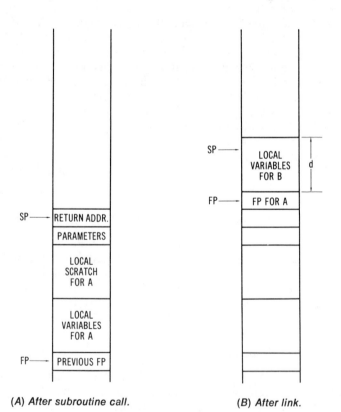

(A) After subroutine call.   (B) After link.

Fig. 3-18. Link and unlink instructions allocate and deallocate

fetching and executing instructions. Execution will not resume until the 68000 receives an interrupt of sufficiently high priority, or an external reset. In practice, STOP is often used to change the interrupt mask, and can be considered an enhancement of the wait for interrupt (WAI) instruction of the 8-bit 6800 microprocessor.

Trap-Generating Instructions

Traps, like interrupts, cause the program counter to be loaded with one of several addresses in memory, based on a "vector number" supplied to the microprocessor. However, with interrupts, all vector numbers are supplied by an external device, but with traps, all vector numbers are furnished internally. As described later (in Chapter 7), traps will be automatically generated by certain error conditions, but they can also be generated under software control, with any of the three instructions described here.

The *trap* (*TRAP*) instruction initiates a trap operation uncondi-

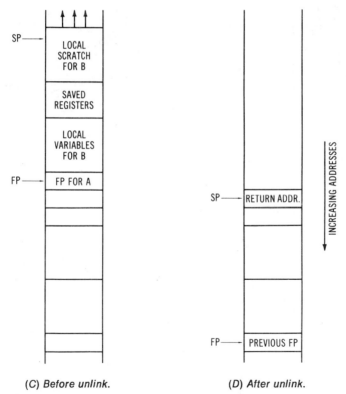

(C) *Before unlink.*   (D) *After unlink.*

local storage for nested subroutine and procedure calls.

Table 3-17. System Control Instructions

Mnemonic	Assembler Syntax	Operand Size	Allowable Addressing Modes Source	Allowable Addressing Modes Destination	Condition Codes X N Z V C
Privileged Instructions					
RESET	RESET				– – – – –
RTE	RTE	16	(SP)+ → SP; (SP)+ → PC		* * * * *
STOP	STOP #d	16	#d → SR, then STOP		* * * * *
ANDI	ANDI #d,SR (1)	16	#d	SR	* * * 0 0
EORI	EORI #d,SR (1)	16	#d	SR	* * * 0 0
ORI	ORI #d,SR (1)	16	#d	SR	* * * 0 0
MOVE	MOVE <ea>,SR (2)	16	Data	SR	* * * * *
	MOVE USP,An (2)	32	USP	An	– – – – –
	MOVE An,USP (2)	32	An	USP	– – – – –
Trap-Generating Instructions					
TRAP	TRAP #<vector>		PC → -(SP); SR → -(SP); #<vector> → PC		– – – – –
TRAPV	TRAPV		If V = 1, then TRAP		– – – – –
CHK	CHK <ea>,Dn	16	If Dn < 0 or Dn > (ea), then TRAP	Data	– * U U U
Status Register Instructions					
ANDI	ANDI.B #d,SR (1)	8	#d	CCR	* * * 0 0
EORI	EORI.B #d,SR (1)	8	#d	CCR	* * * 0 0
ORI	ORI.B #d,SR (1)	8	#d	CCR	* * * 0 0
MOVE	MOVE <ea>,CCR (2)	16	Data	CCR	* * * * *
	MOVE SR,<ea> (2)	16	SR	Data Alterable	– – – – –

Notes: (1) Described with logical instruction group; Table 3-10 and accompanying text.
(2) Described with data movement instruction group; Table 3-7 and accompanying text.

tionally, and supplies a vector number (0 to 15) in the operand. Thus, TRAP can be used to generate any of 16 different software interrupts.

The *trap on overflow* (*TRAPV*) instruction tests the overflow (V) flag in the condition code register, and traps to a specific memory location if V is set. If V is clear, execution continues with the next sequential instruction.

The third trap-generating instruction, *check register against bounds* (*CHK*), also operates conditionally. This instruction checks the contents of a data register, and traps to a specific memory location if the register contains a value that is less than zero or greater than an addressed "upper bound" operand. This kind of testing helps keep data arrays within their allotted bounds.

SUMMARY

In this chapter, we studied each of the 14 addressing modes and learned what each is used for. These 14 modes provide all of the basic addressing capabilities of earlier, 8-bit microprocessors, plus a variety of valuable options. The ability to postincrement or predecrement an address, for example, gives the programmer a fast, efficient way to operate on strings and tables. Further, the inclusion of modes with offsets as well as indexes makes arrays readily accessible.

This chapter also covered each of the 56 instructions that are microcoded into the 68000. As with the addressing modes, many of the instructions are familiar to readers who have programmed the 6800 or other 8-bit microprocessors, but even these instructions are offered in easier-to-use, enhanced versions. For example, Motorola took the load, store, register-transfer, push and pull operations, and combined them in a single instruction type, called MOVE. Other frequently encountered operations that normally require several lines of code were also combined into single instructions. Therefore, in the 68000 we see a test-decrement-and-branch instruction (DBcc), a multi-increment instruction (ADDQ) and a multidecrement instruction (SUBQ).

Focusing special attention on support of high-level languages, the Motorola designers also provided unique instructions for boundary checking (CHK) and for allocating and deallocating stack space for local variables during procedure calls (LINK and UNLK). Further, the immense addressing range of the 68000 (16M bytes) is intended to support multitasking and multiprocessing, so a memory allocation instruction (TAS) is also provided.

With this fundamental understanding and appreciation for the programming capabilities of the 68000, let us move on to a discussion of some of the ways these capabilities can be applied. The next two chapters cover two types of common programming applications —mathematical operations, and processing lists and look-up tables.

BIBLIOGRAPHY

1. *MC68000 16-Bit Microprocessor User's Manual.* Austin, TX: Motorola Semiconductor, Inc., 1980. (See Chapters 2 and 3, and Appendixes B and D.)

2. Starnes, T. W. "Compact Instructions Give the MC68000 Power While Simplifying Its Operation." *Electronic Design,* September 27, 1979, pp. 70–74.

3. ———. "Powerful Instructions and Flexible Registers of the MC68000 Make Programming Easy." *Electronic Design,* April 26, 1980, pp. 171–176.

CHAPTER 4

Mathematical Routines

Readers who have gained their education in microcomputer programming through any of the conventional 4-bit or 8-bit microprocessors are undoubtedly impressed with the arithmetic potential of the 68000. For instance, the very fact that the 68000 has built-in multiply and divide instructions, in both signed and unsigned versions, means hours (or days, or weeks) of time that would be used developing multiplication and division subroutines can be redirected to more stimulating activities, such as playing tennis.

In this chapter, we will build upon the potential offered by the multiply and divide instructions in developing some programs that tackle somewhat tougher math problems. We will begin with programs to perform 32-bit × 32-bit multiply operations on both signed and unsigned numbers. From there, the discussion will deal with how to handle overflow situations in divide operations, then finish up with a program that calculates the square root of a 32-bit number.

MULTIPLICATION

In Chapter 3, we studied the two multiplication instructions, signed multiply (MULS) and unsigned multiply (MULU), and noted that they operate only on word-length (16-bit) values. How difficult is it to multiply values that are 32 bits in length, or longer? It is not very difficult at all, as we shall see. As anyone who has written a multiplication program for an 8-bit microprocessor can tell you, just *having* a multiplication instruction, of any length, makes up for any inconvenience required to extend its capabilities.

Unsigned 32-Bit × 32-Bit Multiply

Multiprecision unsigned numbers can be multiplied by using the MULU instruction to generate a series of 32-bit *cross products*, which are summed to form the final product. This method is the same one we used to multiply decimal numbers by hand with pencil and paper. As you will recall (in these days of hand calculators, it may be a little hazy), you write the multiplicand with the multiplier below it and perform a series of multiplications—one for each digit in the multiplier. Each partial product is written directly below its multiplier digit, causing it to be offset one digit position to the left of its predecessor. When all of the partial products have been calculated, they are added to produce the final product.

For example, the multiplication of 124 by 103 looks like this:

124	Multiplicand
× 103	Multiplier
372	Partial Product #1
000	Partial Product #2
124	Partial Product #3
12772	Final Product

The partial products are offset from each other to account for the *decimal weights* of the multiplier digits. In this example, the 3 is a "ones" digit, the 0 is a "tens" digit and the 1 is a "hundreds" digit. Therefore, the example could be written in this form:

$$103 \times 124 = (3 \times 124) + (0 \times 124) + (100 \times 124)$$

or

$$103 \times 124 = (3 \times 10^0 \times 124) + (0 \times 10^1 \times 124) + (1 \times 10^2 \times 124)$$

In this section, we will develop a subroutine to multiply two 32-bit unsigned numbers, which yields a 64-bit unsigned product. In the absence of a multiply instruction, this would involve 32 multiplication operations, one for each bit in the multiplier. Fortunately, however, the 68000 has an instruction that multiplies 16-bit unsigned numbers directly. This instruction, MULU, allows us to view the 32-bit multiplier and multiplicand as two-digit numbers, where each digit is 16 bits long. Thus, just *four* multiplications will be required to generate the 64-bit product.

Fig. 4-1 contains a symbolic representation of the multiplier (digits AB) and the multiplicand (digits CD), and illustrates how the partial products are derived and how they must be aligned in order to calculate the 64-bit final product. The circled numbers in Fig. 4-1 identify the four 16-bit additions that must be made in calculating the product.

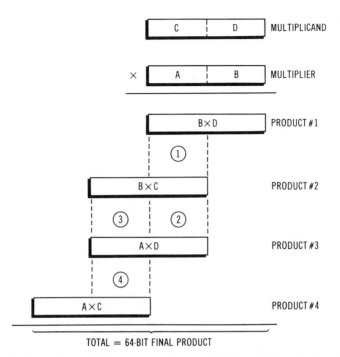

Fig. 4-1. Generating a 64-bit product with four 16-bit by 16-bit multiplications.

Using Fig. 4-1 as a guide, it is possible to develop a subroutine that can multiply two 32-bit unsigned numbers. Example 4-1 shows such a subroutine, labeled MULU32, in which the multiplier and multiplicand are entered in data registers D2 and D1, respectively. The 64-bit unsigned product is returned in these same registers, D1 (low 32 bits) and D2 (high 32 bits).

The operations performed by the MULU32 subroutine are fairly straightforward if you refer to Fig. 4-1 as you look at the instructions and their comments. The MULU32 subroutine begins by saving the contents of three general-purpose registers (D3, D4, and D5) on the stack, then makes a copy of the multiplicand in both D3 and D4. The next instruction swaps the 16-bit halves of D4. This swap is a necessary preparation for generating the second and fourth partial products (see Fig. 4-1), which involve the *high-order word of the multiplicand*. This swap is necessary because the unsigned multiply (MULU) instruction can only multiply the *low-order words* of two data registers. This particular SWAP instruction is the first of several in the subroutine. A SWAP D5 instruction is used two instructions later to prepare for generating the third and fourth partial products.

Example 4-1. A 32-Bit × 32-Bit Unsigned Multiply Subroutine

```
*   THIS SUBROUTINE MULTIPLIES TWO 32-BIT UNSIGNED NUMBERS, TO
*   GENERATE A 64-BIT PRODUCT. ENTER WITH MULTIPLIER IN D2 AND
*   MULTIPLICAND IN D1. THE PRODUCT IS RETURNED IN D1 (LOW 32
*   BITS) AND D2 (HIGH 32 BITS).
*
            ORG       $1000
MULU32      MOVEM.L   D3–D5,–(SP)     SAVE SCRATCH REGISTERS.
            MOVE.L    D1,D3           COPY   MULTIPLICAND INTO D3
            MOVE.L    D1,D4           AND INTO D4,
            SWAP      D4              IN SWAPPED FORM.
            MOVE.L    D2,D5           COPY MULTIPLIER INTO D5,
            SWAP      D5              IN SWAPPED FORM.
            MULU      D2,D1           PARTIAL PRODUCT #1.
            MULU      D4,D2                           #2.
            MULU      D5,D3                           #3.
            MULU      D5,D4                           #4.
            SWAP      D1              SUM1 = PP #2 LOW +
            ADD       D2,D1           PP #1 HIGH.
            CLR.L     D5
            ADDX.L    D5,D4           PROPAGATE CARRY INTO PP #4.
            ADD       D3,D1           SUM2 = SUM1 + PP #3 LOW.
            ADDX.L    D5,D4           PROPAGATE CARRY INTO PP #4.
            SWAP      D1              PUT LOW PROD. IN CORRECT
                                      ORDER.
            CLR       D2              PREPARE FOR SUM3.
            SWAP      D2
            CLR       D3
            SWAP      D3
            ADD.L     D3,D2           SUM3 = PP #2 HIGH + PP #3
                                      HIGH.
            ADD.L     D4,D2           SUM4 = SUM3 + PP #4.
            MOVEM.L   (SP)+,D3–D5     RESTORE REGISTERS.
            RTS
            END
```

Now, with all of the multiplication operands in place, the actual multiplications can be performed. The subroutine has four consecutive MULU instructions, which leave partial products #1, #2, #3, and #4 in data registers D1, D2, D3, and D4, respectively. The only remaining task is to sum up the partial products, with respect to their weights, to obtain the 64-bit final product.

The circled numbers in Fig. 4-1 identify the four pairs of 16-bit words that must be added, in the order in which the MULU32 subroutine adds them. In Example 4-1, the four consecutive MULU instructions are followed by a SWAP instruction, which swaps the word contents of D1 (partial product #1). This swap is a necessary preparation for the first add operation because, like the MULU instruction, the add instructions can add only the low-order words of two data registers.

After making this first addition, any carry out of that operation (in X) is propagated into D4 (partial product #4), using an all-zeros register, D5, as a "dummy" operand for the add extended operation. In the second add operation, the low word of D3 (partial product #3) is added to the low word of D1, which holds the result of the first add operation, and any carry is again propagated into D4.

At this point, the low-order 32 bits of the final product are intact in data register D1, but with the data words out of order. A SWAP D1 instruction remedies the problem, and the 68000 is ready to begin accumulating the high-order 32 bits of the product. This will require adding the high-word contents of data registers D2 and D3 (partial products #2 and #3, respectively) to the low-word contents of data register D4 (partial product #4).

The low words of both D2 and D3 currently hold unneeded data from the first two add operations, so both words are cleared and then swapped into the high-order word position of the registers. Two add long instructions place the low-order 32 bits of the final product in data register D2. After restoring the contents of data registers D3, D4, and D5 from the stack, the subroutine ends with an RTS instruction. The MULU32 subroutine will take a maximum of 460 cycles, or 57.5 μs, to execute.

Because a 32-bit operand can represent unsigned numbers as large as 4.294×10^9, many applications will not require a multiplication subroutine that operates on larger numbers. (And those that do will probably use floating-point math!) However, it is certainly possible to write a subroutine that multiplies 64-bit (or longer) numbers with the basic principles that were used in Example 4-1, but you soon run out of working registers and would have to use memory for temporary storage.

Signed 32-Bit × 32-Bit Multiply

Although the multiplication subroutine in Example 4-1 was described as a subroutine to multiply two unsigned numbers, it will also correctly multiply two signed numbers, as long as they are both positive. That is, Example 4-1 is indeed a "32-bit × 32-bit nonnegative multiply subroutine." This subroutine cannot properly multiply negative numbers because such numbers are represented in *2s-complement* form.

How, then, can two signed numbers be multiplied if one or both are negative? Certainly one valid solution would be to negate the negative operand(s), perform the multiplication, then adjust the product, if required. If just one of the operands is negative, the product must be 2s-complemented. If both of the operands are negative, the (positive) product is correct as it stands.

This simple approach is employed in Example 4-2, in which the low byte of data register D6 is used to hold a "negative indicator."

Example 4-2. A 32-Bit × 32-Bit Signed Multiply Subroutine

```
*   THIS SUBROUTINE MULTIPLIES TWO 32-BIT SIGNED NUMBERS, TO
*   GENERATE A 64-BIT PRODUCT. ENTER WITH MULTIPLIER IN D2 AND
*   MULTIPLICAND IN D1. THE PRODUCT IS RETURNED IN D1 (LOW 32
*   BITS) AND D2 (HIGH 32 BITS PLUS SIGN).
*
             ORG      $2000
MULS32       MOVE.B   D6,—(SP)     SAVE SCRATCH REGISTER.
             CLR.B    D6           NEGATIVE INDICATOR = 0.
             TST.L    D1           MULTIPLICAND NEGATIVE?
             BPL.S    CHKD2          NO.  GO CHECK MULTIPLIER.
             NEG.L    D1             YES.  2'S COMP. MULTIPLICAND
             NOT.B    D6             AND 1'S COMP. INDICATOR.
CHKD2        TST.L    D2           MULTIPLIER NEGATIVE?
             BPL.S    GOMUL          NO.  GO MULTIPLY.
             NEG.L    D2             YES.  2'S COMP. MULTIPLIER
             NOT.B    D6             AND 1'S COMP. INDICATOR.
GOMUL        JSR      MULU32       CALL UNSIGNED MULTIPLY SUBR.
             TST.B    D6           IS SIGN ON PRODUCT CORRECT?
             BEQ.S    DONE           YES, SIGN IS OKAY.  EXIT.
             NEG.L    D1             NO. 2'S COMP. PRODUCT.
             NEGX.L   D2
DONE         MOVE.B   (SP)+,D6     RESTORE SCRATCH REGISTER D6.
             RTS
             END
```

This indicator, initialized to zero, is set to all 1s if just one of the operands is negative, but will remain zero if both operands are either positive or negative. Then, after the MULU32 subroutine is called to perform the 32-bit by 32-bit multiplication, the negative indicator is used to determine whether the product is correct (indicator zero) or needs to be negated (indicator nonzero). The subroutine in Example 4-2 (MULS32) will have an execution time that varies depending on whether the operands are both positive, both negative, or of opposite sign. The execution times of MULS32 (including those of the called subroutine, MULU32) are as follows:

Operands	Maximum Time (Cycles)	Maximum Time (μs)
Both positive	558	69.75
Opposite signs	576	72.00
Both negative	574	71.75

A faster solution, and one that does not cause either operand to be altered, can be obtained by following this algorithm:

If either or both operands are negative, perform the multiplication, then modify the product in one of two ways:
    1. If just one operand is negative, subtract the other operand (i.e., the positive operand) from the most-significant part of the product.

2. *If both operands are negative, subtract both operands from the most-significant part of the product.*

Are you skeptical? Let us test this algorithm by working out the 103 times 124 example once more, but with a negative multiplier (-103). The pencil-and-paper version will look like this:

```
        01111100    Multiplicand = +124
      × 10011001    Multiplier = −103
      ----------
        01111100
        00000000
        00000000
        01111100
        01111100
        00000000
        00000000
        01111100
      ----------
  0100101000011100  Product = +18,972
```

When compared with the correct answer ($-12,772$), our answer appears to be "garbage." Not only is it too large, but it has the wrong sign to boot! Let us see what the preceding algorithm can do for us. The algorithm calls for subtracting the positive operand ($+124$, a single byte) from the high-order byte of the product. In binary, it is easier for us to add than subtract, so the 2s complement of the positive operand is added to the high byte of the product:

```
  0100101000011100    Original Product = +18,972
  +       10000100    2s-Comp. Multiplicand = −124
  ----------------
  1100111000011100    New Product = −12,772
```

The product is now correct. Readers are invited to validate Step 2 of the algorithm by applying this solution to the paper-and-pencil product of -103 times -124. Fig. 4-2 shows the additional steps required to multiply signed numbers of any length.

As you can see from Fig. 4-2, this algorithm allows us to use our previously described unsigned multiplication subroutine (Example 4-1) to perform the initial multiplication. However, there is an additional requirement that the original multiplier and multiplicand be saved for the product "adjustment" instructions. Example 4-3 gives the new, more-efficient 32-bit × 32-bit signed multiply subroutine. This subroutine, MLTS32, is nothing more than the MULU32 subroutine from Example 4-1, with a few additional instructions at the beginning, to save the multiplier and multiplicand (in D7 and D6, respectively), and a few more instructions at the end, to test the operand signs and adjust the product, if required.

Example 4-3. An Improved 32-Bit × 32-Bit Signed Multiply Subroutine

```
*     THIS SUBROUTINE MULTIPLIES TWO 32-BIT SIGNED NUMBERS, TO
*     GENERATE A 64-BIT PRODUCT. ENTER WITH MULTIPLIER IN D2 AND
*     MULTIPLICAND IN D1. THE PRODUCT IS RETURNED IN D1 (LOW 32
*     BITS) AND D2 (HIGH 32 BITS).
*
          ORG       $1000
MLTS32    MOVEM.L   D3–D7,–(SP)     SAVE SCRATCH REGISTERS.
          MOVE.L    D1,D6           COPY MULTIPLICAND INTO D6
          MOVE.L    D2,D7           AND MULTIPLIER INTO D7.
*
*     PERFORM A 32-BIT BY 32-BIT UNSIGNED MULTIPLICATION.
*
          MOVE.L    D1,D3           COPY MULTIPLICAND INTO D3
          MOVE.L    D1,D4           AND INTO D4,
          SWAP      D4              IN SWAPPED FORM.
          MOVE.L    D2,D5           COPY MULTIPLIER INTO D5,
          SWAP      D5              IN SWAPPED FORM.
          MULU      D2,D1           PARTIAL PRODUCT #1.
          MULU      D4,D2                           #2.
          MULU      D5,D3                           #3.
          MULU      D5,D4                           #4.
          SWAP      D1              SUM1 = PP #2 LOW +
          ADD       D2,D1           PP #1 HIGH.
          CLR.L     D5
          ADDX.L    D5,D4           PROPAGATE CARRY INTO PP #4.
          ADD       D3,D1           SUM2 = SUM1 + PP #3 LOW.
          ADDX.L    D5,D4           PROPAGATE CARRY INTO PP #4.
          SWAP      D1              PUT LOW PROD. IN CORRECT
                                    ORDER.
          CLR       D2              PREPARE FOR SUM3.
          SWAP      D2
          CLR       D3
          SWAP      D3
          ADD.L     D3,D2           SUM3 = PP #2 LOW + PP #3
                                    HIGH.
          ADD.L     D4,D2           SUM4 = SUM3 + PP #4.
*
*     THE INSTRUCTIONS TO FOLLOW MODIFY THE PRODUCT, IF
*     REQUIRED.
*
          TST.L     D7              MULTIPLIER NEGATIVE?
          BPL.S     CHKD6           NO.  GO CHECK MULTIPLICAND.
          SUB.L     D6,D2           YES.  SUB. MULTIPLICAND
                                    FROM PROD.
CHKD6     TST.L     D6              IS MULTIPLICAND NEGATIVE?
          BPL.S     DONE            NO.  WE ARE DONE.
          SUB.L     D7,D2           YES.  SUB. MULTIPLIER
                                    FROM PROD.
DONE      MOVEM.L   (SP)+,D3–D7     RESTORE SCRATCH REGISTERS
          RTS
          END
```

The execution times of the MLTS32 subroutine are as follows:

Operands	Maximum Time (Cycles)	Maximum Time (μs)
Both positive	532	66.5
Opposite signs	536	67.0
Both negative	540	67.5

DIVISION

There are many applications for division, but one of the most common is in taking the average of a set of numbers—perhaps the results of a series of laboratory tests. Example 4-4 shows a typical program for such a task. This program, called AVERAGE, averages a specified number of unsigned word values pointed to by A0, with the word count contained in the low word of D0. The average is returned as an integer in the low word of D1 and a fractional remainder in the high word of D1. The AVERAGE program uses two scratch registers, D2 (to hold the word count) and D3 (to receive word values read from memory), but affects no registers other than D1.

Example 4-4. A Word-Averaging Routine

```
*   THIS ROUTINE TAKES THE AVERAGE OF A SPECIFIED NUMBER OF
*   UNSIGNED WORD VALUES IN MEMORY. UPON RETURN, THE INTEGER
*   PORTION OF THE AVERAGE VALUE IS IN THE LOW WORD OF D1 AND
*   THE FRACTIONAL REMAINDER IS IN THE HIGH WORD OF D1.
*   THE ADDRESS OF THE FIRST WORD IS CONTAINED IN A0 AND THE
*   WORD COUNT IS CONTAINED IN THE LOW WORD OF D0.
*
            ORG       $1000
AVERAGE     MOVEM.L   D0/D2/D3/A0,-(SP)    SAVE SCRATCH
                                           REGISTERS
            MOVE      D0,D2                PUT WORD COUNT INTO
                                           D2 AND MAKE D0 =
            SUBQ      #1,D0                COUNT - 1.
            CLR.L     D1                   CLEAR DIVIDEND
            CLR.L     D3                   REGISTER AND WORD-
                                           HOLDING REGISTER.
LOOP        MOVE      (A0)+,D3             FETCH NEXT WORD
            ADD.L     D3,D1                AND ADD IT TO TOTAL.
            DBF       D0,LOOP              ALL WORDS NOW
                                           TOTALED?
            DIVU      D2,D1                  YES.  TAKE THE
                                           AVERAGE.
            MOVEM.L   (SP)+,D0/D2/D3/A0    RESTORE SCRATCH
            END                            REGISTERS.
```

Clearly, the divide operation in Example 4-4 will be aborted if D0 holds zero upon entry, but can it be aborted by an overflow condition? No, overflow cannot possibly occur here, because the ratio of the dividend (word total) to the divisor (word count) will

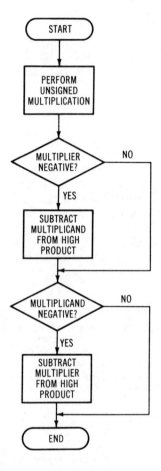

Fig. 4-2. A signed multiplication algorithm.

never exceed 65,536! However, overflow could occur if long-word values, rather than word (or byte) values, were being averaged. For this reason, it is worthwhile to take a look at a procedure in which a valid quotient can be obtained regardless of whether or not overflow occurs.

DIVISION WITH OVERFLOW

As you know from Chapter 3, if overflow occurs during execution of a signed divide (DIVS) or unsigned divide (DIVU) instruction, the 68000 sets the overflow (V) flag and terminates the operation, without affecting divisor or dividend. Overflow will occur when the dividend is so much larger than the divisor that the quotient cannot be contained in a 16-bit word.

In some applications, an overflow represents an error condition. In other applications, an overflow condition is acceptable, but means that a quotient longer than 16 bits must be returned. Since the division is aborted when the 68000 encounters an overflow condition, how can such a longer quotient be obtained? Perhaps the easiest way to obtain this quotient is by splitting the 32-bit dividend into two 16-bit numbers, and then performing two 16-bit by 16-bit divide operations (which *cannot* produce an overflow). If the divisor is a 16-bit number (X) and the dividend is a 32-bit number (Y_1Y_0), the divide operation can be represented as

$$X \overline{\,)\, Y_1Y_0\,}$$

or, more properly, as

$$X \overline{\,)\, (Y_1 \times 2^{16}) + Y_0\,}$$

This division will generate two 16-bit quotient digits (Q_1 and Q_0) and two 16-bit remainder digits (R_1 and R_0), as follows:

$$\begin{array}{c} Q_1 \times 2^{16} \\ X \overline{\,)\, Y_1 \times 2^{16}\,} \end{array} \quad \text{and } R_1 \times 2^{16}$$

$$\begin{array}{c} Q_0 \\ X \overline{\,)\, (R_1 \times 2^{16}) + Y_0\,} \end{array} \quad \text{and } R_0$$

As you can see, the net result of these two operations is a 32-bit quotient, Q_1Q_0, and a 32-bit remainder, $0R_0$ (interim remainder R_1, if generated at all, becomes zero during the second divide operation). If no overflow occurs, Q_1 will be zero, and the result will be returned as $0Q_0$ and $0R_0$.

From the preceding observations, it is possible to develop a division subroutine that will *always* return a valid quotient and remainder, regardless of whether or not an overflow occurs. Example 4-5 gives a subroutine, called DIVUO, that will do the job. This subroutine divides a 32-bit dividend in D1 by a 16-bit divisor in D0, and then checks for overflow. If overflow occurred, the subroutine uses data registers D2 and D3 to perform the correction.

Following these divisions (if they are indeed required), the 68000 executes the instructions at FORMAT, in which the 32-bit quotient is loaded into D1 and the 16-bit remainder is loaded into the low word of D0. If an overflow occurs, D1 will contain Q_1Q_0 and D0 will contain $0R_0$, as shown in Fig. 4-3A. If no overflow occurs, the low word of D1 and D0 will contain Q and R, respectively, and the high words of both of these registers will contain all zeros, as shown in Fig. 4-3B.

Example 4-5. A Division Subroutine That Accounts for Overflow

```
*   THIS DIVIDE SUBROUTINE DETERMINES THE CORRECT QUOTIENT
*   AND REMAINDER, IRRESPECTIVE OF OVERFLOW. ENTER WITH THE
*   16-BIT DIVISOR IN D0 AND THE 32-BIT DIVIDEND IN D1. THE 32-BIT
*   QUOTIENT IS RETURNED IN D1 AND THE 32-BIT REMAINDER IS
*   RETURNED IN D0.
*
        ORG     $2000
DIVUO   MOVEM   D2/D3,-(SP)   SAVE SCRATCH REGISTERS.
        CLR     D3            PUT ZEROS IN LOW WORD OF D3.
        DIVU    D0,D1         HAS OVERFLOW OCCURRED?
        BVC.S   FORMAT          NO.  GO FORMAT RESULTS.
        MOVE    D1,D2           YES.  COPY Y0 INTO D2.
        CLR     D1            D1 CHANGES FROM Y1-Y0 TO
                              Y1-0.
        SWAP    D1            D1 CONTAINS 0-Y1.
        DIVU    D0,D1         DIVIDE PUTS R1-Q1 INTO D1.
        MOVE    D1,D3         D3 CONTAINS Q1.
        MOVE    D2,D1         D1 CHANGES FROM R1-Q1 TO
                              R1-Y0.
        DIVU    D0,D1         DIVIDE PUTS R0-Q0 INTO D1.
*
*   FORMAT QUOTIENT (D1) AND REMAINDER (D0)
*
FORMAT  MOVE.L  D1,D0         D0 CONTAINS R-Q OR R0-Q0.
        SWAP    D1            D1 CONTAINS Q-R OR Q0-R0.
        MOVE    D3,D1         D1 CONTAINS Q-0 OR Q0-Q1.
        SWAP    D1            D1 CONTAINS 0-Q OR Q1-Q0.
        CLR     D0            D0 CONTAINS R-0 OR R0-0.
        SWAP    D0            D0 CONTAINS 0-R OR 0-R0.
        MOVEM   (SP)+,D2/D3   RESTORE SCRATCH REGISTERS.
        RTS
        END
```

SQUARE ROOT

In this final portion of the chapter, we will develop a program to calculate the square root of a 32-bit integer number. To make this calculation, the program will use the classical method of successive approximations.

To illustrate this method, assume that the number whose root is to be determined has the value N. The first approximation for the square root is derived using the value $(N/200) + 2$. N is divided by this value. The result is added to the first approximation and the sum is divided by 2. *That* result becomes our next approximation. For example, to find the square root of 10,000:

N = 10,000; first approximation is $(10,000/200) + 2$, or 52
$$10,000/52 \ = 192, \quad (192 + 52)/2 = 122$$
$$10,000/122 = \ 81, \quad (122 + 81)/2 = 101$$
$$10,000/101 = \ 99, \quad (101 + 99)/2 = 100$$
$$10,000/100 = 100$$

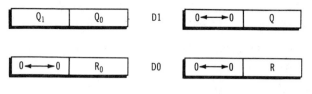

Q_1	Q_0	D1	$0 \leftarrow \rightarrow 0$	Q

$0 \leftarrow \rightarrow 0$	R_0	D0	$0 \leftarrow \rightarrow 0$	R

(A) With overflow. (B) Without overflow.

Fig. 4-3. Division results, with and without overflow.

So, we see, the square root of 10,000 is 100. We know that 100 *is* the square root, rather than simply another intermediate approximation, because when 100 is multiplied by itself it produces the original number, exactly. This particular number, 10,000, happened to have an integer square root, but we cannot expect the solution to be an integer for very many numbers. The square root of 9999, for instance, is not an integer. This means that if the square root of 9999 is to be determined, the 68000 will continue trying to determine the square root of this number. The processor will continue looping through the approximation instructions, because the square of the *integer* approximation will never be equal to 9999. Therefore, there has to be some way to stop the processor once it has determined the closest or "best" square root for the number.

A number of different methods can be used to end the approximation procedure. The method that best suits your needs will depend on how accurate your answer must be, and how much execution time can be alloted to deriving that answer. One solution is to let the 68000 execute the loop 10 times and assume that answer is accurate enough. This method will suit many applications, but is rather arbitrary in nature. Another, more precise, solution is to let the 68000 execute the loop until two successive approximations are identical, or differ by a value of one. This latter solution will be used in our software example.

Example 4-6 gives a subroutine (SQRT32) that calculates the integer square root of a 32-bit number, by successive approximations. In this subroutine, the 32-bit number is contained in data register D0 and the 16-bit square root is returned in data register D1. The subroutine begins by deriving the initial approximation, using the relationship $(N/200) + 2$. The remainder of the subroutine is a loop, starting at NXTAPP, in which the 68000 calculates a new approximation by dividing the 32-bit integer by the preceding approximation, then averaging these approximations. Before averaging the approximations, however, the 68000 tests for the "end" condition, by checking whether the new approximation is either equal to, one greater than, or one less than, the preceding approximation. When one of these three conditions is satisfied, the 68000 returns from the subroutine, with the 16-bit square root in data register D1.

Example 4-6. A 32-Bit Square Root by Successive Approximation Subroutine

```
*   THIS SUBROUTINE CALCULATES THE SQUARE ROOT OF A 32-BIT
*   INTEGER IN D0, AND RETURNS THAT SQUARE ROOT AS A 16-BIT
*   INTEGER IN THE LOW WORD OF D1. THE ORIGINAL NUMBER IN D0
*   IS NOT AFFECTED.
*
            ORG     $2000
SQRT32      MOVEM.L D2/D3,−(SP)     SAVE SCRATCH REGISTERS.
            MOVE.L  D0,D2           COPY DATA VALUE INTO D2.
            DIVU    #200,D2         DIVIDE BY 200,
            ADDQ    #2,D2           THEN ADD 2.
NXTAPP      MOVE.L  D0,D1           LOAD DATA VALUE INTO D1.
            DIVU    D2,D1           DIVIDE IT BY LAST APPROX.
            MOVE    D1,D3           AND PUT NEW APPROX. IN D3.
            SUB     D2,D3           LAST TWO APPROXS. IDENTICAL?
            BEQ.S   DONE              YES.  EXIT.
            CMPI    #1,D3             NO.  CHECK FOR DONE.
            BEQ.S   DONE
            CMPI    #−1,D3
            BEQ.S   DONE
            ADD     D1,D2           ADD LAST TWO APPROXS.
            LSR     #1,D2           AND DIVIDE SUM BY 2.
            BRA.S   NXTAPP
DONE        MOVEM.L (SP)+,D2/D3     RESTORE SCRATCH REGISTERS.
            RTS
            END
```

BIBLIOGRAPHY

1. Fredette, G. "68000 Routine Extracts Square Roots." *EDN*, August 19, 1981, pp. 185–194.

2. Grappel, R. "68000 Routine Divides 32-Bit Numbers." *EDN*, March 4, 1981, pp. 161–162.

3. ———— and Hemenway, J. "EDN Software Tutorial: Pseudorandom Generators." *EDN*, May 20, 1980, pp. 119–122. (This article discusses ways to generate pseudorandom numbers with both hardware and software, and includes a random number generator program for the 68000.)

4. Hwang, K. *Computer Arithmetic*. New York: John Wiley & Sons, Inc., 1979.

5. For some applications, arithmetic operations may be more efficiently performed with hardware. The following articles discuss math processing chips that are available for this purpose:
    (a) Bucklen, W., *et al.* "Single-Chip Digital Multipliers Form Basic DSP Building Blocks." *EDN*, April 1, 1981, pp. 153–163.
    (b) Stauffer, M. K. "Math Processing Chips Boost µC Computing Power." *EDN*, August 20, 1980, pp. 113–120.
    (c) Twaddell, W. "ICs and Semiconductors." *EDN*, July 20, 1980, pp. 74–94.

CHAPTER 5

Lists and Look-Up Tables

There are many ways in which information in memory can be organized for processing. These organizational techniques vary with the application, and are categorized with such names as lists, arrays, strings, look-up tables, and vectors. As expected, the subject can (and does) fill many volumes, but we will concentrate on just two types of organization—*lists* and *look-up tables.*

Lists are probably the most fundamental data storage technique. They consist of units of data (one or more bytes) called *elements,* arranged sequentially in memory. The sequence can be consecutive, in which each element occupies one or more adjoining memory locations; or the sequence can be linked, in which each data element is followed by a pointer to the next element in the list. Further, the elements can be arranged randomly, or in ascending or descending order.

Look-up tables are data structures that have one specific purpose —to find information (either data or addresses) that has a defined relationship to a known value. A telephone directory is a good example of a look-up table; knowing a name, you can look up an associated telephone number.

UNORDERED LISTS

In our ordered society, where telephone-book listings are arranged alphabetically and where house numbers increase (or decrease) systematically as you go up or down a street, unordered *anythings* seem somehow inferior to us. Unordered lists are the bane of the programmer too because they are often difficult to process. To find out whether a certain value is in an unordered list, you must search the list from the beginning, element by element, until you either find the value or you reach the end of the list. But like it or not, unordered lists are a fact of life in many applications, and represent a common way to store random, chronologically derived, or dynamically changing data (especially data from an experiment).

Adding an Entry to an Unordered List

Subroutine ADD2UL, shown in Example 5-1, is a sample of the kind of program that you could use to create an unordered list, or to add a new element to an existing unordered list. For this example, the list is comprised of word values (either signed or unsigned).

Example 5-1. Adding an Entry to an Unordered List

```
*    THIS SUBROUTINE ADDS THE LOW WORD OF DATA REGISTER D0
*    TO AN UNORDERED LIST, IF IT IS NOT ALREADY IN THE LIST.
*    THE STARTING ADDRESS OF THE LIST IS IN ADDRESS REGISTER A0.
*    THE LENGTH OF THE LIST, IN WORDS, IS IN THE LIST'S FIRST
*    WORD LOCATION.
*
           ORG       $2000
ADD2UL     MOVEM.L   D1/A1,—(SP)    SAVE SCRATCH REGISTERS.
           MOVEA.L   A0,A1          COPY STARTING ADDRESS INTO
           MOVE      (A1)+,D1       A1 AND WORD COUNT
           SUBQ      #1,D1          MINUS 1 INTO D1.
NXTEL      CMP       (A1)+,D0       DO ENTRY AND ELEMENT MATCH?
           BEQ.S     ITSIN          YES.  IT'S IN LIST; DONE.
           DBF       D1,NXTEL       NO.  LOOP UNTIL END OF
           MOVE      D0,(A1)        LIST, THEN ADD ENTRY TO
           ADDQ      #1,(A0)        THE END AND INCREMENT
                                    ELEMENT COUNT.
ITSIN      MOVEM.L   (SP)+,D1/A1    RESTORE SCRATCH REGISTERS.
           RTS
           END
```

This subroutine simply searches the list, element by element, for the occurrence of the value that the user wants to add to the list, which is contained in the low word of data register D0. If this value is already in the list, the 68000 returns from the subroutine, because you do not want the value to be duplicated in the list. Otherwise, the value is "tacked on" to the end of the list, as a new element. The starting address of the list is contained in address register A0. The first element in the list (a word) contains an unsigned number that represents the length of the list, in words, so this particular subroutine can be used to build a list that is up to 64K words long.

There is nothing particularly unusual about this subroutine. It copies the starting address of the list from A0 into A1 (so that this address is preserved in A0), and then reads the element count from the first word of the list into D1. This count is then decremented, because the search loop will terminate when the count has decreased to −1, rather than to zero. The search loop, which starts at NXTEL, compares the elements in the list to the value in D0. If the value is already in the list, the 68000 branches to ITSIN, and then returns. Otherwise, if the value is not in the list, it is added to the end of the list and an ADDQ instruction increases the element count (addressed by A0) by one.

How long will it take this subroutine to execute? Obviously, that will depend on the number of elements in the list, and whether or not the search value is already in the list. For all but the smallest lists, the total execution time of the subroutine is largely a function of how many times the three-instruction NXTEL loop is executed. Let us examine the timing for both cases—element is not in the list, and element is in the list—for a list having N elements.

If the search value is not in the list, the NXTEL loop will be executed N times. For the first N−1 executions, the loop will take 26 cycles to execute; for the last cycle, the loop will take 30 cycles to execute. The remaining instructions in the subroutine will be executed only once, and will require 108 cycles. Therefore,

$$\text{Time}_{\text{total}} = 108 + 26(N-1) + 30$$
$$= 26N + 112 \text{ cycles}$$

Thus, to add an element to a 100-element list will take 2712 cycles, or 339.0 μs.

If the search value is in the list, it should take the 68000 an average of N/2 comparisons to find it, because 50% of the time a search value will lie in the lower half of the list and 50% of the time it will lie in the upper half of the list. For all but the last of these N/2 comparisons, the NXTEL loop will take 26 cycles to execute (as in the preceding paragraph); for the last cycle, in which a match is detected, the NXTEL loop will take only 18 cycles to execute. The remaining instructions in the subroutine will require an additional 88 cycles. Therefore, on the average,

$$\text{Time}_{\text{total}} = 88 + 26(N/2 - 1) + 18$$
$$= 13N + 80 \text{ cycles}$$

Thus, to find an element in an unordered 100-element list will take an average of 1380 cycles, or 172.5 μs.

Deleting an Element From an Unordered List

To delete an element from an unordered list, you must find the element to be deleted, and then move all remaining elements in the list up one element (to write over the deletion "victim"). Once this element has been removed, there is one less element in the list, so the element count of the list must be decremented by one.

The DELEUL subroutine given in Example 5-2 performs just such an operation, using the low word of data register D0 to specify the value to be deleted. As in Example 5-1, the starting address of the list is stored in address register A0.

Example 5-2. Deleting an Element From an Unordered List

```
*   THIS SUBROUTINE DELETES THE VALUE IN THE LOW WORD OF DATA
*   REGISTER D0 FROM AN UNORDERED LIST, IF THAT VALUE IS IN
*   THE LIST. THE STARTING ADDRESS OF THE LIST IS IN ADDRESS
*   REGISTER A0. THE LENGTH OF THE LIST, IN WORDS, IS IN THE LIST'S
*   FIRST WORD LOCATION.
*
           ORG       $1000
DELEUL     MOVEM.L   D1/A1,-(SP)    SAVE SCRATCH REGISTERS.
           MOVEA.L   A0,A1          COPY STARTING ADDRESS INTO
           MOVE      (A1)+,D1       A1, AND WORD COUNT
           SUBQ      #1,D1          MINUS 1 INTO D1.
NEXTEL     CMP       (A1)+,D0       DELETE VICTIM FOUND?
           BNE.S     DELETE         YES. GO DELETE THAT
                                    ELEMENT.
           DBF       D1,NEXTEL      NO.   SEARCH UNTIL END OF
           BRA.S     ALLDUN         LIST, THEN EXIT (ELEMENT
                                    NOT IN LIST).
*
*   DELETE AN ELEMENT, BY MOVING ALL SUBSEQUENT ELEMENTS UP
*   BY ONE WORD LOCATION.
*
DELETE     MOVE      (A1)+,-4(A1)   MOVE ONE WORD UP IN LIST.
           DBF       D1,DELETE      HAVE ALL ELEMENTS BEEN
                                    MOVED?
           SUBQ      #1,(A0)        YES.  DECREMENT ELEMENT
                                    COUNT.
ALLDUN     MOVEM.L   (SP)+,D1/A1    RESTORE SCRATCH REGISTERS.
           RTS
           END
```

The first portion of the subroutine (DELEUL to NEXTEL) loads the starting address of the list (where the element count is stored) into A1, and then loads the word count minus one into D1; these instructions are identical to those at the beginning of Example 5-1. The NEXTEL loop compares each element in the list to the value in D0. If a matching element is found, the 68000 branches to the DELETE loop, which moves all subsequent elements up one word location and then decrements the element count.

Finding the Minimum and Maximum Values in an Unordered List

The need to find the minimum and maximum values in a list is a requirement in many applications, particularly those in which test data or statistical information is being processed. One method that can be used to find these values without sorting the list is to initially establish the first element as both the minimum and maximum value, and then sequentially compare each of the remaining elements in the list to that minimum and maximum value. If your program encounters a value that is less than the minimum value, that element becomes the new minimum value unit. Likewise, if your program encounters a value that is greater than the maximum value, that element becomes the new maximum.

Subroutine MINMAX in Example 5-3 applies this method to an unordered list comprised of unsigned word values. When the subroutine is called, the starting address of the list must be contained in A0. Upon return, the minimum and maximum values will be stored in two symbolic memory locations, MINVAL and MAXVAL.

In Example 5-3, the instructions from MINMAX to CHKMIN load the element count, minus one, into data register D1 and store the value of the first data element into both MINVAL and MAX-VAL. At CHKMIN, the next element is loaded into D0, and then

Example 5-3. Finding the Minimum and Maximum Values in an Unordered List

```
*    THIS SUBROUTINE FINDS THE MINIMUM AND MAXIMUM WORD
*    VALUES IN AN UNORDERED LIST. THE MINIMUM VALUE IS RETURNED
*    IN MEMORY LOCATION MINVAL; THE MAXIMUM VALUE IS RETURNED
*    IN MEMORY LOCATION MAXVAL. THE STARTING ADDRESS OF THE
*    LIST IS IN ADDRESS REGISTER A0. THE LENGTH OF THE LIST, IN
*    WORDS, IS IN THE LIST'S FIRST WORD LOCATION.
*
           ORG       $3000
MINVAL     DS.W      1                MINIMUM VALUE LOCATION.
MAXVAL     DS.W      1                MAXIMUM VALUE LOCATION.
MINMAX     MOVEM.L   D0/D1/A0,-(SP)   SAVE SCRATCH REGISTERS.
           MOVE      (A0)+,D1         MOVE ELEMENT COUNT INTO
           SUBQ      #1,D1            D1 AND DECREMENT IT.
           MOVE      (A0),MINVAL      INITIALLY, MAKE FIRST
           MOVE      (A0)+,MAXVAL     ELEMENT BOTH MIN AND
                                      MAX.
CHKMIN     MOVE      (A0)+,D0         LOAD NEXT ELEMENT INTO
                                      D0.
           CMP       MINVAL,D0        IS THIS ELEMENT A NEW MIN?
           BEQ.S     CONT
           BCC.S     CHKMAX
           MOVE      D0,MINVAL          YES. UPDATE MINVAL.
           BRA.S     CONT
CHKMAX     CMP       MAXVAL,D0        IS THIS ELEMENT A NEW
                                      MAX?
           BLS.S     CONT
           MOVE      D0,MAXVAL          YES. UPDATE MAXVAL.
CONT       DBF       D1,CHKMIN        END OF LIST?
           MOVEM.L   (SP)+,D0/D1/A0     YES. RESTORE SCRATCH
           RTS                          REGISTERS.
           END
```

compared to MINVAL. At this point, any of three paths can be taken:

1. If the value in D0 is equal to MINVAL (zero flag is set), the 68000 branches to CONT, to check whether all elements have been processed.
2. If the value in D0 is greater than MINVAL (carry flag is clear), the 68000 branches to CHKMAX, where it is compared to MAXVAL.
3. If the value in D0 is less than MINVAL (carry flag is set), the 68000 "drops through" the BCC.S CHKMAX instruction and stores the word in D0 as the new MINVAL.

Following Step 2 or 3, the loop terminator instruction at CONT (DBF D1,CHKMIN) checks whether all elements in the list have been processed, and branches to CHKMIN if they have not.

As mentioned previously, this particular subroutine processes lists that are comprised of *unsigned* word values. If you wish to find the minimum and maximum in a list of *signed* word values, you can do so by simply replacing BCC.S CHKMAX with BPL.S CHKMAX and replacing BLS.S CONT with BLE.S CONT. All other instructions remain the same.

A SIMPLE SORTING TECHNIQUE

Although unordered data is perfectly acceptable for many applications, ordered data is often easier to analyze, and it certainly makes it much easier to locate an element. How can an unordered list be ordered? A considerable amount of literature exists on the subject. (Two good sources are References 1 and 2.) However, one of the simplest techniques is called the *bubble sort*.

Just as bubbles rise upward into the sky, list elements rise upward in memory during a bubble sort. (Data can be sorted in an increasing or decreasing order; we will discuss only increasing order.) During a bubble sort, elements of a list are accessed sequentially, starting with the first element, and are compared to the next element in the list. If an element is greater than the next sequential element in the list, the elements are exchanged. The next pair of elements is compared, exchanged if required, and so on. By the time the 68000 gets to the last element of the list, the largest element in the list will have "bubbled up" to the last element position of the list.

If the bubble-sort algorithm is used, the microcomputer usually requires several passes to sort a list, as can be seen by the following example. Consider a 5-element list that is initially arranged in the following order:

05 03 04 01 02

After one pass through the list, the elements will be in the following order:

03 04 01 02 05

Element 05, the largest element of the list, has "bubbled up" to the top of the list. The next pass will produce the order:

03 01 02 04 05

Element 04 is bubbled up the list to a position that is just before element 05. The result of the final pass is:

01 02 03 04 05

This example not only demonstrates how the bubble-sort algorithm operates, but it also gives an indication of what type of performance you can expect from it. Note that three passes were required to sort a partially ordered, 5-element list. If the list were totally ordered at the outset, it would still take one pass through the algorithm to deduce this fact. Conversely, if the list were initially arranged in descending order (the worst case), the bubble-sort algorithm would require five passes to order the list, four passes to sort, and one additional pass to detect that no additional elements need to be exchanged. From this observation, we can state that the 68000 will have to make from one to N number of passes through an N-element list, in order to sort it. On the average, N/2 passes are required to sort an N-element list.

What constitutes a "pass," in terms of instructions and time? Well, that will depend on how your programming algorithm is set up. Certainly, one way of bubble-sorting a list is to process the *entire* list, over and over, until your program finally makes a pass through the list in which no elements were exchanged. That approach will do the job, but it is time-consuming "overkill." Why? Because it is continuing to make comparisons on elements that have bubbled up to the end of the list in previous passes, and therefore need not be compared. A much quicker and more efficient approach is to make comparisons on only those elements that have not yet bubbled up to the end of the list.

Note that for any given list, both approaches just described will involve the same number of sorting passes, but there are drastic differences in the amount of *time* each will take to get the job done. If we use the previously mentioned statistic that an average of N/2 passes are required to sort an N-element list, here is how the two approaches compare: The first approach, in which all elements are compared in every pass, will perform N/2 sorting passes through N elements. The second approach, in which only the previously unsorted elements are compared, will also perform N/2 sorting passes, but each pass will involve one less comparison than the preceding pass! That is, during the first pass, N elements will be compared, during the second pass N−1 elements will be compared, and so on. During the final pass just two elements will be compared. To get a feel for the time savings you will realize by using the second approach, consider this: To sort a 100-element list, the first approach will require about 4950 comparisons, whereas the second approach will require only about 3675 comparisons, which is about one-quarter fewer comparisons!

Bubble-Sorting a List Having 16-Bit Elements

With the preceding background in bubble-sort theory, we are prepared to tackle an actual problem—sorting a list that is made up of 16-bit unsigned elements. Fig. 5-1 is a flowchart showing what steps are needed to do the job. If you understand the description of the bubble-sort algorithm, this flowchart should present no problem. Note, however, that the flowchart does include an indicator that will let the 68000 know when the list has been entirely sorted. This indicator, called the *exchange flag,* is tested at the end of each sorting pass. The exchange flag is "turned on" (set to logic 1) if at least one exchange occurred during the preceding pass; otherwise it is "turned off" (reset to logic 0), at which point the sorting ends.

The actual subroutine for this flowchart is given in Example 5-4. As you can see from the listing, upon entry the starting address of the list to be sorted must be in address register A0. While the subroutine is executing, A0 retains the address of the first data element in the list. This address is moved to A1 at the beginning of each sorting pass. Besides A0 and A1, the SORT subroutine also uses four data registers. Register D1 holds the exchange flag in bit 7. Register D3 is used to hold the count of unsorted elements. It supplies data register D0 with this count at the beginning of each pass, and gets decremented by a DBF instruction upon completion of the pass. Register D2 is used to hold an element during the compare procedure.

By the way, you should take note of the two instructions that follow the DBF. The instruction NOT.B D1 1s-complements the exchange flag (in D1), and the instruction BPL.S LOOP initiates a new sorting pass if the NOT operation has changed the flag to 0. That is, the branch to LOOP is taken *only* if the exchange flag was "on" (set to 1) before the NOT instruction was executed.

In many applications, the elements of a list will not fit into a simple 8-bit, 16-bit, or 32-bit format, and programmers must develop sort routines to handle lists with even longer elements. The

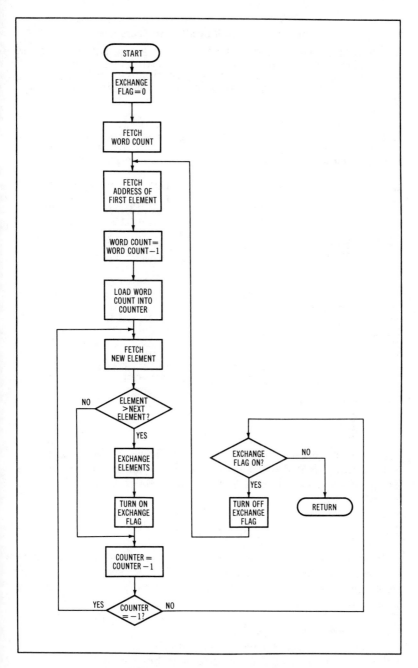

Fig. 5-1. Bubble-sort algorithm.

Example 5-4. A 16-Bit Bubble-Sort Subroutine

```
*   THIS SUBROUTINE ARRANGES THE 16-BIT ELEMENTS OF A LIST IN
*   ASCENDING ORDER IN MEMORY, USING BUBBLE SORT. THE
*   STARTING ADDRESS OF THE LIST IS IN ADDRESS REGISTER A0. THE
*   LENGTH OF THE LIST, IN WORDS, IS IN THE LIST'S FIRST WORD
*   LOCATION.
*
        ORG     $4000
SORT    MOVEM.L D0-D3/A0/A1,-(SP)   SAVE SCRATCH REGISTERS.
        CLR.B   D1                  EXCHANGE FLAG = 0.
        MOVE    (A0)+,D3            LOAD WORD COUNT INTO
                                    D3.
LOOP    MOVEA.L A0,A1               LOAD ELEMENT ADDR. INTO
                                    A1.
        SUBQ    #1,D3               DECREMENT WORD COUNT
        MOVE    D3,D0               AND LOAD IT INTO
                                    COUNTER D0.
COMP    MOVE    (A1)+,D2            FETCH WORD INTO D2.
        CMP     (A1),D2             IS NEXT WORD GT.
                                    THIS WORD?
        BLS.S   DECCTR                 YES.  CONTINUE.
        MOVE    (A1),-2(A1)            NO.  EXCHANGE THESE
        MOVE    D2,(A1)                TWO WORDS.
        TAS     D1                  TURN ON EXCHANGE FLAG.
DECCTR  DBF     D0,COMP             END OF LIST?
        NOT.B   D1                     YES.  IS EXCHANGE FLAG
                                       ON?
        BPL.S   LOOP                IF SO, START OVER.
        MOVEM.L (SP)+,D0-D3/A0/A1   RESTORE SCRATCH
                                    REGISTERS.
        RTS
        END
```

preceding comments should give you sufficient background to develop a program that will sort elements of any length. For additional background, see the bubble-sort routine in Reference 4, which sorts a mailing list.

ORDERED LISTS

Now that we have learned how to order a list, let us discuss how to search the list for a known value and, then, see how two common operations—adding elements and deleting elements—can be programmed.

Searching an Ordered List

Earlier in this chapter we learned that in order to locate a given value in an unordered list, the list must be searched sequentially, element by element. For an N-element list, this requires an average of N/2 comparisons. If a list is *ordered*, however, any of a number of search techniques can be employed. For all but the shortest lists, most of these techniques will be faster and more efficient than the sequential search technique.

One of the most widely known search techniques for ordered lists is called the *binary search*. Its name is derived from the fact that it divides the list into a series of progressively narrower halves, to eventually "zero in" on one element location in the list. A binary search starts in the middle of the list and determines which half of the list the entry value is in. It then takes *that* half of the list and divides it into halves . . . , and so on.

The flowchart in Fig. 5-2 shows the kinds of operations needed to conduct a binary search on an ordered list. Upon completion of the search, *the result is returned as an address*. If the search value is found in the list, it will be the address of the matching element. If the value is not in the list, it will be the address of the last element that was compared. You can find out which of these two addresses has been returned by checking whether the final value of the index is zero (no match) or nonzero (match).

Example 5-5 shows a subroutine that can be used to search an ordered list that is comprised of unsigned word values. The instructions from BSRCH to CALCI conduct initial tests against the lower and upper bounds of the list, to check whether the search value is out-of-bounds or lies at these extremes. If the search value falls within the boundaries of the list, the remaining instructions (CALCI onward) search the list, using the algorithm that was flowcharted in Fig. 5-2.

Example 5-5. A 16-Bit Binary-Search Subroutine

```
*   THIS SUBROUTINE SEARCHES AN ORDERED LIST FOR THE WORD
*   VALUE CONTAINED IN DATA REGISTER D0. THE STARTING ADDRESS
*   OF THE LIST IS IN ADDRESS REGISTER A0 AND THE WORD COUNT
*   IS IN THE LIST'S FIRST WORD LOCATION.
*   RESULT INDICATIONS ARE RETURNED IN REGISTERS A1 (ALL 32
*   BITS) AND D1 (LOW 16 BITS), AS FOLLOWS:
*        1.  IF THE VALUE IS IN THE LIST, D1 IS NONZERO AND A1
*            HOLDS THE ADDRESS OF THE MATCHING WORD IN THE
*            LIST.
*        2.  IF THE VALUE IS NOT IN THE LIST, D1 IS ZERO AND A1
*            HOLDS THE ADDRESS OF THE LAST WORD TO BE
*            COMPARED.
*
        ORG     $1000
BSRCH   MOVEA.L A0,A1         PUT LIST STARTING ADDR. INTO A1.
        CLR.L   D1           CLEAR INDEX REGISTER.
*
*   CHECK WHETHER SEARCH VALUE IS AT OR BEYOND BOUNDS OF
*   LIST.
```

```
                CMP      2(A1),D0      SEARCH VALUE LT OR EQ LOWER
                                       BOUND?
                BHI.S    TRYHI           NO.  CHECK UPPER BOUND.
                BNE.S    CALCA           YES.  SEE IF VALUE + LOWER
                                         BOUND.
                MOVEQ    #2,D1
CALCA           ADDQ.L   #2,A1
                RTS
TRYHI           MOVE     (A1),D1       FETCH WORD COUNT AND
                LSL      #1,D1         CONVERT IT TO BYTE INDEX.
                CMP      0(A1,D1),D0   SEARCH VALUE GT UPPER BOUND?
                BLS.S    EQHI
                ADDA.L   D1,A1           YES.  FORM ADDR & CLEAR D1.
                CLR      D1
                RTS
EQHI            BNE.S    CALCI           NO.  SEE IF VALUE = UPPER
                                         BOUND.
                ADDA.L   D1,A1
                RTS
*
*       SEARCH VALUE IS NOT AT OR BEYOND BOUNDS OF LIST.
*       PROCEED WITH THE SEARCH.
*
CALCI           LSR      #1,D1         DIVIDE INDEX BY 2.
                ANDI.B   #$FE,D1       FORCE INDEX TO A WORD
                                       BOUNDARY.
                BEQ.S    RETRN         INDEX = 0?
                ADDA.L   D1,A1           NO. CALCULATE SEARCH ADDRESS.
COMP            CMP      (A1),D0       SEARCH VALUE FOUND IN LIST?
                BNE.S    CHKLOW
RETRN           RTS                      YES.  EXIT WITH ADDRESS IN A1.
CHKLOW          BCC.S    CALCI           NO.  SEARCH VALUE IS HIGHER.
                LSR      #1,D1           NO.  SEARCH VALUE IS LOWER
                ANDI.B   #$FE,D1       CALCULATE NEW INDEX.
                BEQ.S    RETRN
                SUBA.L   D1,A1         CALCULATE NEW SEARCH ADDRESS
                BRA.S    COMP          AND GO COMPARE.
                END
```

As in previous examples in this chapter, the starting address of the list is passed to the subroutine in A0; the subroutine will not alter this address. The result address is returned in A1 and the match/no-match indication is returned in D1. Since the BSRCH subroutine operates on *word* values, each time a new index is calculated it is forced to an *even* value, by ANDing the last-significant byte of the (16-bit) index with the immediate value $FE.

How much more efficient is a binary search than a straight sequential comparison, the kind we used in Example 5-1? A mathematical analysis[1(a)] has shown that whereas a sequential search of an N-element list requires an average of $N/2$ comparisons, a binary search requires $\log_2 N$ comparisons. For a 100-element list, a sequential

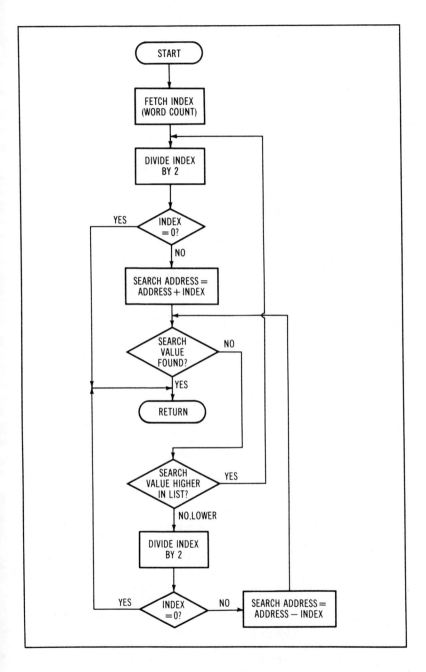

Fig. 5-2. Binary-search algorithm.

search will average 50 comparisons, but a binary search will do the same job with about 7 comparisons!

Adding an Entry to an Ordered List

The process of adding an entry to an ordered list can be divided into four basic steps:

1. Find out where the entry must be added.
2. Clear a location for the entry by moving all higher-valued elements down one position to the next higher-address element location.
3. Insert the entry at the newly vacated element position.
4. Update the list length by adding one to it.

The subroutine just developed, BSRCH (Example 5-5), gives us a good clue as to where the element must be added, in that it returns the address of the last element to be compared. All we need to determine to complete Step 1 is whether the entry must be inserted immediately *preceding*, or immediately *following*, the last-compared element. That determination can be made by simply comparing the entry value to the last-compared element.

Knowing the steps that are needed to add an entry to an ordered list, we can develop a subroutine to do the job. One solution is given in the ADD2OL subroutine in Example 5-6. This subroutine begins by calling BSRCH, to find out whether the search value is already in the list. As you know, BSRCH returns an address in A1 and a match/no-match indicator in D1.

Upon return from BSRCH, the ADD2OL subroutine interrogates D1, and exits if D1 is nonzero (since that means the entry is already in the list). If D1 is zero, however, the subroutine calculates the address of the end of the list. By subtracting the contents of A1 from this address, and right-shifting the result, the 68000 calculates the number of words that must be moved down in memory (the move count) to make room for the element to be inserted in the list. If the entry is less than the last-compared value, the last-compared word must be moved down also, so the move count is increased by one.

If an entry is greater than the last word in the list, it must be tacked on to the end. Otherwise, this value will have to be inserted in the list, which will require moving all subsequent elements down one word position. The two-instruction loop at MOVEL moves elements down, one by one, starting with the last word in the list. Upon completion of the move, the instructions starting at ADDIT add the entry to the list and increase the word count by one.

Example 5-6. Adding an Entry to an Ordered List

```
*   THIS SUBROUTINE ADDS THE LOW WORD OF DATA REGISTER D0 TO
*   AN ORDERED LIST, IF THIS VALUE IS NOT ALREADY IN THE LIST.
*   THE STARTING ADDRESS OF THE LIST IS IN ADDRESS REGISTER A0
*   AND THE WORD COUNT IS IN THE LIST'S FIRST WORD LOCATION.
*   THE BSRCH SUBROUTINE (EXAMPLE 5-5) IS CALLED TO CONDUCT
*   THE SEARCH.
*
            ORG       $2000
ADD2OL      MOVEM.L   D1/D2/A1/A2,−(SP)   SAVE SCRATCH REGISTERS.
            JSR       BSRCH               SEARCH LIST FOR ENTRY.
            TST       D1                  IS ENTRY IN THE LIST?
            BNE.S     ITISIN                YES. EXIT.
            MOVE.L    A0,D2                 NO.  CALCULATE ADDR.
            ADD.L     (A0),D2               OF END OF LIST.
            MOVEA.L   D2,A2               LOAD END + 2 INTO A2.
            ADDQ.L    #2,A2
            SUB.L     A1,D2               CALCULATE NO. OF WORDS
                                          TO BE MOVED
            LSR.L     #1,D2
            SUBQ.L    #1,D2               AND SUBTRACT 1 FROM
                                          THAT COUNT.
            CMP       (A1),D0             SHOULD COMPARE LOC. BE
                                          MOVED TOO?
            BCS.L     INCCNT                YES.  GO INCREMENT
                                            MOVE COUNT.
            TST.L     D2                    NO.  ADD ENTRY TO END
                                            OF LIST?
            BEQ.S     ADDIT                 YES.  GO ADD IT TO END.
            BRA.S     MOVEL
INCCNT      ADDQ.L    #1,D2               INCREMENT MOVE COUNT.
MOVEL       MOVE      −(A2),2(A2)         MOVE NEXT WORD DOWN.
            DBF       D2,MOVEL            ALL WORDS MOVED?
ADDIT       MOVE      D0,(A2)               YES.  INSERT ENTRY IN
            ADDQ      #1,(A0)               LIST AND INCREMENT
                                            ELEMENT COUNT.
ITISIN      MOVEM.L   (SP)+,D1/D2/A1/A2   RESTORE SCRATCH
                                          REGISTERS.
            RTS
            END
```

Deleting an Element From an Ordered List

It is much easier to delete an element from an ordered list than it is to add one, because all the 68000 has to do is find the proper element, move all subsequent elements up one location, and decrement the count, which is in the first element of the list.

Example 5-7 shows a typical delete subroutine, called DELOL, which uses the BSRCH subroutine (Example 5-5) to locate the intended deletion "victim." As usual, the starting address of the list is contained in address register A0. The value to be deleted is in the low word of data register D0.

Example 5-7. Deleting an Element From an Ordered List

```
*    THIS SUBROUTINE DELETES THE VALUE IN THE LOW WORD OF DATA
*    REGISTER D0 FROM AN ORDERED LIST, IF THE VALUE IS IN THE LIST.
*    THE STARTING ADDRESS OF THE LIST IS IN ADDRESS REGISTER A0.
*    THE LENGTH OF THE LIST, IN WORDS, IS IN THE LIST'S FIRST WORD
*    LOCATION.
*    THE BSRCH SUBROUTINE (EXAMPLE 5-5) IS CALLED TO CONDUCT
*    THE SEARCH.
*
          ORG      $3000
DELOL     MOVEM.L  D1/D2/A1,-(SP)   SAVE SCRATCH REGISTERS.
          JSR      BSRCH            SEARCH LIST FOR ENTRY.
          TST      D1               IS ENTRY IN THE LIST?
          BEQ.S    EXIT               NO.  RETURN.
          MOVE.L   A0,D2              YES.  CALCULATE ADDR. OF
          ADD.L    (A0),D2            END OF LIST.
          SUB.L    A1,D2            CALCULATE NO. OF WORDS
                                    TO BE MOVED.
          LSR.L    #1,D2
          SUBQ.L   #1,D2            AND SUBTRACT 1 FROM THAT
                                    COUNT.
          BEQ.S    DECCNT
DELETE    MOVE     2(A1),(A1)+      MOVE WORD UP IN LIST.
          DBF      D2,DELETE        ALL WORDS MOVED?
DECCNT    SUBQ     #1,(A0)            YES.  DECREMENT ELEMENT
                                       COUNT.
EXIT      MOVEM.L  (SP)+,D1/D2/A1   RESTORE SCRATCH REGISTERS.
          RTS
          END
```

If BSRCH locates the entry value in the list, the DELOL subroutine uses its address, and the address of the end of the list, to calculate the number of words that must be moved up in the list. The two-instruction loop at DELETE performs the move operation. When all words have been moved, the element count in the first word of the list is decremented by one, to reflect the deletion.

LOOK-UP TABLES

Many microprocessor programs include applications that require a particular value to be obtained before processing can resume. This value may be a mathematical derivative of a test or calculation result, such as the sine of a calculated angle or the Celsius equivalent of a temperature that has been measured in Fahrenheit. Or, the required value may be a parameter that has some defined relationship to a program input, but which cannot be calculated, such as a telephone number that corresponds to a name. Applications like these usually call for a *look-up table*. As the name implies, a look-up table is used to obtain an item of information (an *argument*) based on a known value (a *function*).

Look-up tables often replace complicated or time-consuming conversion operations, such as calculating the square root or cube root of a number, or deriving a trigonometric function (sine, cosine, etc.) of an angle. Look-up tables are especially efficient when a function is limited to a very small range of arguments. By using a look-up table, the microcomputer does not have to perform complex calculations each time an argument is required. In fact, you will find that as a rule, look-up tables reduce execution time in all but the most trivial of relationships. (You would not use a look-up table to store arguments that are always twice the value of a function, for instance.) But since look-up tables typically require large amounts of memory storage space, they are most efficient in applications where storage space can be sacrificed for execution speed.

Look-Up Tables Can Replace Equations

You can save processing time and programming development time by providing the results of complex equations in a look-up table. In this section we will examine one common application—finding the sine of an angle that is expressed in degrees.

The sine of all angles between 0° and 360° can be graphed, as shown in Fig. 5-3. Mathematically, this curve can be approximated by using the formula

$$\text{sine } (X) = X - \frac{X^3}{3!} + \frac{X^5}{5!} - \frac{X^7}{7!} + \frac{X^9}{9!}$$

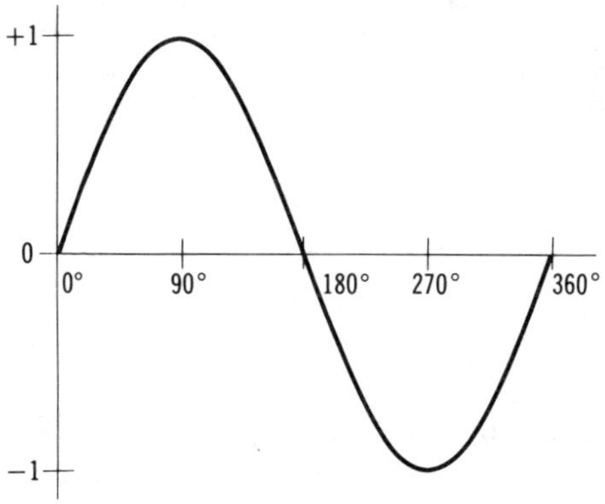

Fig. 5-3. The sine of all angles between 0° and 360°.

It is certainly possible to write a program to perform this approximation, but such a program may require a couple of milliseconds to calculate the sine. If your application requires very precise sines, you may be forced to write this program. However, applications with less stringent requirements can use an angle-to-sine look-up table.

Note from Fig. 5-3 that the sine of any angle between 0° and 180° is positive and that the sine of any angle greater than 180° and less than 360° is negative. Therefore,

$$0° < X < 180°, \text{ sine is positive}$$
$$180° < X < 360°, \text{ sine is negative}$$

As you can see in Fig. 5-3, the sine of 91° is the same as the sine of 89° and the sine of 179° is the same as the sine of 1°. Therefore, it can be concluded that for angle X

$$0° \leq X \leq 90°, \text{ take sine}(X)$$
$$90° \leq X \leq 180°, \text{ take sine}(180° - X)$$
$$\text{or sine}(90° - (X - 90°))$$

For example,

$$\text{sine}(170°) = \text{sine}(90° - (170° - 90°))$$
$$= \text{sine}(90° - 80°)$$
$$= \text{sine}(10°)$$

Further, angles in quadrants III and IV have sines with the same magnitude, but the opposite sign, as the angles in quadrants I and II, respectively. This observation allows us to state the following:

$$180° \leq X \leq 270°, \text{ take } -\text{sine}(X - 180°)$$
$$270° \leq X \leq 360°, \text{ take } -\text{sine}(360° - X)$$
$$\text{or } -\text{sine}(90° - (X - 270°))$$

For example,

$$\text{sine}(190°) = -\text{sine}(190° - 180°)$$
$$= -\text{sine}(10°)$$

Or, for an angle between 270° and 360°,

$$\text{sine}(290°) = -\text{sine}(90° - (290° - 270°))$$
$$= -\text{sine}(90° - 20°)$$
$$= -\text{sine}(70°)$$

The preceding relationships show that the sine of any angle between 0° and 360° can be expressed as some function of the sine of an angle between 0° and 90°. For a look-up table application this is significant, because it means that *the look-up table need only contain the sine values for angles from 0 to 90°!*

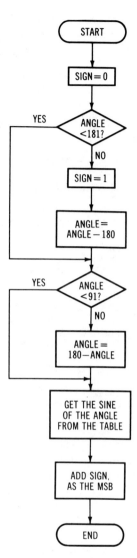

Fig. 5-4. Flowchart for angle-to-sine look-up subroutine.

These relationships also allow us to construct a flowchart for an angle-to-sine conversion subroutine. This flowchart, shown in Fig. 5-4, derives the sine as a sign-and-magnitude value.

Example 5-8 gives the 68000 angle-to-sine conversion subroutine. This subroutine accepts angles from 0° to 360°, in data register D0, and returns an 8-bit sign-and-magnitude sine value in data register D1. In this subroutine, called SINANG, the 68000 begins by checking whether the angle is less than 181°. If it is, program execution branches to SINPOS; otherwise, the 68000 sets the sign bit to one (sines above 180° are negative) and subtracts 180° from the angle.

Example 5-8. Finding the Sine of an Angle

```
*   THIS PROGRAM CALCULATES THE BINARY SINE VALUE FOR THE
*   ANGLE (0 TO 360 DEGREES) CONTAINED IN THE LOW WORD OF
*   DATA REGISTER D0, USING A LOOK-UP TABLE. THE SIGNED SINE
*   IS RETURNED IN THE LOW BYTE OF DATA REGISTER D1. D0 IS
*   UNAFFECTED.
*
          ORG      $1000
SINANG    MOVE     D0,−(SP)        SAVE SCRATCH REGISTERS.
          MOVE.L   A0,−(SP)
          CLR.B    D1              INITIALIZE SINE BYTE TO ZERO.
          CMPI     #180,D0         ANGLE LESS THAN 181 DEGS?
          BLS.S    SINPOS            YES.  CONTINUE WITH SIGN = 0.
          TAS      D1                NO.  SET SIGN BIT = 1.
          SUBI     #180,D0         SUBTRACT 180 DEGS FROM ANGLE.
SINPOS    CMPI     #91,D0          ANGLE LESS THAN 91 DEGS?
          BMI.S    GETSIN            YES.  GO LOOK UP SINE.
          NEG      D0                NO.  SUBTRACT ANGLE FROM 180.
          ADDI     #180,D0
GETSIN    LEA      SINTAB,A0       LOAD TABLE ADDRESS INTO A0.
          OR.B     0(A0,D0),D1     COMBINE SINE WITH SIGN BIT.
          MOVE.L   (SP)+,A0        RESTORE SCRATCH REGISTERS.
          MOVE     (SP)+,D0
*
*   THE SINE LOOK-UP TABLE FOLLOWS
*
SINTAB    DC.B     0,2,4,6,8,$B,$D, $F,$11,$14,$16
             .     (Rest of the table follows, 91 bytes total.)
             .
             .
```

With the sign bit now in bit 7 of register D1, the CMPI instruction at SINPOS compares the current value of the angle to 91°. If the angle is greater than or equal to 91°, its value must be subtracted from 180°. The simplest way to perform this subtraction would be with the instruction SUBI D0,#180, but the 68000 does not support this form of the SUBI instruction (only the form SUBI #data,Dn is legal), so we must make the subtraction by 2s-complementing D0, then adding 180° to the result. The final two instructions load the address of the look-up table (SINTAB) into A0, then look up the sine, using address register indirect with index addressing, and OR it with the sign bit in D1. The SINTAB table contains 91 byte-length sine values, to accommodate angles from 0° to 90°. The values used to form SINTAB are shown in Table 5-1.

The SINANG subroutine occupies 19 words in memory. Its execution time depends on which quadrant the look-up angle resides in.

Table 5-1. A Sine Look-Up Table With Angles in 1° Increments

Angle	Sine		Angle	Sine	
	Decimal	Binary		Decimal	Binary
0.00	.0000	00000000	45.00	.7071	01011010
1.00	.0175	00000010	46.00	.7193	01011100
2.00	.0349	00000100	47.00	.7313	01011101
3.00	.0523	00000110	48.00	.7431	01011111
4.00	.0698	00001000	49.00	.7547	01100000
5.00	.0872	00001011	50.00	.7660	01100010
6.00	.1045	00001101	51.00	.7771	01100011
7.00	.1219	00001111	52.00	.7880	01100100
8.00	.1392	00010001	53.00	.7986	01100110
9.00	.1564	00010100	54.00	.8090	01100111
10.00	.1736	00010110	55.00	.8191	01101000
11.00	.1908	00011000	56.00	.8290	01101010
12.00	.2079	00011010	57.00	.8387	01101011
13.00	.2250	00011100	58.00	.8480	01101100
14.00	.2419	00011110	59.00	.8572	01101101
15.00	.2588	00100001	60.00	.8660	01101110
16.00	.2756	00100011	61.00	.8746	01101111
17.00	.2924	00100101	62.00	.8829	01110001
18.00	.3090	00100111	63.00	.8910	01110010
19.00	.3256	00101001	64.00	.8988	01110011
20.00	.3420	00101011	65.00	.9063	01110100
21.00	.3584	00101101	66.00	.9135	01110100
22.00	.3746	00101111	67.00	.9205	01110101
23.00	.3907	00110010	68.00	.9272	01110110
24.00	.4067	00110100	69.00	.9336	01110111
25.00	.4226	00110110	70.00	.9397	01111000
26.00	.4384	00111000	71.00	.9455	01111001
27.00	.4540	00111010	72.00	.9511	01111001
28.00	.4695	00111100	73.00	.9563	01111010
29.00	.4848	00111110	74.00	.9613	01111011
30.00	.5000	01000000	75.00	.9659	01111011
31.00	.5150	01000001	76.00	.9703	01111100
32.00	.5299	01000011	77.00	.9744	01111100
33.00	.5446	01000101	78.00	.9781	01111101
34.00	.5592	01000111	79.00	.9816	01111101
35.00	.5736	01001001	80.00	.9848	01111110
36.00	.5878	01001011	81.00	.9877	01111110
37.00	.6018	01001101	82.00	.9903	01111110
38.00	.6157	01001110	83.00	.9926	01111111
39.00	.6293	01010000	84.00	.9945	01111111
40.00	.6428	01010010	85.00	.9962	01111111
41.00	.6561	01010011	86.00	.9976	01111111
42.00	.6691	01010101	87.00	.9986	01111111
43.00	.6820	01010111	88.00	.9994	01111111
44.00	.6947	01011000	89.00	.9998	01111111
45.00	.7071	01011010	90.00	1.0000	01111111

Not including execution times for the JSR and RTS instructions, the execution times are:

- For angles between 0° and 90°, SINANG will execute in 59 cycles, or 7.375 μs.
- For angles between 91° and 270°, SINANG will execute in 69 cycles, or 8.625 μs.
- For angles between 271° and 360°, SINANG will execute in 79 cycles, or 9.875 μs.

Look-Up Tables Can Perform Code Conversions

Look-up tables are also used to hold coded data, such as display codes, printer codes, and messages. As an example, Example 5-9 shows a subroutine that performs multiple look-ups. It converts a hexadecimal digit in the low byte of D0 to its ASCII, BCD, and Gray Code equivalents. The converted values will be returned in three consecutive byte locations in memory, starting at the address pointed to by address register A0.

Example 5-9. A Code-Conversion Subroutine

```
*   THIS SUBROUTINE USES THREE LOOK-UP TABLES TO CONVERT A
*   HEX DIGIT IN THE LOW BYTE OF D0 TO ITS ASCII, BCD, AND GRAY
*   CODE EQUIVALENTS. THE CONVERTED VALUES ARE RETURNED IN
*   THREE CONSECUTIVE BYTES IN MEMORY, STARTING AT THE
*   ADDRESS IN A0. D0 AND A0 ARE UNAFFECTED BY THE SUBROUTINE.
*
*
            ORG       $1000
LOOKUP  MOVE      D0,−(SP)              SAVE SCRATCH REGISTERS.
        MOVE.L    A1,−(SP)
        EXT.W     D0                    FORM INDEX.
        LEA       ATABLE,A1             A1 POINTS TO TABLE.
        MOVE.B    0(A1,D0),(A0)         FETCH ASCII CODE.
        MOVE.B    $10(A1,D0),1(A0)      FETCH BCD CODE.
        MOVE.B    $20(A1,D0),2(A0)      FETCH GRAY CODE.
        MOVE.L    (SP)+,A1              RESTORE SCRATCH REGISTERS.
        MOVE      (SP)+,D0
        RTS
ATABLE  DC.B      '0123456789ABCDEF'
        DC.B      0,1,2,3,4,5,6,7,8,9,$10,$11,$12,$13,$14,$15
        DC.B      0,1,3,2,6,7,5,4,$C,$D,$F,$E,$A,$B,9,8
        END
```

Of course, the LOOKUP subroutine in Example 5-9 will only convert a single hexadecimal digit. Many applications, such as data processing and data encryption, require strings of data to be converted from one form to another. Reference 4 contains a 68000 program that may be of value in those types of applications. This program employs a look-up table to convert a string of data in a memory buffer to another string in another memory buffer.

JUMP TABLES

Look-up tables can contain more than just data. In many cases, the elements of the table are addresses. An error routine, for example, can use a look-up table to find the starting address of an operator error message, based on a code in a data register. Similarly, an interrupt routine can use a look-up table to call one of several service routines, based on which device in the system generated the interrupt service request. Another routine may use a look-up table to call one of several control programs, based on a control key pressed by an operator. In all of these applications (there are many more as well), the look-up table containing the addresses is referred to as a *jump table*. Jump tables are used in applications where the control path is dependent upon the state of a specific condition.

Example 5-10 illustrates how a jump table can service the needs of five different users in a multiterminal microcomputer system. This subroutine, SELUSR, interprets the contents of data register D0 as a user identification code, and uses this code to call one of five user service subroutines. SELUSR checks the validity of the entered code, and traps to the CHK exception routine if the code is greater than four. (More about exceptions in Chapter 7.) However, with a valid code, the subroutine will convert the user code to an index, then use that index to fetch the address of a user routine (USER0 through USER4) into A0. The fetch employs program counter relative with index addressing; this mode is induced by the RORG directive preceding the subroutine. With the correct address in A0, a simple indirect jump transfers program control to the user subroutine.

Example 5-10. A Multiuser Selection Subroutine

```
*   THIS SUBROUTINE CALLS ONE OF FIVE USER SUBROUTINES, BASED
*   ON A USER IDENTIFICATION CODE IN THE LOW BYTE OF DATA
*   REGISTER D0.  THE SUBROUTINE AFFECTS THE A0 AND D0
*   REGISTERS.
        RORG      $1000
SELUSR  EXT.W     D0              EXTEND USER CODE TO WORD.
        CHK       #4,D0           INVALID ID CODE?
        LSL       #2,D0           NO.  CALCULATE INDEX (ID × 4).
        LEA       UADDR,A0        FETCH TABLE ADDR. INTO A0.
        MOVEA.L   0(A0,D0.W),A0   FETCH ADDR OF USER
        JMP       (A0)            SUBROUTINE AND JUMP TO THAT
                                  SUBROUTINE.
UADDR   DC.L      USER0,USER1,USER2,USER3,USER4
        END
```

REFERENCES

1. Sorting and searching techniques are described in the following articles:
   (a) Bentley, J. L. "An Introduction to Algorithm Design." *Computer*, February 1979, pp. 66–78.
   (b) Vile, R. C. "Sorting Revealed." *MICRO*, July 1980, pp. 13–29. (This highly entertaining and informative article covers bubble sort, insertion sort, selection sort, shell sort, and quicksort, and gives BASIC programs for each type.)
   (c) Hemenway, J. and Grappel, R. D. "EDN Software Tutorial: Sorting Algorithms." *EDN*, September 20, 1980, pp. 153–157. (Includes BASIC programs for exchange sort, insertion sort, and selection sort.)
   (d) Walker, B. "Sorting With Binary Trees." *BYTE*, October 1980, pp. 96–110, 250–263. (Excellent article, with programs given in BASIC and Pascal.)

2. Knuth, D. E. *The Art of Computer Programming. Volume 3: Sorting and Searching.* Reading, MA: Addison-Wesley Publishing Co., 1973.

3. Look-up tables are discussed in:
   (a) Leventhal, L. A. "Cut Your Processor's Computation Time." *Electronic Design*, August 16, 1977, pp. 82–89.
   (b) Titus, J. A. *et al.* "Interfacing Fundamentals: Lookup Tables." *Computer Design*, February 1979, pp. 130–134.

4. Starnes, T. W. "Powerful Instructions and Flexible Registers of the MC68000 Make Programming Easy." *Electronic Design*, April 26, 1980, pp. 171–176.

CHAPTER 6

68000 Microprocessor Chip Hardware

The 68000 microprocessor is housed in a 64-pin dual in-line package (DIP), with the pinouts shown in Fig. 6-1. Note that each pin has been assigned a symbolic name, and that some of these names have a bar drawn over them (e.g., $\overline{AS}$, $\overline{UDS}$, $\overline{LDS}$, and $\overline{DTACK}$). This convention is intended to distinguish between signals that are active in the low or logic-0 state (with a bar) and signals that are active in the high or logic-1 state (without a bar). To eliminate the "logic 0/logic 1" and "high/low" confusion, we will hereafter refer to signals as being *asserted* if they are true and *negated* if they are false.

For ease of understanding, the external signal lines of the 68000 will be described in functional groups. These groups are shown in Fig. 6-2.

CLOCK, POWER, AND GROUND LINES

The 68000 microprocessor operates from +5 volts, connected to two pins labeled Vcc, and using two ground pins labeled GND. The *clock* (*CLK*) input is a TTL-level signal that can have a frequency of up to 10 MHz.

THE DATA BUS AND ADDRESS BUS

The 68000 is called a *16-bit* microprocessor because its basic unit of information, the word, is 16 bits wide. No more than 16 bits of information can be transferred to or from memory and I/O devices

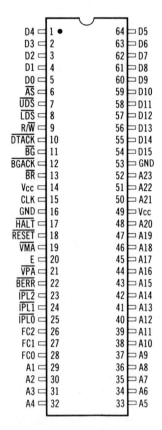

Fig. 6-1. The pinouts of the 68000 microprocessor.

at one time. To transfer more than 16 bits requires additional transfer cycles. All information transfers between the 68000 and external devices are conducted on the bidirectional, 16-bit *data bus* (D0–D15).

Which device in the system is to receive the information from, or transmit the information to, the 68000 microprocessor? The 68000 identifies an external device by transmitting its unique address throughout the system over 23 *address bus* lines (A1–A23). Since the address bus is 23 bits wide, the 68000 can select any of 8,388,608 word locations. (Two additional signals, $\overline{\text{UDS}}$ and $\overline{\text{LDS}}$, select bytes within a word. These signals are discussed with the asynchronous bus control signals.) The 68000 notifies all system devices that a valid address is on the address bus by asserting the *address strobe* ($\overline{\text{AS}}$) signal. Remember, since AS has a bar over it, "asserting" $\overline{\text{AS}}$ means putting it in the logic-0 state.

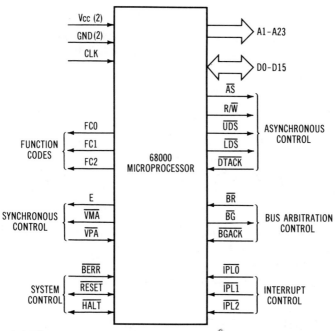

Fig. 6-2. The external signal lines of the 68000 shown in functional groups.

FUNCTION CODE SIGNALS

Whenever the 68000 communicates with an external device (memory or I/O), it accompanies the address information with "qualitative" information on three *function code signals (FC0, FC1, and FC2)*. The function code outputs inform external devices whether the 68000 is addressing data or program memory space (and whether the processor is in the user state or the supervisor state), or is servicing an interrupt. Table 6-1 shows the various combinations of these three signals. Note that the high-order function code signal, FC2, reflects the state of the supervisor (S) bit in the status register.

The function code signals indicate that *program space* is being accessed when the program counter (PC) is the address source or when reset vectors are being fetched. The function code signals indicate that *data space* is being accessed when most operands are read (the PC is *not* the address source), when all operands are written, or when vectors other than reset are being fetched.

The function code signals can be used with the address bus signals to write-protect certain portions of memory. They can also be used by an external device, such as a memory management unit, to ensure that certain operations are only conducted when the proces-

Table 6-1.
Function Code Signals Inform External Devices
of the Operating State of the 68000

Function Code Output				
FC2	FC1	FC0	Classification	Privilege State
0	0	0	(Reserved)	User
0	0	1	Data Space	User
0	1	0	Program Space	User
0	1	1	(Reserved)	User
1	0	0	(Reserved)	Supervisor
1	0	1	Data Space	Supervisor
1	1	0	Program Space	Supervisor
1	1	1	Interrupt Acknowledge	Supervisor

sor is in the correct state. Further, the function code signals can be externally decoded and used to extend the address space of the 68000 to four 16M-byte segments, for a total of 64M bytes! Fig. 6-3 shows a simple circuit that will perform this memory segmentation.

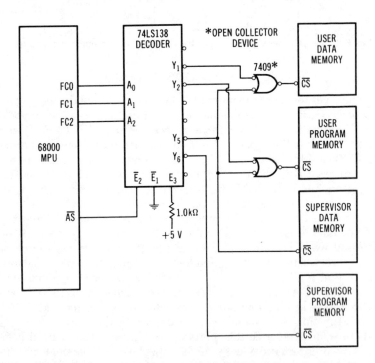

Fig. 6-3. Segmenting memory with the function code signals.

ASYNCHRONOUS CONTROL SIGNALS

Some conventional 8-bit microprocessors, such as the 6800 and the 6502, have control lines to communicate only with synchronous devices. That is, these microprocessors are designed to interface with external devices which must accept output data, or supply input data, within a specified amount of time. Communicating with slower devices, or asynchronous devices, requires special interface hardware and software. However, the 68000 can be interfaced to either synchronous or asynchronous devices, and has a set of control lines for each device type.

The Asynchronous Control Lines

As you know, the 68000 can operate on individual bytes within a word, so we normally refer to the 16M-byte addressing capability of the processor, rather than to its 8M-word addressing capability. How are individual bytes addressed? They are addressed by the address bus and two special control signals, *upper data strobe* ($\overline{UDS}$) and *lower data strobe* ($\overline{LDS}$). When $\overline{UDS}$ is asserted (a logic 0) by the 68000, information is transferred on the high-order eight lines of the data bus, D8 through D15. When $\overline{LDS}$ is asserted, information is transferred on the low-order eight lines of the data bus, D0 through D7. During word transfers, both strobe signals ($\overline{UDS}$ and $\overline{LDS}$) are asserted, and information is transferred on all 16 data bus lines, D0 through D15.

How can an addressed external device know whether the 68000 wants to input (read) information from it or output (write) information to it? The external device "knows" the direction of transfer by the state of the *read/write control signal* ($R/\overline{W}$). The $R/\overline{W}$ line is a logic 1 during a read cycle and a logic 0 during a write cycle.

Once an external device has either placed data onto the data bus (for a read operation) or has gated data off of the data bus (for a write operation), the device notifies the 68000 that the data has been transferred by asserting *data transfer acknowledge* ($\overline{DTACK}$). When the processor senses $\overline{DTACK}$ during a read operation, it latches the data and then terminates the bus cycle. Because cycle termination hinges on reception of $\overline{DTACK}$, the speed at which the 68000 can transfer data depends on how fast the addressed device can be accessed. In effect, *the 68000 slows down for devices having long access times and speeds up for devices having short access times!* Of course, the maximum rate will be determined by the frequency of the clock used to drive the processor.

Fig. 6-4 summarizes the signals involved in addressing asynchronous memory. In addition to the 68000, and the odd-byte and even-byte memory circuits, Fig. 6-4 contains a *watchdog timer*. This timer

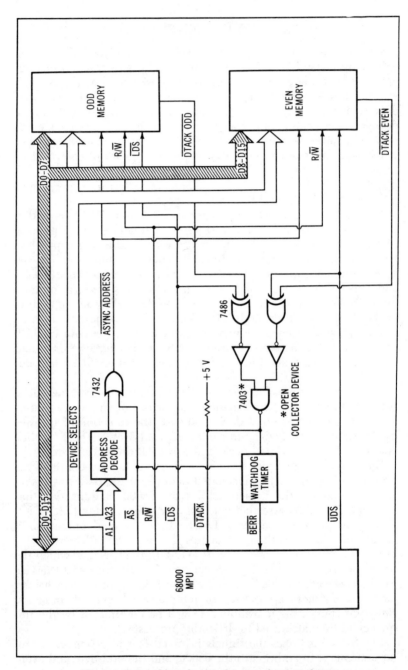

Fig. 6-4. Byte addressing on the asynchronous bus.

is designed to wait a specified amount of time between the assertion of $\overline{AS}$ and the reception of $\overline{DTACK}$. If the memory circuits return the proper combination of $\overline{DTACK\ ODD}$ and $\overline{DTACK\ EVEN}$ within the allotted time, the $\overline{DTACK}$ signal to the microprocessor is asserted. Otherwise, the timer asserts a bus error ($\overline{BERR}$) signal, which causes the 68000 to initiate exception processing. In this way, the timer prevents a faulty device from "hanging up" the system indefinitely.

Timing for Asynchronous Data Transfers

Now that the asynchronous control signals have been discussed, let us look at how they interact during data transfer operations. Fig. 6-5 shows the timing of these signals during normal word-length read and write cycles, and during a "slow" (delayed $\overline{DTACK}$) read cycle. These waveforms are referenced to the 68000 input clock signal, CLK. With an 8-MHz input, CLK has a period of 125 ns, and changes state every 62.5 ns. A normal (undelayed) read cycle lasts four clock cycles, or 500 ns at 8 MHz. Due to internal propagation delays, and the need to drive $R/\overline{W}$ to a logic 0, a normal (undelayed) write cycle takes one additional clock cycle, for a total of 625 ns at 8 MHz.

The 68000 can accept $\overline{DTACK}$ anytime after it asserts $\overline{AS}$, but expects to receive $\overline{DTACK}$ before state 5 (read) or state 7 (write). If $\overline{DTACK}$ is not sensed before this machine state, the 68000 will automatically insert "wait" states into the read or write cycle. The rightmost portion of Fig. 6-5 shows how wait states are added to a read cycle.

The timing for byte transfers is similar to that for word transfers, except that only one of the data strobes ($\overline{UDS}$ or $\overline{LDS}$) will be asserted, and only one-half of the data bus will carry valid data. The other half of the data bus will remain in the high-impedance state. The active data strobe is derived from an internal signal, A0, the least-significant bit of the program counter. For byte transfer timing, refer to section 4.2.1 of the MC68000 User's Manual.[1]

SYNCHRONOUS CONTROL SIGNALS

The 68000 has three control signals that can be used to interface the microprocessor with synchronous peripheral devices, such as those in the 8-bit 6800 and 6500 families. The three synchronous control signals are enable (E), valid peripheral address ($\overline{VPA}$), and valid memory address ($\overline{VMA}$).

The *enable* (E) signal is a clock that 8-bit peripherals use to synchronize data transfers. This free-running clock corresponds to the E or $\phi 2$ signals in existing 6800 and 6500 systems. The E clock

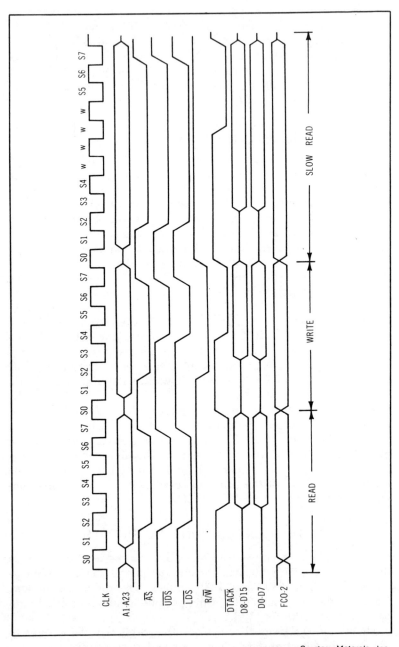

Courtesy Motorola, Inc.

Fig. 6-5. The timing for asynchronous word transfers.

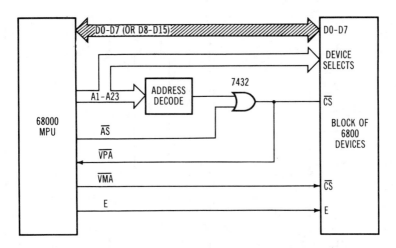

Fig. 6-6. Accessing 6800 peripherals on the synchronous bus.

signal has a frequency that is one-tenth of the 68000 input clock (CLK), so in an 8-MHz 68000 system, E has a frequency of 800 kHz. Further, E has a 60/40 duty cycle; it is a logic 0 for six CLK cycles and a logic 1 for four CLK cycles.

Valid peripheral address ($\overline{VPA}$) is an input signal that notifies the 68000 that a 6800 peripheral is being addressed, and that the data transfer operation should be synchronized with the enable (E) clock. Normally, $\overline{VPA}$ is derived from a decoded address and the address strobe ($\overline{AS}$) signal. You may note that $\overline{VPA}$ is the synchronous equivalent of the asynchronous $\overline{DTACK}$ signal.

If $\overline{AS}$ is still asserted when the 68000 receives $\overline{VPA}$, the processor responds by asserting *valid memory address* ($\overline{VMA}$), which is used by the addressed peripheral device to complete the device selection.

Fig. 6-6 illustrates the signals that are normally used to interface the 68000 microprocessor to 6800 peripheral devices. Fig. 6-7 shows the timing for a synchronous read and write cycle. Chapter 8 contains a further discussion of interfacing the 68000 to 8-bit synchronous devices.

BUS ARBITRATION SIGNALS

The bus arbitration signals are used in direct memory access (DMA) and multiprocessor applications, to transfer control of the system buses from a 68000 microprocessor to an external device. In these applications, external devices that wish to become the "bus master" inform the 68000 of this requirement by asserting the *bus request* ($\overline{BR}$) input signal. The 68000 is always at a lower bus pri-

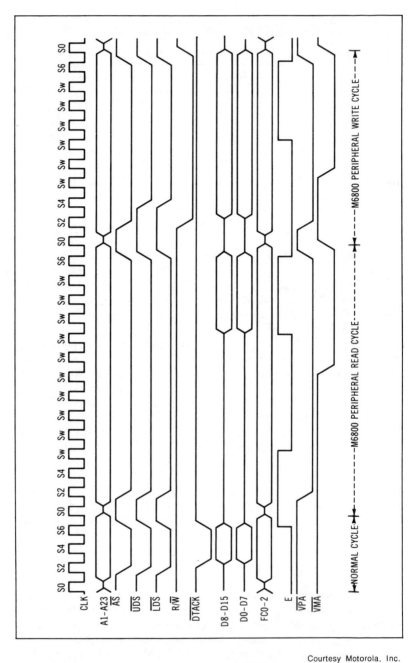

Courtesy Motorola, Inc.

Fig. 6-7. The timing for synchronous (8-bit) data transfers.

ority than external devices, and will relinquish bus control after completing the current bus cycle. In the meantime, upon sensing $\overline{BR}$, the 68000 synchronizes internally and then indicates its acceptance of the request by asserting *bus grant* ($\overline{BG}$). If several devices have asserted $\overline{BR}$, some external circuitry is needed to resolve the conflict, and allow only one of the requesting devices to receive $\overline{BG}$.

Upon receiving bus grant, the requesting device waits for the processor to complete its current bus cycle (i.e., waits for $\overline{AS}$ and $\overline{DTACK}$ to be negated), then asserts *bus grant acknowledge* ($\overline{BGACK}$) back to the 68000. In effect, the 68000 and the requesting device are conducting the following dialog: By asserting $\overline{BR}$, the requesting device is saying, "I want the bus." Through $\overline{BG}$, the 68000 replies, "You can have the bus." At the end of the current bus cycle, the device issues $\overline{BGACK}$, thereby announcing to the microprocessor (and to the rest of the system), "Okay, I've got control of the bus."

At the end of this dialog, the new bus master removes its request, by negating $\overline{BR}$. In a similar manner, the processor negates $\overline{BG}$ and waits for the external device to complete its bus operations. At that time, the device will negate $\overline{BGACK}$ and the processor will resume normal operation. The timing for this entire sequence is shown in Fig. 6-8.

SYSTEM CONTROL SIGNALS

The 68000 has three system control signals. One of these signals is an input, the other two are bidirectional.

Reset ($\overline{RESET}$) is a bidirectional signal that allows the processor or an external device to reset the system. A processor-generated reset, induced by a RESET instruction, asserts $\overline{RESET}$ for 124 clock cycles. This gives all external devices time to reset, but does not affect the internal state of the 68000 itself.

During catastrophic failure, the entire system (the processor and all external devices) can be reset if both $\overline{RESET}$ and the other bidirectional system control signal, *halt* ($\overline{HALT}$), are both asserted to the 68000 for more than 100 ms. This causes the 68000 to initiate a "power-on reset" sequence, during which the processor enters the supervisor state and jumps to a reset routine from a vector in lowest memory. This reset sequence is discussed in Chapter 7, along with other exceptions.

However, $\overline{HALT}$ need not necessarily accompany $\overline{RESET}$. By itself, $\overline{HALT}$ can be used as an input to the 68000, to single-step the processor through bus cycles for debugging purposes. The circuit in Fig. 6-9 will perform this function. If the RUN/SINGLE-STEP switch is in the SINGLE-STEP position, the processor will complete the cur-

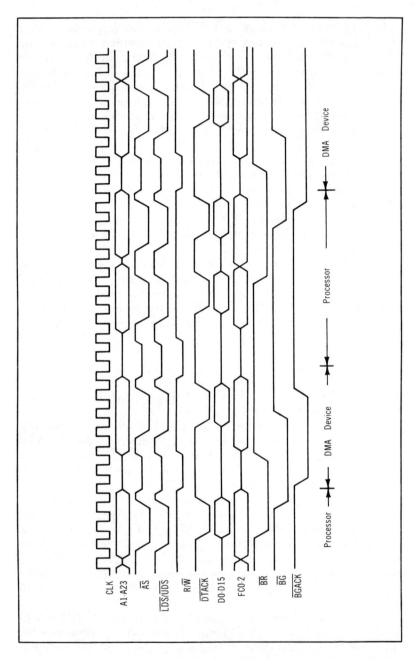

Courtesy Motorola, Inc.

Fig. 6-8. Bus arbitration timing.

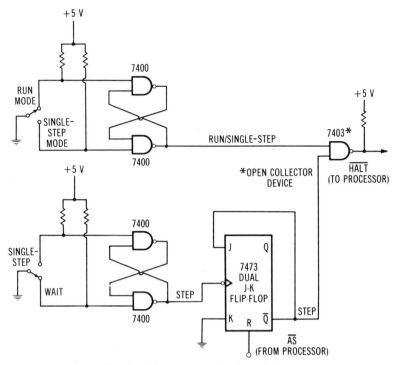

Fig. 6-9. Single-step using the halt line.

rent bus cycle, and then halt. This will happen each time you set the SINGLE-STEP/WAIT switch to SINGLE-STEP. While the processor is *halted,* the address bus, data bus, and function code lines are in the high-impedance state, and the bus control lines are negated (the bus arbitration lines are available, however). Reference 3 at the end of this chapter describes another type of single-step circuit, with control based on $\overline{\text{DTACK}}$, rather than $\overline{\text{HALT}}$.

The $\overline{\text{HALT}}$ signal can also be asserted by the 68000, as an output. It will be an output when the processor has stopped executing instructions due to a "double bus fault" exception condition (see Chapter 7).

The $\overline{\text{HALT}}$ signal can also be used (as in input) with the system control input signal, *bus error* ($\overline{\text{BERR}}$). The purpose of $\overline{\text{BERR}}$ is to inform the processor that there is a problem somewhere within the system. That is, $\overline{\text{BERR}}$ signals the occurrence of an unanticipated event (e.g., a spurious interrupt or an illegal memory access request) or the nonoccurrence of an anticipated event (e.g., a device has failed to return $\overline{\text{DTACK}}$ or $\overline{\text{VPA}}$).

Upon sensing $\overline{\text{BERR}}$, the 68000 can either initiate a bus error exception sequence (see Chapter 7) or try running the bus cycle again. The processor will try rerunning the bus cycle if $\overline{\text{HALT}}$ is being externally asserted when $\overline{\text{BERR}}$ is received. For a cycle rerun, the processor will complete the bus cycle, then halt and put the address, data, function code, and control lines in the high-impedance state. When the external logic negates $\overline{\text{BERR}}$ and $\overline{\text{HALT}}$, the processor will rerun the previous bus cycle. (The only exception is a TAS instruction, which cannot be rerun.)

INTERRUPT CONTROL LINES

External devices can send an interrupt request to the 68000 microprocessor by encoding the priority level of the request onto three *interrupt control inputs, $\overline{\text{IPL0}}$, $\overline{\text{IPL1}}$, and $\overline{\text{IPL2}}$*. At the end of the current instruction cycle, the 68000 will compare the encoded priority level (1 through 7, with 7 being highest priority) with the 3-bit interrupt mask in the status register. This mask is shown in Fig. 1-3 and described in its accompanying text.

If the encoded value on the interrupt control inputs is equal to or less than the value of the interrupt mask, the 68000 will simply "ignore" the request and resume instruction execution. However, if the interrupt request has a higher value than the interrupt mask, the 68000 will place the input priority level on the address bus (A1, A2, and A3), issue an interrupt acknowledge (by asserting function lines FC0, FC1, and FC2), and initiate an interrupt acknowledge sequence. Details of this sequence are given in Chapter 7.

REFERENCES

1. *MC68000 16-Bit Microprocessor User's Manual.* Austin, TX: Motorola Semiconductor, Inc., 1980, Chapter 4.

2. Stockton, J. and Scherer, V. "Learn the Timing and Interfacing of MC68000 Peripheral Circuits." *Electronic Design,* November 8, 1979, pp. 58–64.

3. Starnes, T. W. "Handling Exceptions Gracefully Enhances Software Reliability." *Electronics,* September 11, 1980, pp. 153–157.

CHAPTER 7

Processing States, Privilege States, and Exceptions

This chapter describes the processing states and privilege states of the 68000, and then discusses how the 68000 processes interrupts, traps, and other "exceptions."

PROCESSING STATES

The 68000 microprocessor is always in one of three processing states—normal, exception, or halted. Until now, our discussion has primarily focused on the *normal state,* in which the 68000 fetches instructions from memory, executes them, and records the results in memory or in a register. A special case of the normal state is the stopped state, which the 68000 enters in response to a STOP instruction. As you will recall from Chapter 3, STOP is a privileged instruction that causes the 68000 to stop fetching and executing instructions until it receives a sufficiently high priority interrupt or an external reset.

The *exception state* is the way that the 68000 responds to deviations from normal instruction processing. Such deviations, or *exceptions,* can be caused by interrupts, trap instructions, tracing, noncatastrophic hardware failures, and a variety of other conditions, both internal and external to the microprocessor. We will take a detailed look at exceptions, and how the 68000 processes them, later in this chapter.

The 68000 enters the *halted state* if a catastrophic hardware failure occurs, such as two consecutive bus errors. Such failures imply that the system is unusable, so the only way the 68000 can be restarted from the halted state is with an external reset. Be careful not to confuse the halted state with the previously mentioned, software-induced stopped state.

PRIVILEGE STATES

From time to time throughout this book, we have mentioned the two states of privilege in which the 68000 can operate. These states, called the *supervisor state* and the *user state,* provide a measure of security to the system by allowing certain "privileges" in the supervisor state that are not available in the user state (see Table 7-1).

Table 7-1. Privileges of the User and Supervisor States of the 68000

	User State	Supervisor State
Enter state by:	Clearing S bit in status register.	Trap, reset, interrupt, privileged instruction.
Function code output FC2 =	0	1
System stack pointer:	User stack pointer.	Supervisor stack pointer.
Other stack pointers:	Registers A0–A6.	User stack pointer and registers A0–A6.
Status register access: (read) (write)	Entire status register. Condition codes only.	Entire status register. Entire status register.
Instructions available:	All, except: RESET RTE STOP #d ANDI.W #d,SR EORI.W #d,SR ORI.W #d,SR MOVE <ea>,SR MOVE USP,An MOVE An,USP	All, including those listed at left.

Programs running in the less-privileged user state can execute all of the 68000 instructions, except those that alter the upper eight bits of the status register (the "system byte"), stop the processor, or issue a system reset. Further, user state programs can perform stack operations, but they cannot read from or write to the system stack *pointers.*

Programs running in the more-privileged supervisor state have access to the full capabilities of the 68000. That is, supervisor programs can access both system stack pointers and, through the privileged instructions, can manipulate the status register as required. Control over the status register permits supervisor programs to change the interrupt mask and turn the trace mode on or off.

In most systems, programs other than those designed for system control execute in the user state. Operating system chores, such as task or context switches, should be performed when the 68000 is in the supervisor state.

How to Change the Privilege State

The privilege state is selected by the supervisory (S) bit in the status register. The 68000 operates in the supervisor state when S = 1, and operates in the user state when S = 0.

Transition from one privilege state to another can be made in a number of ways. The processor will go *from the supervisor state to the user state* if the S bit is cleared to 0. This can be done with any MOVE, ANDI, or EORI instruction that uses the status register (SR) as the destination and has a zero in bit 13 of the source operand. Here are a few examples:

Instruction	Action Taken
MOVE #$0400,SR	Turn off trace; change to user state; load interrupt mask with 100_2; clear condition codes.
ANDI #$DFFD,SR	Clear overflow (V); change to user state; no other changes.
EORI #$2000,SR	Change to user state; no other changes.

The processor will also go back to the user state upon returning from an exception (performed with an RTE instruction), if the exception occurred in the user state. A discussion of exceptions is upcoming in this chapter.

The processor will go *from the user state to the supervisor state* if the S bit is set to 1. Typically, this is done under software control with one of the trap instructions, but it will also occur due to a bus error, an interrupt, attempted execution of a privileged instruction, or any other exception. Fig. 7-1 gives a simplified summary of the conditions that cause the privilege state to change.

EXCEPTIONS

As mentioned at the beginning of this chapter, *an exception is a deviation from normal processing, due to an internal or external condition, that places the processor in the supervisor state.* These exceptions (summarized in Table 7-2) will be described shortly, but before doing so it is worthwhile to examine the way in which the 68000 processes them.

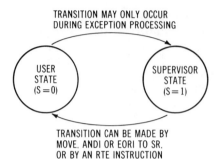

TRANSITION MAY ONLY OCCUR
DURING EXCEPTION PROCESSING

USER STATE (S = 0)

SUPERVISOR STATE (S = 1)

TRANSITION CAN BE MADE BY
MOVE. ANDI OR EORI TO SR.
OR BY AN RTE INSTRUCTION

Fig. 7-1. Transitions from one privilege state to the other.

How the 68000 Processes Exceptions

Except for reset, every exception, whether induced by an internal event (a trap instruction, for instance) or an external event (an interrupt or a hardware failure), will cause the 68000 to take five identifiable steps. We will cover reset later, but the five steps for all other exceptions are as follows:

1. Upon entering the exception state, the 68000 saves the 16-bit contents of the status register in a nonaddressable internal register.

2. The supervisory (S) bit in the status register is set to 1, putting the microprocessor in the supervisor state, and the trace (T) bit is cleared to 0, turning off the trace mode. If the exception is due to an interrupt, the interrupt mask is updated with the incoming priority level, to lock out interrupts that have the

Table 7-2. Summary of Exceptions, Internal and External

Source	Exception Type	Caused By
Internal	Instruction	TRAP, TRAPV, CHK, DIVS, DIVU.
	Privilege Violation	Privileged instruction in user state.
	Trace	Trace mode.
	Illegal Address	Odd address with word or long word.
	Illegal Instruction.	Invalid bit pattern.
	Unimplemented Instruction	Op-word pattern 1010 or 1111.
External	Reset	$\overline{\text{RESET}}$ input asserted.
	Interrupts	Sufficiently high-priority interrupt.
	Bus Error.	$\overline{\text{BERR}}$ input asserted.
	Spurious Interrupt	$\overline{\text{BERR}}$ input asserted during interrupt acknowledge.

Vector Number(s)	Address			Assignment
	Dec	Hex	Space	
0	0	000	SP	Reset: Initial SSP
—	4	004	SP	Reset: Initial PC
2	8	008	SD	Bus Error
3	12	00C	SD	Address Error
4	16	010	SD	Illegal Instruction
5	20	014	SD	Zero Divide
6	24	018	SD	CHK Instruction
7	28	01C	SD	TRAPV Instruction
8	32	020	SD	Privilege Violation
9	36	024	SD	Trace
10	40	028	SD	Line 1010 Emulator
11	44	02C	SD	Line 1111 Emulator
12*	48	030	SD	(Unassigned, reserved)
13*	52	034	SD	(Unassigned, reserved)
14*	56	038	SD	(Unassigned, reserved)
15	60	03C	SD	Uninitialized Interrupt Vector
16-23*	64	04C	SD	(Unassigned, reserved)
	95	05F		—
24	96	060	SD	Spurious Interrupt
25	100	064	SD	Level 1 Interrupt Autovector
26	104	068	SD	Level 2 Interrupt Autovector
27	108	06C	SD	Level 3 Interrupt Autovector
28	112	070	SD	Level 4 Interrupt Autovector
29	116	074	SD	Level 5 Interrupt Autovector
30	120	078	SD	Level 6 Interrupt Autovector
31	124	07C	SD	Level 7 Interrupt Autovector
32-47	128	080	SD	TRAP Instruction Vectors
	191	0BF		—
48-63*	192	0C0	SD	(Unassigned, reserved)
	255	0FF		—
64-255	256	100	SD	User Interrupt Vectors
	1023	3FF		—

*Vector numbers 12,13,14,16 through 23 and 48 through 63 are reserved for future enhancements by Motorola. no user peripheral devices should be assigned these numbers.

Courtesy Motorola, Inc.

Fig. 7-2. Address assignments for exceptions.

same priority or a lower priority, until this interrupt has been serviced.

3. The 68000 determines the *vector number* of the exception, and multiplies this number by four to convert it to a *vector address*. The 68000 can recognize 255 different vector numbers, 0 and 2 through $FF. Fig. 7-2 summarizes the vector number and vec-

tor address for each exception condition. For interrupts, the vector number is provided by the interrupting external device. For all other exceptions, the vector number is calculated internally, by the microcode contained in the 68000.

4. The current program counter value and the internally saved copy of the status register are pushed onto the supervisor stack. In most cases, the program counter value is the address of the next unexecuted instruction.

5. With this information saved, the 68000 loads the program counter with the contents of the calculated vector address and begins executing the exception's service routine.

Fig. 7-3 is a flowchart of the preceding sequence of operations. The makeup of an exception service routine will, of course, depend on which exception is being processed. However, *every* exception service routine must be terminated with a return from exception (RTE) instruction, which pulls the status register and program counter values from the supervisor stack, allowing normal (pre-exception) instruction execution to resume.

Multiple Exceptions

How does the 68000 react if two or more exception conditions arise simultaneously? What happens, for example, if an interrupt occurs while a trace exception is being processed? The answers to these questions are found in Table 7-3, which lists the exception types by decreasing priority. That is, the conditions in Group 0 will be processed before those in Groups 1 and 2, and the conditions in Group 1 will be processed before those in Group 2. Therefore, if a bus error occurs during trace processing, the trace processing will be suspended (at the end of the current clock cycle) until bus error processing has been completed.

Table 7-3. Exception Grouping and Priority

Group	Exception	Exception Processing Will Begin:
0	Reset Bus Error Illegal Address	At the end of a clock cycle.
1	Trace Interrupt	At the end of an instruction cycle.
	Illegal Instruction Unimplemented Instruction Privilege Violation	At the end of a bus cycle.
2	TRAP, TRAPV, CHK, Divide by Zero	Within an instruction cycle.

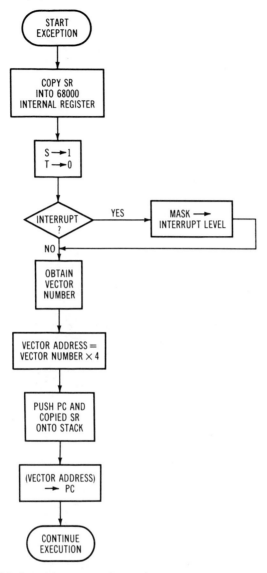

Fig. 7-3. General sequence for exception processing (except reset).

Conditions within each group in Table 7-3 are also listed in order of decreasing priority. Therefore, if an interrupt occurs while a trace exception is being processed, the trace will be processed, then the interrupt will be serviced and, finally, the 68000 will resume executing instructions in the program.

One special condition, *double bus fault,* should be mentioned here. A double bus fault represents a catastrophic failure within the system, and will occur if a bus error or illegal address exception is generated while a previous Group 0 exception (reset, bus error, or illegal address) is being processed. Upon receiving two such consecutive errors, the 68000 removes itself from the system by entering the halted state. Once halted, only an external reset can cause the microprocessor to be restarted.

INTERNALLY GENERATED EXCEPTIONS

We will now describe each of the exceptions that can be generated by some condition *internal* to the 68000 microprocessor, beginning with the instructions that can cause an exception.

Instructions That Can Cause Exceptions

In the course of discussing the 68000 instruction set in Chapter 3, we encountered several instructions that can cause exception processing to be initiated. One of these instructions (TRAP) always causes an exception; the others (TRAPV, CHK, DIVS, and DIVU) may or may not produce an exception, based on some condition.

Trap (TRAP) forces an exception to one of 16 user-defined trap routines, as selected by the immediate operand in the instruction. Specifically, instructions TRAP #0 through TRAP #15 cause program control to be unconditionally transferred to the routines whose addresses are contained in long-word locations $80 through $BC, respectively. Table 7-4 lists the assignments for the 16 possible trap instructions. The trap instructions act as a set of software interrupts, and are useful for calling the operating system, simulating interrupts during debugging, signaling completion of a task, or indicating that an error condition has been encountered in a program.

Trap on overflow (TRAPV) will cause a trap, through vector address $1C, if the overflow (V) bit in the condition code register is set to 1. A single routine at the operating system level may then handle every overflow occurrence.

Check register against bounds (CHK) determines whether the low word of a specified data register is within the bounds of 0 and a specified 2s-complement upper limit (in memory or another data register). If the register contents are outside of these bounds, the 68000 initiates a trap through vector address $18. The CHK instruction may be used to verify that a stack does not get too large, that a string of characters will fit into an allocated space, that an array entry fits within the dimensions of the array, or that a task does not access data outside of its designated storage area.

As far as exceptions go, the instructions *divide signed (DIVS)*

Table 7-4. Vector Addresses for TRAP

Instruction	Transfers Program Control Through Vector Address:
TRAP #0	$80
TRAP #1	$84
TRAP #2	$88
TRAP #3	$8C
TRAP #4	$90
TRAP #5	$94
TRAP #6	$98
TRAP #7	$9C
TRAP #8	$A0
TRAP #9	$A4
TRAP #10	$A8
TRAP #11	$AC
TRAP #12	$B0
TRAP #13	$B4
TRAP #14	$B8
TRAP #15	$BC

and *divide unsigned* (*DIVU*) are the most conditional of all, because they can only cause an exception on one condition—if the divisor is zero. A zero divisor causes a trap through vector address $14.

You will recall from Chapter 3 that an attempt to divide by zero is one of two conditions that will prevent the divide operation from taking place. The operation will also be stopped if an overflow occurs during the division. (In both cases, the divisor and dividend are left intact, however.) When this happens, the 68000 simply sets the V bit in the status register, then continues execution with the next instruction. Since overflow is an error condition, your divide software must make some provision for dealing with it. One option is to design the divide routine so that it gives a valid quotient regardless of whether or not overflow occurs. This option is illustrated in Chapter 4 (Example 4-5). You can also choose to call the supervisor on overflow, by following the DIVS or DIVU with a *TRAPV* instruction.

Privilege Violations

The 68000 initiates exception processing, through vector address $20, if a user program attempts to execute one of the privileged instructions. The privileged instructions are described in Chapter 3 (Table 3-17 and accompanying text) and are listed in the "user state" column of Table 7-1.

Tracing

Like the halt feature, the trace feature is provided to assist in program development and debugging. With the trace feature turned on

(T = 1 in the status register), the 68000 generates an exception after each instruction is executed, thereby causing the processor to "single-step" through a program. The trace exception causes program control to be transferred to a user-supplied routine in memory, through vector address $24.

Like all exceptions, a trace exception causes the 68000 to turn off the trace bit (T = 0) and push the current contents of the program counter and status register onto the supervisor stack. Upon return from the exception, tracing will resume *unless* your trace service routine cleared the T bit of the status register that was saved on the stack. The T bit can be cleared by preceding the RTE with the instruction ANDI #$7FFF,(SP).

The trace routine is typically used to give a printout of register contents after each instruction. Depending on how it is programmed, the trace routine can also print out other meaningful parameters, such as the execution time of each instruction.

The trace feature also provides an easy way to add *breakpoints* to a system. This can be done by comparing the address saved on the stack (due to the trace exception) to a table of breakpoint addresses. If the addresses are the same, the contents of the registers could be displayed or printed out. Otherwise, the 68000 would simply return from the trace routine and execute the next instruction in the program. Reference 1 at the end of this chapter gives another possible use for the trace exception routine—to build a table of memory locations that are most frequently referenced by an executing program.

Illegal Address

An *illegal address* is an odd-numbered address that references a word or long-word operand. It traps through vector address $0C. An illegal address can occur on any kind of memory reference, but it is most prevalent when you are using one of the more complex addressing modes, such as the address register indirect with index mode, in which several terms are added to produce the effective address.

For the illegal address exception (and one of the externally generated exceptions, bus error), the 68000 pushes seven words of context information onto the supervisor stack. These words are shown in Fig. 7-4. As you can see, the first three words to be pushed are the program counter and the status register. These are followed by the instruction register (i.e., the op-word of the instruction that generated the illegal address), the illegal address itself, and a "super status word." The super status word provides specific information about the attempted memory access—whether it was a read or a write, whether the 68000 was processing an instruction (normal state or processing a Group 2 instruction) or processing a Group 0 or Group 1 exception, and the state of the function code outputs when the illegal access was attempted. Refer to Table 7-3 for the exception groups.

As mentioned earlier, if one of the instructions in the illegal address exception routine generates an illegal address, the 68000 will enter the *double bus fault* condition, which causes the processor to

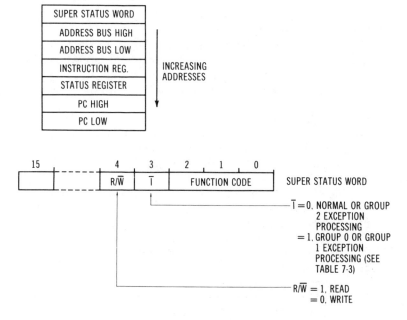

Fig. 7-4. Illegal address and bus error stacking.

halt. An externally generated bus error (discussed later in this chapter) during illegal address exception processing will also cause a double bus fault.

What happens if an odd address is inadvertently stored into the illegal address vector locations ($0C–$0F)? If this improbable and unfortunate situation occurs, and the 68000 happens to attempt a word or long-word memory reference at an odd address, the following sequence of events will take place:

1. Upon sensing the illegal address, the 68000 will initiate illegal address exception processing. After forcing the supervisor state (S = 1), turning off the trace mode (T = 0), and calculating the vector address, the 68000 pushes seven words of informa-

171

tion onto the stack (Fig. 7-4) and loads the contents of the vector address location into the program counter.

2. At this point, the 68000 would normally begin executing the instructions in the illegal address exception routine. However, in this case the program counter has received an *odd* address from the vector locations. Because this instruction address is odd, it is illegal, and the 68000 will initiate illegal address exception processing again. That is, the 68000 will return to Step 1.

3. Will this second consecutive illegal address cause a double bus fault condition? No, it will not cause a double bus fault, because the illegal address occurred during the initialization sequence rather than within the exception service routine. Instead, the 68000 will repeatedly initiate illegal address exception processing, and push seven words onto the stack each time.

4. Since the stack builds downward in memory, any of several events can cause this repetitive sequence to be eventually terminated. These events include the following:

   (a) The 68000 may "run out of" read/write memory, and attempt to push information into nonexistent memory or read-only memory. This should cause external circuitry to initiate bus error exception processing.

   (b) The 68000 may attempt to push information into program memory, rather than data memory, which should also induce bus error exception processing.

   (c) If the stack works its way down to the low 1024 bytes in memory, new values will eventually get stored into the illegal address vector pointer (locations $0C–$0F). If this new address is odd, the preceding sequence will continue. If it is even, the program counter will attempt to execute an "instruction" at this new, random address, with undefined results.

   (d) If the stacking in (c) attempts a write into the reset vectors, at the bottom of memory, a bus error should occur because these locations must be in read-only memory.

Illegal Instruction

An *illegal instruction* is a 16-bit binary pattern that does not represent one of the legal op-words in the 68000 instruction set. The legal bit patterns are summarized in Appendix C of the MC68000 User's Manual. Needless to say, no good assembler will generate an illegal bit pattern, but programmers (even good ones) can inadvertently produce such a pattern in the course of making "fixes" to the object code.

172

Unimplemented Instructions

The design specification for the 68000 included several instructions that were not implemented in the initial production version. These included string manipulation, field manipulation, code translation, floating-point arithmetic, long-word multiply, and special divide algorithm instructions.[2] However, Motorola has reserved about 20% of the total microcode space to accommodate these enhancements (or perhaps others) in future versions.

The unused microcode space includes two of the 16 possible "op-codes" (the four high-order bits of an operation word). Rather than "burying" these unimplemented op-codes, 1010_2 and 1111_2, in the internals of the microprocessor, Motorola has provided a unique vector number in the exception map for each of these op-codes. This gives users the opportunity to add emulation instructions to their programs. These instructions can either anticipate some future Motorola enhancement to the 68000 (such as string or floating-point instructions) or just provide some miscellaneous, handy function for the users' application.

How do you go about using the two unimplemented op-codes? It is quite simple. To use one of these op-codes, you simply insert a word value into your program that has a most-significant hex digit of $A ($1010_2$) or $F ($1111_2$). The insert can be most easily made with a define constant directive, such as DC $A000 or DC $F000. When the 68000 encounters an instruction op-word that begins with $A or $F, it will recognize it as an unimplemented instruction, and trap to a service routine through address $28 (for 1010) or $2C (for 1111).

As an example of the unimplemented instructions, let us emulate a set of *floating-point instructions*, using the op-code 1010. Assume that there are four different floating-point instructions—add, subtract, multiply, and divide. Further, assume that each of these instructions operates on two data registers—a source register and a destination register. Fig. 7-5 shows the bit format for the floating-point op-words. From this diagram you can see that if the instruction to be emulated is a floating-point multiply of D4 times D5, with the product being stored in D5, the way to insert this instruction in a program is with the directive DC $AA14.

What will the floating-point service routine look like? Well, a portion of this routine, the instruction decode sequence, is shown in Example 7-1. The routine itself (FLTP) is preceded by two directives that initialize the 1010 vector address with the address of FLTP. To decode the correct operation (add, subtract, multiply, or divide), the original instruction must be retrieved and put in a register to allow bits 3 and 4 to be manipulated and interrogated.

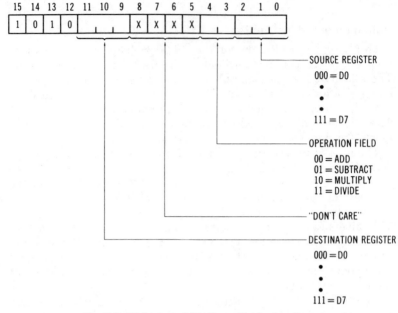

Fig. 7-5. Bit format of floating-point instructions.

The program counter value saved on the stack can be used to retrieve the 1010 instruction, by subtracting 2 from the stacked PC value and accessing that word location.

Example 7-1. A Floating-Point Math Initialization Routine

```
*   THIS EXCEPTION SERVICE IS EXECUTED IF THE 68000 ENCOUNTERS
*   A "1010" INSTRUCTION IN A PROGRAM. IT WILL DECODE THE
*   OPERATION FIELD OF THE INSTRUCTION (BITS 3 AND 4) AND USE
*   THIS NUMBER AS AN INDEX, TO JUMP TO A FLOATING-POINT ADD,
*   SUBTRACT, MULTIPLY, OR DIVIDE ROUTINE ELSEWHERE IN MEMORY.
*   REGISTERS A1 AND D1 ARE AFFECTED.
*
*   INITIALIZE 1010 VECTOR
*
            ORG      $28
            DC.L     FLTP           1010 VECTOR POINTS TO FLTP.
*
            ORG      $1000
FLTP        MOVEA.L  2(SP),A1       GET PC ADDR. OF INSTR. AFTER
                                    1010.
            MOVE     -2(A1),D1      FETCH 1010 INSTRUCTION INTO
            MOVE     D1,-(SP)       D1 AND SAVE A COPY OF IT ON
                                    THE STACK.
            ANDI     #$0018,D1      MASK OUT ALL BUT OP FIELD
                                    (3 & 4).
            LSR      #1,D1          CALCULATE INDEX (OP FIELD ×
                                    4).
```

```
        LEA        OPADDR,A1      FETCH OPERATION TABLE
                                  ADDRESS.
        MOVEA.L    0(A1,D1.W),A1  FETCH ADDRESS OF PROPER
        JMP        (A1)           ROUTINE AND JUMP TO THAT
                                  ROUTINE.
OPADDR  DC.L       FLTPADD,FLTPSUB,FLTPMUL,FLTPDIV
        END
```

Once the op-word has been fetched in D1, a copy of it is saved
on the stack, for later register decoding by the add, subtract, multiply, or divide routine. This done, an ANDI instruction masks out
all but the operation field (bits 3 and 4), and a one-bit right shift
converts it into an OPADDR table index. All that remains is to fetch
the address of the operation routine (FLTPADD, FLTPSUB, FLTP-
MUL, or FLTPDIV) into A1, then jump to that routine. The address is fetched with a MOVEA instruction, using program counter
relative with index addressing. You will note that this routine, FLTP,
is very similar to the multiuser selection subroutine, SELUSR, in
Example 5-10, in that both use an input code to derive an index
into a look-up table. The main difference is that SELUSR must check
to determine whether the ID code is valid, whereas FLTP needs no
such check because it decodes a two-bit field to select one of four
math routines. If the field in FLTP was *three* bits long, and only
five of the eight possible combinations were valid, a validity check
would be required.

EXTERNALLY GENERATED EXCEPTIONS

Having now completed our discussion of internally generated exceptions, let us discuss conditions *external* to the 68000 that can
cause exception processing to be initiated. There are three such conditions—reset, interrupts, and bus error.

Reset

The $\overline{\text{RESET}}$ input has the highest priority level of all exceptions
(refer to Table 7-3), and is designed for system initiation and re-
covery from catastrophic failures, such as loss of power. In essence,
$\overline{\text{RESET}}$ informs the 68000 that any processing in progress is mean-
ingless, and should be aborted.

Upon receiving the asserted $\overline{\text{RESET}}$ signal, the 68000 reverts to
the supervisor state (S = 1), turns off the trace mode (T = 0), and
sets the interrupt mask to the highest level, level 7, so that no interrupt can disrupt the reset process. Unlike other exceptions, a reset
saves neither the program counter nor the status register. The reset
exception vector is four words long, and occupies addresses $00
through $07; these addresses *must* reside in read-only memory.

During the reset process, the 68000 fetches the first two words into the system stack pointer and the second two words into the program counter, then begins executing the instructions pointed to by the program counter (the power-up/restart routine).

Fig. 7-6 is a flowchart of exception processing for the reset condition. Note that it includes a provision for a double bus fault if a bus error or address error occurs during reset processing.

Interrupts

Readers who are accustomed to programming interrupt polling sequences for earlier 8-bit microprocessors will be pleased to learn that the 68000 has a minicomputer-like *prioritized interrupt structure*, which will accept seven different levels of interrupt requests. Further, these interrupts may be vectored or nonvectored.

Interrupt priorities range from level 1 (lowest priority) to level 7 (highest priority, nonmaskable). When an external device wishes to interrupt the 68000, it encodes the priority level of the interrupt request onto three interrupt control lines, $\overline{IPL0}$, $\overline{IPL1}$, and $\overline{IPL2}$. Unless a trace, illegal address, bus error, or reset exception is being processed, the 68000 will finish executing the current instruction, and then compare the encoded priority level with the 3-bit interrupt mask in the status register (see Fig. 1-3 in Chapter 1).

If the encoded value on the interrupt control lines is equal to or less than the value of the interrupt mask, the 68000 will simply "ignore" the request and resume normal instruction execution. (The only exception to this is level 7, which will acknowledge another level 7 interrupt request.) However, if the interrupt request has a value that is higher than the interrupt mask, the 68000 will initiate exception processing.

For the most part, interrupt processing follows our general exception processing sequence (Fig. 7-3), but has enough additional steps to warrant its own step-by-step description. Following are the steps in the interrupt processing sequence; they are flowcharted in Fig. 7-7:

1. Upon receiving a sufficiently high-priority interrupt request, the 68000 saves the 16-bit contents of the status register in a nonaddressable internal register.
2. The 68000 places itself in the supervisor state $(S = 1)$ and turns off the trace mode $(T = 0)$.
3. The priority level of the interrupt being acknowledged (1 through 7) is placed in the interrupt mask of the status register, and output to all devices in the system on address lines A1, A2, and A3. To qualify the address bus information as an

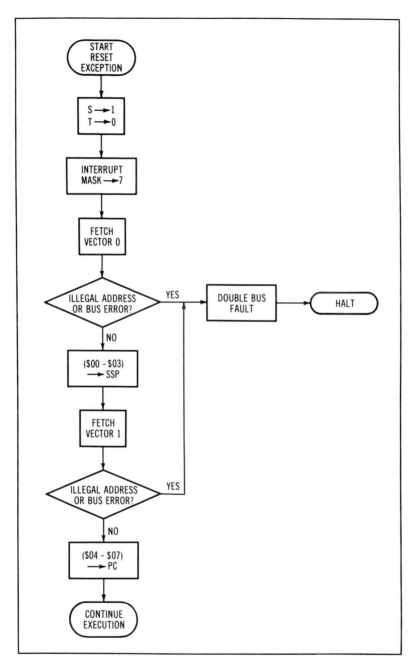

Fig. 7-6. Sequence for reset exception processing.

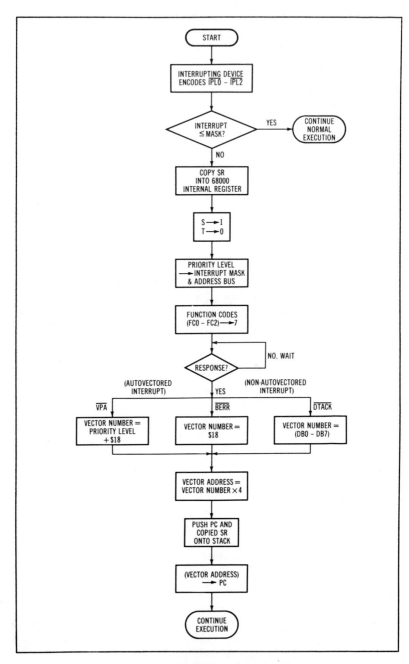

Fig. 7-7. Interrupt processing sequence.

interrupt acknowledge, the 68000 asserts all three function code lines (FC0, FC1, and FC2).

4. At this point, the 68000 waits for the system to respond with either an error signal ($\overline{\text{BERR}}$) or either of two nonerror signals ($\overline{\text{VPA}}$ or $\overline{\text{DTACK}}$). If neither $\overline{\text{VPA}}$ nor $\overline{\text{DTACK}}$ is asserted within a predetermined time interval, an external "watchdog timer" should assert bus error ($\overline{\text{BERR}}$) to inform the 68000 that the interrupt request was a *spurious interrupt*. A spurious interrupt causes the 68000 to generate a vector number of $18.

5. If the interrupt request was not spurious, the two valid responses to interrupt acknowledge are $\overline{\text{VPA}}$ and $\overline{\text{DTACK}}$. Here is what each of these responses means:

   (a) Devices that are specifically designed to support the 68000 will respond to the interrupt acknowledge by placing one of 192 *user interrupt* vector numbers ($40–$FF) on the least-significant byte of the data bus, DB0 through DB7, and asserting $\overline{\text{DTACK}}$.

   (b) Earlier devices, such as those that support the 6800 and 6500 families, cannot supply a vector number. These devices respond to the interrupt acknowledge by asserting $\overline{\text{VPA}}$, which causes the 68000 to look at the priority level, and add a base address of $18 to this level to form an *autovector* number. Since the priority levels range from 1 to 7, the autovector numbers will range from $19 to $1F.

6. The 68000 now multiplies the vector number by four to convert it to a vector address. For a spurious interrupt, the vector address will be $60. For the user interrupts, the vector address will range from $100 to $3FC. For the autovectors, the vector address will range from $64 (level 1) to $7C (level 7).

7. The current program counter value and the internally saved copy of the status register are pushed onto the supervisor stack.

8. The 68000 loads the program counter with the contents of the calculated vector address and begins executing the interrupt service routine.

Bus Error

From previous discussions in this book, you know that the bus error ($\overline{\text{BERR}}$) signal is an externally generated input that notifies the 68000 of an error somewhere within the system. We have discussed the following applications of $\overline{\text{BERR}}$:

1. Asserted alone, $\overline{\text{BERR}}$ is used to signify that any of a variety of errors has occurred in the system. For example, a watchdog timer may assert $\overline{\text{BERR}}$ to indicate that an addressed memory or peripheral device has failed to send a $\overline{\text{VPA}}$ or $\overline{\text{DTACK}}$ re-

sponse to the 68000. Further, a memory management unit may assert $\overline{BERR}$ to indicate that the executing program attempted an illegal memory access (e.g., an attempt to write into read-only memory).

2. Asserted with $\overline{HALT}$, $\overline{BERR}$ will cause the 68000 to rerun the bus cycle, then halt.

3. Asserted during processing of a Group 0 exception (reset, illegal address, or bus error), $\overline{BERR}$ will cause a *double bus fault*, thereby placing the processor in the halted state.

4. Asserted during interrupt processing, $\overline{BERR}$ will initiate processing of a *spurious interrupt* exception, through vector address $60.

Condition 4, spurious interrupt processing, will cause the 68000 to stack the current contents of the program counter and status register, a total of three words. Conditions 1, 2, and 3 will cause the 68000 to stack *seven* words—program counter, status register, instruction register, address bus (low and high), and a "super status word." These words are discussed in the description of the illegal address exception (Fig. 7-4 and accompanying text).

As you can see, only Condition 1 will actually cause bus error exception processing to take place. That is, *bus error exception processing will be initiated if $\overline{BERR}$ (alone) is asserted when the 68000 is processing instructions in the normal state, or is processing a Group 1 or Group 2 exception other than an interrupt.* Bus error exception processing causes the 68000 to internally generate a vector number of $02, and initiate execution through vector address $08.

REFERENCES

1. Grappel, R. "MC68000 Charts Its Own Memory Usage." *EDN*, November 20, 1980, pp. 115, 117. (This article describes a program that uses the trace mode to build a table of the memory locations which are most frequently referenced by an executing program.)

2. Tredennick, N. "Implementation Decisions for the MC68000 Microprocessor." *Proceedings of the 3rd Rocky Mountain Symposium on Microcomputers*, Pingree Park, CO, August 1979, pp. 30–35.

BIBLIOGRAPHY

1. *MC68000 16-Bit Microprocessor Users Manual*. Austin, TX: Motorola Semiconductor, Inc., 1980, Chapter 5.

2. Starnes, T. W. "Handling Exceptions Gracefully Enhances Software Reliability." *Electronics*, September 11, 1980, pp. 153–157.

CHAPTER 8

Fundamentals of Interfacing

Chapter 6 described the signal lines with which external devices can be connected to the 68000 microprocessor to form a microcomputer system. We studied the timing relationships between these signals, and described how the 68000 can communicate with either 16-bit asynchronous devices or 8-bit synchronous devices via separate control lines on the microprocessor integrated circuit. In this chapter, we will take a brief look at the support chips that can be interfaced to the 68000. A simple interfacing example is also included.

68000 SUPPORT CHIPS

Table 8-1 lists the support chips for the 68000 that are either available now or are expected to be in production by the end of 1984. These chips all connect to the *asynchronous* control lines of the microprocessor.

The 68120 IPC is a general-purpose, user-programmable input/output controller. Based on an 8-bit 6801 one-chip microcomputer, the IPC can be configured as an I/O preprocessor or as a "slave" processing unit for distributed processing. In addition to the 6801 MCU, the IPC contains a system interface, a serial communications interface, 21 parallel I/O lines, a 16-bit timer, a dual-ported 128K-byte read/write memory, 2K bytes of ROM, and six semaphore registers. Model 68121 has all the features of the 68120, but contains no ROM. The 68122 CTC is an IPC that is programmed as a serial I/O subsystem. It is used to connect up to 32 terminals to a 68000-based system.

Table 8-1. 68000 Peripheral Chips

Part No.	Description	Developed By
68120/68121	Intelligent Peripheral Controller (IPC)	Motorola
68122	Cluster Terminal Controller (CTC)	Motorola
68230	Parallel Interface/Timer (PI/T)	Motorola
68430	DMA Interface (DMAI)	Signetics/Phillips
68440	Dual-Channel DMA Controller (DDMA)	Motorola
68450	DMA Controller (DMAC)	Hitachi
68451	Memory Management Unit (MMU)	Motorola
68452	Bus Arbitration Module (BAM)	Motorola
68454	Intelligent Multiple-Disk Controller (IMDC)	Signetics/Phillips
68459	Disk Phase-Locked Loop (DPLL)	Signetics/Phillips
68561	Multi-Protocol Communications Controller II (MPCC-II)	Rockwell
68562	Dual Universal Serial Communications Controller (DUSCC)	Signetics/Phillips
68564	Serial I/O Controller (SIO)	Mostek
68590	Local Area Network Controller for Ethernet (LANCE)	Mostek
68652/2652	Multi-Protocol Communications Controller (MPCC)	Signetics/Phillips
68653/2653	Polynomial Generator/Checker (PGC)	Signetics/Phillips
68661/2661	Enhanced Programmable Communications Interface (EPCI)	Signetics/Phillips
68681	Dual Universal Asynchronous Receiver/Transmitter (DUART)	Signetics/Phillips
68881	Floating-Point Co-Processor (FPC)	Motorola
68901	Multi-Functional Peripheral (MFP)	Mostek

The 68230 PI/T is a general-purpose parallel interface device. It contains two multimode double-buffered I/O ports, a third 8-bit I/O port, a 24-bit programmable timer, and circuitry for generating prioritized interrupt vectors.

Direct Memory Access (DMA) is supported by three different chips: the single-channel 68430 DMAI, the two-channel 68440 DDMA and the four-channel 68450 DMAC.

The 68451 MMU provides address translation and memory protection for the entire 16M-byte addressing space of the 68000. An MMU can be used to define multiple segments as small as 256 bytes within this space. For each segment, the MMU defines the logical address space (the program and data space for the supervisor or user state), using the function code lines. It also specifies an offset to the physical address, and the segment's memory protection characteristics. The MMU will generate a bus error exception if an unauthorized access of a segment is attempted. Another chip that reflects the large-system potential of the 68000 is the 68452 BAM, which allows up to eight bus masters (see Chapter 6) to share the system's resources, and can be expanded indefinitely to support more masters.

The 68454 IMDC and the 68459 DPLL form a two-chip set for disk control. The IMDC provides intelligent control for up to four drives (Winchester-type hard disks or floppy disks, in any combination), while the DPLL will have two versions—one for hard disks and one for floppies.

Of the remaining ten chips in Table 8-1, nine are data communications devices. These chips provide support for standard protocols—asynchronous, byte control (Bisync) and bit-oriented (SDLC)—as well as Ethernet.

The 68881 Floating Point Co-processor (FPC) is a high-performance companion part to the 68020, the 16/32-bit version of the 68000. The co-processor is designed to interface so closely with the 68020 that it actually operates coincidentally on the same instruction sequence. That is, the co-processor takes instructions dealing with complex arithmetic routines, and solves those while the processor is proceeding with the main program.

6800 SUPPORT CHIPS

Many applications do not require the sophisticated features of the 68000 support chips, and can be implemented with less expensive support chips from the earlier 8-bit microprocessors, such as the 6800 and the 6500. Table 8-2 lists some of the more commonly used 6800 support circuits. Any of these chips can be interfaced to the

68000 using the synchronous control lines[1] or the asynchronous control lines[2, 3].

Table 8-2. Available 6800 Peripheral Chips

Part No.	Description
MC6821	Peripheral Interface Adapter (PIA)
MC6840	Programmable-Timer Module (PTM)
MC6843	Floppy Disk Controller (FDC)
MC6844	Direct Memory Access Controller (DMAC)
MC6845	CRT Controller (CRTC)
MC6847	Video Display Generator (VDG)
MC6850	Asynchronous Communications Interface Adapter (ACIA)
MC6852	Synchronous Serial Data Adapter (SSDA)
MC6854	Advanced Data Link Controller (ADLC)
MC6859	Data Security Device
MC6860	0- to 600-bps Digital Modem
MC6862	2400-bps Modulator
MC68488	IEEE-488 Bus Interface Adapter (GPIA)

For the remainder of this chapter, let us consider how one of the more popular of these chips, the 6821 Peripheral Interface Adapter (PIA), can be interfaced to a 68000 microprocessor.

INTERFACING A 6821 PIA TO THE 68000

The 6821 PIA provides all of the necessary circuitry to interface a 6800 or 68000 microprocessor to a printer, display, keyboard, bank of switches, or a variety of other peripheral devices. The PIA communicates with the microprocessor on the system buses (data, address, and control), and it communicates with attached peripherals via two 8-bit ports, called Port A and Port B. Each of the 16 lines that comprise the two ports can be independently programmed, at system initialization time, to function as either an input line or an output line.

Within the PIA, each bidirectional port (Port A and Port B) is supported by:

- A *data direction register*. Each bit of the data direction register determines whether its corresponding port line shall function as an input (0) or an output (1).
- A *control register* that holds the interrupt status flags of the port, and selects internal logic connections within the PIA.
- A *peripheral data register* that holds data being transferred between the microprocessor and an attached peripheral.
- Two *interrupt control* lines that are configured by the contents of the control register.

184

Six registers within the PIA are addressable—two peripheral registers, two data direction registers, and two control registers. Each peripheral register "shares" a byte location in memory with a data direction register, however, so a PIA will respond to four (rather than six) memory addresses. Readers unfamiliar with this or other characteristics of the 6821 PIA are referred to the PIA data sheet in *The Complete Motorola Microcomputer Data Library*.[2]

Like all 8-bit devices, the 6821 PIA is designed to transfer information eight bits at a time. Transferring more than eight bits will require additional transfer operations, if you have only one PIA. Since the 68000 has a 16-bit data bus, this microprocessor is designed to transfer information 16 bits at a time. *We can employ the PIA for 16-bit transfers by simply connecting two of these devices in parallel*, one to transfer the high-order bits and the other to transfer the low-order bits.

An Interface to Transfer 16-Bit Data

Fig. 8-1 shows an example of how two 6821 PIAs can be interfaced to the synchronous bus of the 68000 to transfer 16 bits of information at a time. Note that in this particular system, 6800 peripheral devices are assumed to reside within the addressing range $FEF800 through $FEFF00, because valid peripheral address ($\overline{VPA}$) will be asserted only if address strobe ($\overline{AS}$) is asserted and the output of the 13-input NAND gate (74LS133) is a logic 0. Furthermore, the PIAs shown in Fig. 8-1 are only selected when address lines A3, A4, and A5 are logic 1s. Therefore, these particular devices will respond to addresses in the range $FEF838 to $FEFFFF. Two other address lines, A1 and A2, are also connected to these PIAs. They are used to select the internal registers, as follows:

A2	A1	Register Selected
0	0	PRA/DDRA
0	1	CRA
1	0	PRB/DDRB
1	1	CRB

Since each PIA occupies four bytes in memory, the two PIAs in Fig. 8-1 will occupy eight bytes (four words)—four even-numbered bytes for the "high-order" PIA, and four odd-numbered bytes for the "low-order" PIA. Let us assume that our PIAs occupy addresses $FEFF00 through $FEFF07, as shown in Fig. 8-2.

Some Simple 16-Bit Transfers, Using PIAs

For illustration purposes, assume that the PIAs in Fig. 8-1 are connected to two 16-bit peripherals. The peripheral connected to

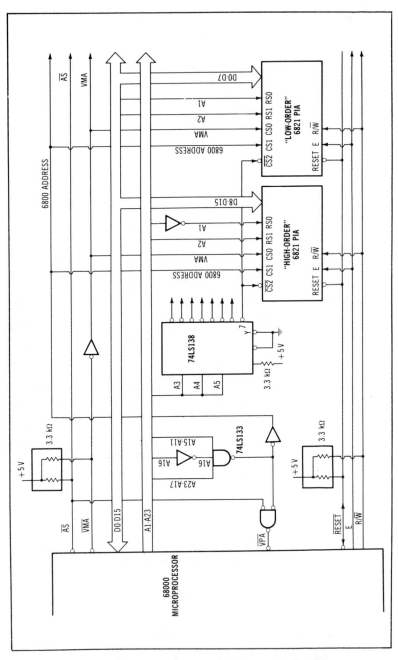

Fig. 8-1. Interface between a 68000 and two 6821 PIAs.

	HIGH-ORDER PIA	LOW-ORDER PIA	
$FEFF00	PRA/DDRA	PRA/DDRA	$FEFF01
$FEFF02	CRA	CRA	$FEFF03
$FEFF04	PRB/DDRB	PRB/DDRB	$FEFF05
$FEFF06	CRB	CRB	$FEFF07

Fig. 8-2. PIA registers in memory.

Port A of both PIAs is an input-only device (perhaps a bank of switches). When this device has placed a word of input data on the Port-A data lines (PA0–PA7) of both PIAs, it notifies the 68000 by asserting a *DATA READY* signal on pin CA1 of the high-order PIA. After reading the word into memory, the 68000 informs the peripheral that the word has been read by asserting a $\overline{DATA\ TAKEN}$ signal on pin CA2 of the high-order PIA.

The peripheral connected to Port B of both PIAs is an output-only device (perhaps a group of LEDs). When the peripheral is prepared to accept a word of data, it notifies the 68000 by asserting a *PERIPHERAL READY* signal on pin CB1 of the high-order PIA. The 68000 then outputs a data word to the Port-B data lines (PB0–PB7) of both PIAs, and notifies the peripheral that it has done so by asserting an $\overline{OUTPUT\ READY}$ signal on pin CB2 of the high-order PIA. Fig. 8-3 illustrates the data paths just described.

In order for a PIA to communicate with attached peripheral devices, it must be *programmed* to suit the characteristics of these particular devices. PIAs are so configured at system initialization time, as part of the power-up reset sequence. Example 8-1 is an initialization routine for the two PIAs we are discussing here. The high-order PIA is configured as follows:

- DDRA is loaded with all 0s, making A an input port.
- CRA is loaded with %00100110 ($26), to enable handshaking.

Example 8-1. Initializing Two PIAs

```
PIAD   EQU   $FEFF00            ADDRESS OF PRA/DDRA.
PIAC   EQU   PIAD+2             ADDRESS OF CRA.
PIBD   EQU   PIAD+4             ADDRESS OF PRB/DDRB.
PIBC   EQU   PIAD+6             ADDRESS OF CRB.
*
       MOVEA.L  PIAD,A0         POINT TO HIGH-ORDER PIA.
*   CONFIGURE THE HIGH-ORDER PIA
       MOVE.L   #$26FF26,D0     SET UP PARAMETERS
       MOVEP.L  D0,0(A0)        AND MOVE THEM TO THE PIA.
*   CONFIGURE THE LOW-ORDER PIA
       MOVE.L   #$04FF04,D0     SET UP PARAMETERS
       MOVEP.L  D0,1(A0)        AND MOVE THEM TO THE PIA.
```

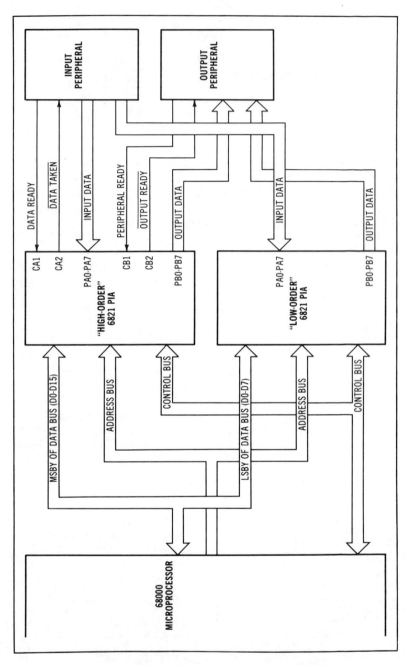

Fig. 8-3. Two 6821 PIAs interfaced to two peripherals.

- DDRB is loaded with all 1s ($FF), making B an output port.
- CRB is loaded with %00100110 ($26), to enable handshaking.

Then, the low-order PIA is configured as follows:

- DDRA is loaded with all 0s, making A an input port.
- CRA is loaded with %00000100 ($04), to select PRA.
- DDRB is loaded with all 1s ($FF), making B an output port.
- CRB is loaded with %00000100 ($04), to select PRB.

Once the PIAs have been configured, transferring information to and from their attached peripherals is relatively simple. To transfer a single 16-bit word to the output peripheral, for example, involves waiting for the peripheral ready line to be asserted, then moving the data word to the peripheral register B of the PIAs. This sequence is shown in Example 8-2, in which the output word is contained in the low-order 16 bits of data register D0. The "no-op" instruction MOVE PIBD,PIBD at the end of the program simply performs the read operation needed to clear the "peripheral ready" flag in bit 7 of the control register.

Example 8-2. Writing a 16-Bit Word to a Peripheral

```
*   OUTPUT THE WORD CONTAINED IN DATA REGISTER D0.
OUTW  TST.B  PIBC        PERIPHERAL READY?
      BPL.S  OUTW        WAIT UNTIL IT IS,
      MOVE   D0,PIBD     THEN OUTPUT THE WORD.
      MOVE   PIBD,PIBD   CLEAR PERIPHERAL READY.
```

Transferring multiple words to the output peripheral is nearly as easy as transferring just one word, as you can see by examining Example 8-3. This program writes the contents of D0 to the output peripheral continuously, incrementing the word in D0 after each transfer operation.

Example 8-3. Incrementing a 16-Bit Word and Writing It to a Peripheral Continuously

```
*   OUTPUT THE WORD CONTAINED IN DATA REGISTER D0
*   CONTINUOUSLY, INCREMENTING IT AFTER EACH TRANSFER
*   OPERATION.
OUTD0  TST.B  PIBC        PERIPHERAL READY?
       BPL.S  OUTD0       WAIT UNTIL IT IS,
       MOVE   D0,PIBD     THEN OUTPUT ONE WORD.
       ADDQ   #1,D0       INCREMENT D0.
       MOVE   PIBD,PIBD   CLEAR PERIPHERAL READY
       BRA.S  OUTD0       AND START AGAIN.
```

The program in Example 8-4 shows a typical input transfer operation, in which 35 words are read into consecutive memory locations. Address register indirect with postincrement addressing is used in the transfer instruction, so that the address is automatically updated to point to the next location in memory. Note that counter D0 is initialized with a value of 34, rather than 35, because the terminating instruction (DBF D0,IN35) will cause program control to "fall through" the loop when D0 has been decremented to −1, rather than zero.

Example 8-4. Reading Data From an Input Peripheral and Storing It in Memory

```
*   READ 35 WORDS INTO MEMORY, STARTING AT THE LOCATION BEING
*   POINTED TO BY ADDRESS REGISTER A0.
        MOVE.L   #34,D0         SET UP COUNTER D0.
IN35    TST.B    PIAC           DATA READY?
        BPL.S    IN35           WAIT UNTIL IT IS
        MOVE     PIAD,(A0)+     THEN INPUT WORD.
        DBF      D0,IN35        LOOP UNTIL DONE.
```

REFERENCES

1. *MC68000 16-Bit Microprocessor User's Manual.* Austin, TX: Motorola Semiconductor, Inc., 1980, Chapter 6.

2. Morales, A. J. "Interface 6800-μP Peripherals to the 68000." *EDN*, March 4, 1981, pp. 159, 161. (This article shows how to interface 6800 peripherals to the asynchronous control lines of the 68000 for faster operation.)

3. Morales, A. J. "Access Memory Directly in 16-Bit μC Systems." *Electronic Design*, June 11, 1981, pp. 221-227. (Shows how to use an MC6844 device for DMA.)

4. *The Complete Motorola Microcomputer Data Library.* Phoenix, AZ: Motorola Semiconductor Products, Inc., 1978.

BIBLIOGRAPHY

1. Grappel, R. and Hemenway, J. "Effective Storage and Backup Call for a Capable Controller." *EDN*, March 4, 1981, pp. 135–144. (This article describes interfacing of Shugart Winchester disk drive and floppy-disk drive to the 68000.)

2. Groves, S. "Balancing RAM Access Time and Clock Rate Maximizes Microprocessor Throughput." *Computer Design*, July 1980, pp. 118–126. (A major portion of the material in this article was derived from Motorola Engineering Bulletin EB-83: *The Inter-Relationship Between Access Time and Clock Rate in an MC68000 System.* Austin, TX: Motorola Semiconductor, Inc., March 4, 1980.)

3. Hemenway, J. and Grappel, R. "To Construct a Real-Time Clock, Combine Hardware and Software." *EDN*, October 5, 1980, pp. 115–120.

4. ———. "Use MC68000 Interrupts to Supervise a Console." *EDN*, June 5, 1980, pp. 183–186.

5. Johnson, R. C. "Microsystems Exploit Mainframe Methods." *Electronics,* August 11, 1981, pp. 119-127. (A report on memory management techniques, including coverage of the 68451 MMU circuit.)

6. Stockton, J. and Scherer, V. "Learn the Timing and Interfacing of MC68000 Peripheral Circuits." *Electronic Design,* "November 8, 1979, pp. 58–64.

7. The following are two recent surveys of support chips.
   (a) Bursky, D. "Support Circuits—the 'Power' Behind Powerful Processors." *Electronic Design,* November 22, 1980, pp. 123–140.
   (b) Huffman, G. "As μC-System Complexity Grows, Support Chips Assume Host Tasks." *EDN,* November 5, 1980, pp. 214–230.

8. The 68120 Intelligent Peripheral Controller is described in these articles:
   (a) Collins, D. "Single-Chip μC Customizable for Many Interfaces," *Electronic Engineering Times,* February 16, 1981, pp. 40-43.
   (b) Melear, C. "Enhanced Microcomputer Helps Host in DP Systems," *Electronic Design,* May 14, 1981, pp. 185–191.
   (c) Wiles, M. F. and Lamb, S. "Special-Purpose Processor Makes Short Work of Host's I/O Chores," *Electronics,* May 19, 1981, pp. 165–168.

9. The following articles contain diagnostic programs to test read/write memory:
   (a) Grappel, R. D. "M68000 Diagnostic Program Tests Memory," *EDN,* April 15, 1981, pp. 157-158.
   (b) Strom, S. "Subroutine Tests RAM Nondestructively," *Electronics,* May 19, 1981, pp. 170-171.

CHAPTER 9

68000 System
Development Support

The features of a microprocessor and its price and availability are important factors in the success of the product. Clearly, another factor is the amount of hardware support, at both the chip and board level, that is available for the microprocessor because this determines how easily the product can be integrated into a customer's application or end product. However, for all but the simplest applications, the hardware represents the least expensive part of a microprocessor-based project. It is *software* that will require the most significant investment in terms of both time and money.

For industrial microprocessor applications, software development represents an average of 60% to 90% of the total project cost.[1] Software costs range from $1000 to $10,000 for small, dedicated control applications, and up to $100,000 or more for sophisticated systems. When you consider that each line of debugged code currently costs between $10.00 and $20.00 to generate, and that the average program contains thousands of lines of assembly language or high-level code,[2] these costs are not surprising. They do make one point crystal clear, however—for a microprocessor to succeed in today's market, it must be backed by cost-effective system development products, from both the chip manufacturer and other companies. This chapter gives an overview of the system development support for the 68000 in terms of both hardware and software.

According to a recent market survey,[3] about one-half of all microcomputer software development is performed with cross assemblers and other software running on minicomputers or mainframe com-

Fig. 9-1. The Motorola MEX68KDM Design Module.

puters. Another one-fourth occurs on single-board computers, "home-brew" systems, and other "custom" devices. The remaining fourth takes place on what are generally termed microcomputer development systems. Let us now survey the support that is available for the 68000 in these three areas, beginning with a discussion of the products that are available from Motorola.

MOTOROLA SYSTEM SUPPORT PRODUCTS

To support EXORciser® owners, Motorola Microsystems (2200 W. Broadway, Mesa, AZ 85201) is offering the *MEX68KDM Design Module,* which is designed to interface to the company's EXORciser/micromodule bus. The MEX68KDM, shown in Fig. 9-1, includes an 8K-byte system monitor (called MACSbug®), 32K bytes of dynamic read/write memory, two serial RS-232C ports, two 16-bit parallel I/O ports, three 16-bit counter/timers, sockets for up to 48K bytes of ROM/EPROM user memory, and a breadboard area for user-designed I/O. A bus adapter module permits 16-bit memory to be used on the 8-bit EXORciser data bus. The MACSbug monitor provides extensive debug routines, so the user can examine and change memory locations and registers, set breakpoints, trace and display instructions, and control many other processor operations.

® EXORciser and MACSbug are trademarks of Motorola, Inc.

Fig. 9-2. The Motorola EXORmacs Development System.

When used with a cross assembler (such as the one described in Chapter 2), the MEX68KDM Design Module provides an inexpensive way to develop 68000 software on a host computer, such as an IBM System/370, a DEC PDP-11, or an EXORciser. However, those who need the power and flexibility of a multiuser development system, and the efficiency of a resident assembler and compiler, are advised to investigate the *EXORmacs® Development System* (see Fig. 9-2).

Offered by Motorola Semiconductor Products, Inc. (P.O. Box 20912, Phoenix, AZ 85036), the basic EXORmacs system includes a microcomputer chassis with four system modules, a CRT display console, and either a 1M-byte dual-drive floppy disk or a 32M-byte hard disk. The hard disk includes Motorola's 68000 disk operating system, called VERSAdos®. The card cage in the chassis can accommodate up to 15 modules, with four slots occupied by these system modules:

- DEbug Module contains MACSbug firmware, bus arbitration logic, a parallel printer port, and two RS-232C ports.
- MPU Module contains the MC68000 MPU chip, a four-segment memory management unit (for memory allocation and multitasking), and map-switching logic.
- 256K bytes of dynamic read/write (R/W) memory.
- Universal Disk Controller supports one or two 32M-byte hard disks and up to 2M bytes of floppy-disk mask storage.

® EXORmacs and VERSAdos are trademarks of Motorola, Inc.

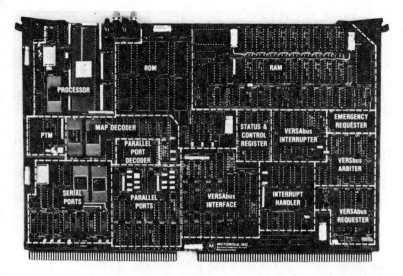

Fig. 9-3. The Motorola VERSAmodule Monoboard Microcomputer (VMM), showing modular functional elements.

The EXORmacs software development package provides the VERSAdos operating system, a structured macro assembler, a linkage editor, a CRT text editor, and a Pascal compiler. EXORmacs is designed using Motorola's VERSAbus® (described in Reference 4), which supports multiprocessing and 32-bit data.

Motorola is also backing the VERSAbus with a comprehensive line of board-level products, called the VERSAmodule® family. The heart of the family is the *VERSAmodule Monoboard Microcomputer* (*VMM*), shown in Fig. 9-3. The VMM uses an 8-MHz 68000 microprocessor and supports the full 16M-byte address space. It has eight sockets, which will accept up to 64K bytes of ROM or PROM, and can be ordered with either 32K bytes or 128K bytes of dynamic R/W memory on board. The VMM also contains three 16-bit timer/counters, two serial ports and four parallel I/O ports (each with eight data lines and two handshake lines). Like the MEX68KDM Design Module, the VMM is a cost-effective tool, but unlike the Design Module, the VMM can also be easily incorporated into end products.

THE VME BUS

In 1981, Motorola, Mostek, Signetics/Phillips and Thomson-EFCIS of France announced support of a bus intended for mid- to

---

® VERSAbus and VERSAmodule are trademarks of Motorola, Inc.

high-end industrial and EDP applications. This *VME bus*[5] is a subset of the VERSAbus that includes some features from the IEEE-P896 bus subcommittee recommendations. The VME bus is designed around the widely-available DIN Eurocard standard, and provides a 24-bit address bus and a 16-bit data bus on a primary 96-pin connector. Both widths can be extended to 32 bits on an optional, second 96-pin connector. Of the 192 pins provided by these two connectors 64 pins are available for user-defined I/O.

Being to Eurocard standard, VME modules come in two sizes: 100 mm × 160 mm (single Eurocard) and 233.35 mm × 160 mm (double Eurocard). Because of their size, modules of this type typically house only one function per board, closely matching hardware to an application.

OTHER 68000-RELATED PRODUCTS

The acceptance of the 68000 is reflected in the ever-growing number of companies *other* than the chip manufacturers who are offering support products for this microprocessor. This section presents a sampling of the market, but is not intended to be an exhaustive survey.

Software Development Systems

Scientific Enterprises, Inc. (9375 S.W. Commerce Circle, Wilsonville, OR 97070) offers a development system called the Software Synthesizer®, which supports the 68000. This system centers around two elements—the Software Synthesis Language (SSL) and a 16-bit Perkin-Elmer minicomputer system. The minicomputer system includes 256K bytes of memory, a 32M-byte Winchester disk system, four video terminal work stations, and a 13M-byte cartridge tape drive for disk backup and archiving. SSL is a unique, high-level language that allows a program to be developed as a set of software components, in much the same way as hardware is constructed from individual components.

TeleSoft (10639 Roselle Street; San Diego, CA 92121) offers a 68000-based desktop computer system whose primary aim is to support development of programs written in the Ada language. This system, called the TeleSoft-Workstation®, consists of a 12-inch CRT display with detached keyboard, a Q-Bus® backplane, 256K bytes of R/W memory and four serial I/O ports. Various mass storage devices are available, ranging from a mini-floppy disk option inte-

---

® Software Synthesizer is a trademark of Scientific Enterprises, Inc.

® TeleSoft-Workstation is a trademark of Renaissance TeleSoftware, Inc. Q-Bus is a trademark of Digital Equipment Corporation.

grated into the WorkStation to double density 8-inch floppy disks, Winchester hard disks and streaming tape drive units. TeleSoft backs its WorkStation with a variety of software packages, including a multitasking operating system and Pascal and Ada compilers.

The 68000 was also selected for the 9826A, a desktop computer from Hewlett-Packard (1501 Page Mill Road; Palo Alto, CA 93304). A software-compatible successor to the popular HP 9825A, the 9826A includes a 7-inch CRT that can display 25 lines of 50 characters each, as well as graphics, with the character set comprising 256 5-by-7-dot characters. The 9826A also includes 64K bytes of R/W memory; a double-sided, double-density 5¼-inch floppy disk drive with a capacity of 256K bytes; a real-time clock; a built-in IEEE-488 interface; and a ROM-based high-level language, either HP's enhanced Basic or HPL. A Pascal option is planned as of this writing.

MicroDaSys, Inc. (P.O. Box 36215, Los Angeles, CA 90036) is offering two 68000-based systems—a two-board, called the 68K®, and a Miniframe® system. The two-board set consists of a CPU board and R/W memory board. The CPU board has two microprocessors (a Motorola 6809, to take care of I/O operations, and a 68000), memory management circuitry, eight RS-232C serial I/O ports, eight parallel ports, and a floppy-disk interface. The memory board has 128K bytes of R/W memory and space for an additional 512K (using 4116s) or 2M (using 6664s) bytes. The Miniframe system comes in a rack-mountable enclosure, and includes the two-board set (but with 256K bytes of read/write memory), plus power supplies, a fan, RS-323 connectors, and two Shugart single/double-density eight-inch floppy-disk drives.

Several companies are also offering a "best-of-two-worlds" approach, with 68000-based products that interfere to *Multibus®* compatible boards. These products include:

- The CTS-300 microcomputer from Codata Systems Corp.; 285 N. Wolfe Road; Sunnyvale, CA 94086. The CTS-300 processes full ANSI standard Fortran 77 and Pascal software under its UNIX-like MERLIN operating system.
- The CMS-16 microcomputer series from CM Technologies Inc.; 525 University Avenue; Palo Alto, CA 94301. One of the microcomputers in this series, the CMS-16/DS1, links to PDP-11 minicomputers.
- The OB68K1 single-board computer from Omnibyte Corp.; 245 W. Roosevelt Road; West Chicago, IL 60185.
- The FT-68M single-board computer from Forward Technology Inc.; 2595 Martin Ave.; Santa Clara, CA 95050.

® 68K and Miniframe are trademarks of MicroDaSys, Inc.
® Multibus is a trademark of Intel Corporation.

Emulogic, Inc.
362 University Avenue
Westwood, MA 02090

Phillips Industries
TQIII-2-51
Eindhoven, The Netherlands

68000-Based Graphics Systems

The versatile processing features and 16M-byte addressing range of the 68000 make it an ideal microprocessor for handling large database applications, such as the two graphics systems we will describe here. Both of these systems are well suited for use in designing cir-

Courtesy Chromatics, Inc.

Fig. 9-4. The Chromatics CGC 7900 Color Graphics Computer.

base applications, such as the two graphics systems we will describe here. Both of these systems are well suited for use in designing circuit boards and very large-scale integrated circuits, schematics and mapping, architectural engineering, and business graphics.

The first of these systems is the CGC 7900 Color Graphics Computer, offered by Chromatics, Inc. (2558 Mountain Industrial Boulevard, Tucker, GA 30084). The CGC 7900 (Fig. 9-4) includes a 19-inch color CRT display with an on-screen resolution of 1024 by 768 pixels (picture elements), 1024 by 1024 within-the-graphics memory, floppy-disk drives, and 128K bytes of read/write memory. Most of this memory is available to the user. The CGC 7900 features high-speed image generation, an eight-color overlay mode, and a "palette" of 16 million colors, of which up to 256 different colors can be displayed simultaneously. The 151-key keyboard includes 34 keys dedicated to graphics functions, 24 program function keys, and a cursor pad. Options include a dual-screen buffer, which allows rapid alternation between two different displays, a 10M-byte Winchester disk drive, a real-time clock, joystick, and light pen.

Equally impressive is the Graphics System 8000 from Lexidata Corp. (755 Middlesex Turnpike, Billerica, MA 01865). The 8000 contains two separate microprocessors. A 68000 controls all input devices (keyboard, data pad, digitizers, trackball, and joystick) and manages the graphics data base. A Lexidata 12-bit bipolar bit-slice display processor controls the raster frame buffer. With the system, Lexidata offers a 19-inch monitor (color or black-and-white) with a resolution of either 640 by 512 pixels or 1280 by 1024 pixels. In color applications, the 640-by-512-pixel monitor can display 1024 different colors simultaneously from a palette of 16.7 million possible colors; 16 colors from a 4096-color palette can be displayed simultaneously on a 1280-by-1024-pixel monitor. The 8000 operates with a wide range of popular 16- or 32-bit minicomputers via either DMA parallel interfaces or an optional RS-232 link.

68000 SOFTWARE SUPPORT

The development hardware we have just examined indicates the acceptance and recognition the 68000 is receiving in the marketplace. Another measure of this acceptance is reflected in the software support for the 68000. As with hardware support, software support remained at a low level until Motorola made the chips available, but has been increasing rapidly ever since.

Operating Systems

The highest level of system software support is represented by the *operating systems* that are available for use with the 68000. An oper-

Table 9-1. Operating System Support for the 68000

Company	OS Name	Languages Supported	Target Computer, OS Size, Maximum Number of Users	Primary Applications*		
				D	PC	GP
The Boston Systems Office, Inc. 469 Moody Street Waltham, MA 02154	UMDS-10	Assembly	DEC 11/03, 16K bytes, 2 users.	•		•
	UMDS-30	Assembly, Pascal	DEC 11/23, 40K bytes, 2 users.	•		•
Emulogic, Inc. 362 University Avenue Westwood, MA 02090	ECL-3211	Assembly, BASIC, C, FORTRAN, Pascal	PDP-11/2 or /23, 4K bytes, 1 user.	•		•
Creative Solutions, Inc. 14625 Tynewick Terrace Silver Springs, MD 20906	Multi-FORTH	Assembly, FORTH	Any computer using 68000, 8K bytes, 16 users.	•	•	•
Hemenway Associates, Inc. 101 Tremont Street Boston, MA 02108	SP/68000	Macro Assembler, Pascal/I, BASIC, FORTRAN-66	68000 boards, 16K bytes, 1 user.	•		•
	MSP/68000		68000 boards, 32K bytes, 1 user.	•	•	•
	M²SP/68000		68000 boards, 48K bytes, 16 users.	•	•	•

Table 9-1. (cont)

	Operating System	Languages	Computer/Requirements			
Industrial Programming 100 Jericho Quadrangle Jericho, NY 11753	MTOS-68K	Assembly, Pascal	Any computer using 68000, 8K bytes, 1 user.	•	•	
Microsoft 10800 NE 8th Street Bellevue, WA 98004	XENIX	Assembly, BASIC, C, FORTRAN-77, COBOL-74	Any computer using LSI-11, 66K bytes, 20 users.	•		•
Motorola Microsystems 3102 North 56th Street Phoenix, AZ 85018	VERSAdos	Structured Macro Assembler, Pascal, FORTRAN-77	EXORmacs, 64K to 120K bytes, 8 users.	•	•	•
Technical Systems Consultants, Inc. 1200 Kent Avenue West Lafayette, IN 47906	UniFLEX	Macro, Relocating, and Cross Assemblers, BASIC, C, Pascal	Any computer using 68000, more than 1 user.	•		•

* Under *Primary Applications*, PC means Process Control, D means Development and GP means General-Purpose.

Table 9-2. Application and Utility Software for the 68000

Company	Product
Alcyon Corp. 8474 Commerce Avenue San Diego, CA 92121	C language compiler to run on PDP-11 under UNIX operating system.
Control Systems, Inc. 1317 Central Avenue Kansas City, KS 66102	UCSD Version 2.0 Pascal compiler-interpreter.
Creative Solutions, Inc. 4801 Randolph Road Rockville, MD 20852	Forth language package to run on Motorola MEX68KDM Design Module.
Genrad/Futuredata 5730 Buckingham Parkway Culver City, CA 90230	Pascal cross compiler.
Hemenway Associates, Inc. 101 Tremont Street, Suite 208 Boston, MA 02108	Floating-point math package, Pascal/I compiler.
Telesoft, Inc. 10639 Roselle Street San Diego, CA 92121	Pascal compiler, translator, Ada compiler.
Ruben Engineering Corp. 60 Aberdeen Avenue Cambridge, MA 02138	Cross assembler and linker to run on PDP-11.
System-Kontakt, Inc. 6 Preston Court Bedford, MA 01730	Cross assembler, Pascal compiler to run on PDP-11.
Whitesmith's Ltd. P.O. Box 1132 Ansonia Station, New York, NY 10023	C and Pascal compilers to run under UNIX/V32, VERSAdos and other operating systems.
Xidat, Inc. 885 N. San Antonio Road Suite O Los Altos, CA 94022	Mainsail language software.

ating system (OS) is a group of programs that control a microcomputer, and acts as the mediator between the computer and its users. The operating system schedules the use of the microcomputer and thereby relieves users of the task of writing code that deals directly with system hardware resources (disk drives, printers, system consoles, and so on).

Table 9-1 lists the features of some operating systems that can be used for developing 68000 software. It was primarily derived from the information given in several excellent survey articles.[6] Note that nearly all of these operating systems support Pascal, which not only indicates the growing popularity of this language, but its usefulness with the 68000.

Table 9-1 also characterizes the primary applications for each of the listed operating systems, in terms of three categories:

1. A *development* operating system develops software to be used either on another "target" microcomputer or on itself. The target need not be the same microprocessor type if the software is developed using cross assemblers or compilers.
2. A *process-control* (or real-time) operating system serves to control industrial processes that place timing constraints on the responses of the OS. Interrupts from external processes signal the microcomputer system, and if the system does not respond in a specified time, the processes are impaired or seriously degraded.
3. *General-purpose* operating systems are usually associated with business or scientific applications.

One other classification that cuts across the three just mentioned is that of multiuser versus single user. A *multiuser operating system* provides computational services to many on-line users, by time sharing system resources among users, in a round-robin fashion. Conversely, a *single-user operating system* allows a single user to submit jobs sequentially for execution.

Other Software Packages

Table 9-2 lists some available software packages other than operating systems. Note that most of these are also designed around the Pascal language.

REFERENCES

1. Wintz, P. "Fundamentals of μP Development Systems." *Digital Design,* November 1980, pp. 30–36.

2. Lee, E. S. "Are Development Systems Really Necessary?" *EDN,* September 5, 1980, page 143.

3. Santoni, A. "Microcomputer Development Systems." *EDN,* September 5, 1980, pp. 141–151.

4. The Motorola VERSAbus is also described in:
   (a) Balph, T. and Kister, J. "μP Bus Gears Up to a 32-Bit Future." *Electronic Design,* July 5, 1980, pp. 97-101.

(b) Warren, C. "Compare μC-Bus Specs to Find the Bus You Need." *EDN*, June 10, 1981, pp. 141–153. (This article contains a valuable cross-reference table covering 20 different buses, including VERSAbus and EROXbus.)

c. ———. "High-Performance Buses Clear a Path for Future μCs." *EDN*, June 24, 1981, pp. 127-187. (This article includes handy reference listings of the specs for Multibus, VERSAbus, Z-Bus and P896 futurebus.)

5. Kaplinsky, C. "Decentralizing μP Bus Grows Easily From 16 to 32 Bits." *Electronic Design*, November 12, 1981, pp. 173-179. (Describes the VME bus.)

6. The following are recent surveys of microcomputer operating systems:
   (a) Hemenway, J. "Microcomputer Operating System Comes of Age." *Mini-Micro Systems*, October 1980, pp. 97–119.
   (b) ———. "μC Operating Systems Directory." *EDN*, November 5, 1980, pp. 275–338.
   (c) Schindler, M. "Microcomputer Operating Systems Branch into Mainframe Territory." *Electronic Design*, March 19, 1981, pp. 179–219.

BIBLIOGRAPHY

1. Board-level products for evaluation and development are described in the following articles:
   (a) Bursky, D. "μC Boards Pack the CPUs and the Support for Every System—But How Much is Enough?" *Electronic Design*, March 15, 1980, pp. 85–89.
   (b) Kister, J. E. and Naugle, R. H. "Develop Software for 16-Bit μC Without Making Costly Commitments." *Electronic Design*, September 13, 1979. (Describes the Motorola MEX68KDM Design Module.)

2. This series of articles presents an excellent discussion of board-level products in general, and the VERSAmodule product line in particular:
   (a) Gorin, J. and Stern, L. "The Case for Board-Level Microcomputers." *Mini-Micro Systems*, November 1980, pp. 81–93.
   (b) ———. "Requirements for High-Performance Microcomputers." *Mini-MicroSystems*, March 1981, pp. 127–136.
   (c) ———. "Making High-Level Systems With Board-Level Products." *Mini-Micro Systems*, May 1981, pp. 165–175.

3. The EXORmacs development system is described in these articles:
   (a) DeLaune, J. and Scanlon, T. "Supporting the 68000." *Mini-Micro Systems*, August 1980, pp. 95–102.
   (b) Kister, J. and Robinson, I. "Development System Supports Today's Processors—and Tomorrow's." *Electronics*, January 31, 1980, pp. 81–88.

4. Microcomputer languages are described in:
   (a) Cherlin, M. "High-Level Languages for Microcomputers." *Mini-Micro Systems*, April 1980, pp. 89–110.
   (b) Schindler, M. "Pick a Computer Language That Fits the Job." *Electronic Design*, July 19, 1980, pp. 62–72.

5. The following are tutorials on operating systems:
   (a) Anderson, D. A. "Operating Systems." *Computer*, June 1981, pp. 69–82.
   (b) Ripps, D. L. *On Operating Systems*. Industrial Programming Inc., 100 Jericho Quadrangle, Jericho, NY 11753, 1980.

ASCII Character Set (7-Bit Code)

LSD	MSD	0 000	1 001	2 010	3 011	4 100	5 101	6 110	7 111
0	0000	NUL	DLE	SP	0	@	P	`	p
1	0001	SOH	DC1	!	1	A	Q	a	q
2	0010	STX	DC2	"	2	B	R	b	r
3	0011	ETX	DC3	#	3	C	S	c	s
4	0100	EOT	DC4	$	4	D	T	d	t
5	0101	ENQ	NAK	%	5	E	U	e	u
6	0110	ACK	SYN	&	6	F	V	f	v
7	0111	BEL	ETB	´	7	G	W	g	w
8	1000	BS	CAN	(	8	H	X	h	x
9	1001	HT	EM	)	9	I	Y	i	y
A	1010	LF	SUB	*	:	J	Z	j	z
B	1011	VT	ESC	+	;	K	[	k	{
C	1100	FF	FS	,	<	L	\	l	¦
D	1101	CR	GS	–	=	M	]	m	}
E	1110	SO	RS	.	>	N	^	n	~
F	1111	SI	US	/	?	O	—	o	DEL

Instruction Execution Times

This appendix contains tables that list the instruction execution times as a *count* of the number of external clock (CLK) periods. To find the actual execution time for a particular instruction, the count in the table must be multiplied by the clock period of your microprocessor. For example, if you are using an 8-MHz 68000, multiply the count by 125 ns.

The timing data in these tables also includes the number of bus read and write cycles for each instruction. This information is enclosed in parentheses following the execution period counts. It is given in the form (R/W), where "R" is the number of read cycles and "W" is the number of write cycles.

All tables in this appendix are reproduced with the permission of Motorola, Inc.

Table B-1. Effective Address Calculation Timing

Addressing Mode	Byte, Word	Long
Register		
Dn — Data Register Direct	0(0/0)	0(0/0)
An — Address Register Direct	0(0/0)	0(0/0)
Memory		
An@ — Address Register Indirect	4(1/0)	8(2/0)
An@+ — Address Register Indirect With Postincrement	4(1/0)	8(2/0)
An@− — Address Register Indirect With Predecrement	6(1/0)	10(2/0)
An@(d) — Address Register Indirect With Displacement	8(2/0)	12(3/0)
An@(d, ix)* — Address Register Indirect With Index	10(2/0)	14(3/0)
xxx.W — Absolute Short	8(2/0)	12(3/0)
xxx.L — Absolute Long	12(3/0)	16(4/0)
PC@(d) — Program Counter With Displacement	8(2/0)	12(3/0)
PC@(d, ix)* — Program Counter With Index	10(2/0)	14(3/0)
#xxx — Immediate	4(1/0)	8(2/0)

* The size of the index register (ix) does not affect execution time.

Table B-2. Move Byte and Word Instruction Clock Periods

Source	Dn	An	An@	An@+	An@-	An@(d)	An@(d,ix)*	xxx.W	xxx.L
Destination									
Dn	4(1/0)	4(1/0)	8(1/1)	8(1/1)	8(1/1)	12(2/1)	14(2/1)	12(2/1)	16(3/1)
An	4(1/0)	4(1/0)	8(1/1)	8(1/1)	8(1/1)	12(2/1)	14(2/1)	12(2/1)	16(3/1)
An@	8(2/0)	8(2/0)	12(2/1)	12(2/1)	12(2/1)	16(3/1)	18(3/1)	16(3/1)	20(4/1)
An@+	8(2/0)	8(2/0)	12(2/1)	12(2/1)	12(2/1)	16(3/1)	18(3/1)	16(3/1)	20(4/1)
An@-	10(2/0)	10(2/0)	14(2/1)	14(2/1)	14(2/1)	18(3/1)	20(3/1)	18(3/1)	22(4/1)
An@(d)	12(3/0)	12(3/0)	16(3/1)	16(3/1)	16(3/1)	20(4/1)	22(4/1)	20(4/1)	24(5/1)
An@(d,ix)*	14(3/0)	14(3/0)	18(3/1)	18(3/1)	18(3/1)	22(4/1)	24(4/1)	22(4/1)	26(5/1)
xxx.W	12(3/0)	12(3/0)	16(3/1)	16(3/1)	16(3/1)	20(4/1)	22(4/1)	20(4/1)	24(5/1)
xxx.L	16(4/0)	16(4/0)	20(4/1)	20(4/1)	20(4/1)	24(5/1)	26(5/1)	24(5/1)	28(6/1)
PC@(d)	12(3/0)	12(3/0)	16(3/1)	16(3/1)	16(3/1)	20(4/1)	22(4/1)	20(4/1)	24(5/1)
PC@(d,ix)*	14(3/0)	14(3/0)	18(3/1)	18(3/1)	18(3/1)	22(4/1)	24(4/1)	22(4/1)	26(5/1)
#xxx	8(2/0)	8(2/0)	12(2/1)	12(2/1)	12(2/1)	16(3/1)	18(3/1)	16(3/1)	20(4/1)

*The size of the index register (ix) does not affect execution time.

Table B-3. Move Long Instruction Clock Periods

Source	Destination								
	Dn	An	An@	An@+	An@ −	An@(d)	An@(d,ix)*	xxx.W	xxx.L
Dn	4(1/0)	4(1/0)	12(1/2)	12(1/2)	14(1/2)	16(2/2)	18(2/2)	16(2/2)	20(3/2)
An	4(1/0)	4(1/0)	12(1/2)	12(1/2)	14(1/2)	16(2/2)	18(2/2)	16(2/2)	20(3/2)
An@	12(3/0)	12(3/0)	20(3/2)	20(3/2)	20(3/2)	24(4/2)	26(4/2)	24(4/2)	28(5/2)
An@+	12(3/0)	12(3/0)	20(3/2)	20(3/2)	20(3/2)	24(4/2)	26(4/2)	24(4/2)	28(5/2)
An@ −	14(3/0)	14(3/0)	22(3/2)	22(3/2)	22(3/2)	26(4/2)	28(4/2)	26(4/2)	30(5/2)
An@(d)	16(4/0)	16(4/0)	24(4/2)	24(4/2)	24(4/2)	28(5/2)	30(5/2)	28(5/2)	32(6/2)
An@(d, ix)*	18(4/0)	18(4/0)	26(4/2)	26(4/2)	26(4/2)	30(5/2)	32(5/2)	30(5/2)	34(6/2)
xxx.W	16(4/0)	16(4/0)	24(4/2)	24(4/2)	24(4/2)	28(5/2)	30(5/2)	28(5/2)	32(6/2)
xxx.L	20(5/0)	20(5/0)	28(5/2)	28(5/2)	28(5/2)	32(6/2)	34(6/2)	32(6/2)	36(7/2)
PC@(d)	16(4/0)	16(4/0)	24(4/2)	24(4/2)	24(4/2)	28(5/2)	30(5/2)	28(5/2)	32(5/2)
PC@(d, ix)*	18(4/0)	18(4/0)	26(4/2)	26(4/2)	26(4/2)	30(5/2)	32(5/2)	30(5/2)	34(6/2)
#xxx	12(3/0)	12(3/0)	20(3/2)	20(3/2)	20(3/2)	24(4/2)	26(4/2)	24(4/2)	28(5/2)

*The size of the index register (ix) does not affect execution time.

Table B-4. Arithmetic, Logical, and Compare Instruction Clock Periods

Instruction	Size	op <ea>, An	op <ea>, Dn	op Dn, <M>
ADD	Byte, Word	8(1/0)+	4(1/0)+	8(1/1)+
	Long	6(1/0)+**	6(1/0)+**	12(1/2)+
AND	Byte, Word	–	4(1/0)+	8(1/1)+
	Long	–	6(1/0)+***	12(1/2)+
CMP	Byte, Word	6(1/0)+	4(1/0)+	–
	Long	6(1/0)+	6(1/0)+	–
DIVS	–	–	158(1/0)+*	–
DIVU	–	–	140(1/0)+*	–
EOR	Byte, Word	–	4(1/0)***	8(1/1)+
	Long	–	8(1/0)***	12(1/2)+
MULS	–	–	70(1/0)+*	–
MULU	–	–	70(1/0)+*	–
OR	Byte, Word	–	4(1/0)+	8(1/1)+
	Long	–	6(1/0)+**	12(1/2)+
SUB	Byte, Word	8(1/0)+	4(1/0)+	8(1/1)+
	Long	6(1/0)+**	6(1/0)+**	12(1/2)+

+ Add effective address calculation time.
* Indicates maximum value.
** Total of 8 clock periods for instruction if the effective address is register direct.
*** Only available effective address mode is data register direct.

210

Table B-5. Immediate Instruction Clock Periods

Instruction	Size	op #, Dn	op #, An	op #, M
ADDI	Byte, Word	**8**(2/0)	—	**12**(2/1)+
	Long	**16**(3/0)	—	**20**(3/2)+
ADDQ	Byte, Word	**4**(1/0)	**8**(1/0)*	**8**(1/1)+
	Long	**8**(1/0)	**8**(1/0)	**12**(1/2)+
ANDI	Byte, Word	**8**(2/0)	—	**12**(2/1)+
	Long	**16**(3/0)	—	**20**(3/1)+
CMPI	Byte, Word	**8**(2/0)	**8**(2/0)	**8**(2/0)+
	Long	**14**(3/0)	**14**(3/0)	**12**(3/0)+
EORI	Byte, Word	**8**(2/0)	—	**12**(2/1)+
	Long	**16**(3/0)	—	**20**(3/2)+
MOVEQ	Long	**4**(1/0)	—	—
ORI	Byte, Word	**8**(2/0)	—	**12**(2/1)+
	Long	**16**(3/0)	—	**20**(3/2)+
SUBI	Byte, Word	**8**(2/0)	—	**12**(2/1)+
	Long	**16**(3/0)	—	**20**(3/2)+
SUBQ	Byte, Word	**4**(1/0)	**8**(1/0)*	**8**(1/1)+
	Long	**8**(1/0)	**8**(1/0)	**12**(1/2)+

+Add effective address calculation time.
*Word only.

Table B-6. Single-Operand Instruction Clock Periods

Instruction	Size	Register	Memory
CLR	Byte, Word	4(1/0)	8(1/1)+
	Long	6(1/0)	12(1/2)+
NBCD	Byte	6(1/0)	8(1/1)+
NEG	Byte, Word	4(1/0)	8(1/1)+
	Long	6(1/0)	12(1/2)+
NEGX	Byte, Word	4(1/0)	8(1/1)+
	Long	6(1/0)	12(1/2)+
NOT	Byte, Word	4(1/0)	8(1/1)+
	Long	6(1/0)	12(1/2)+
Scc	Byte, False	4(1/0)	8(1/1)+
	Byte, True	6(1/0)	8(1/1)+
TAS	Byte	4(1/0)	10(1/1)+
TST	Byte, Word	4(1/0)	4(1/0)+
	Long	4(1/0)	4(1/0)+

+ Add effective address calculation time.

Table B-7. Shift and Rotate Instruction Clock Periods

Instruction	Size	Register	Memory
ASR, ASL	Byte, Word	**6 + 2n**(1/0)	**8**(1/1)+
	Long	**8 + 2n**(1/0)	–
LSR, LSL	Byte, Word	**6 + 2n**(1/0)	**9**(1/1)+
	Long	**8 + 2n**(1/0)	–
ROR, ROL	Byte, Word	**6 + 2n**(1/0)	**8**(1/1)+
	Long	**8 + 2n**(1/0)	–
ROXR, ROXL	Byte, Word	**6 + 2n**(1/0)	**8**(1/1)+
	Long	**8 + 2n**(1/0)	–

+ Add effective address calculation time.
n is the shift count.

Table B-8. Bit Manipulation Instruction Clock Periods

Instruction	Size	Dynamic		Static	
		Register	Memory	Register	Memory
BCHG	Byte	–	8(1/1)+	–	12(2/1)+
	Long	8(1/0)*	–	12(2/0)*	–
BCLR	Byte	–	8(1/1)+	–	12(2/1)+
	Long	10(1/0)*	–	14(2/0)*	–
BSET	Byte	–	8(1/1)+	–	12(2/1)+
	Long	8(1/0)*	–	12(2/0)*	–
BTST	Byte	–	4(1/0)+	–	8(2/0)+
	Long	6(1/0)	–	10(2/0)	–

+ Add effective address calculation time.
* Indicates maximum value.

Table B-9. Branch and Trap Instruction Clock Periods

Instruction	Displacement	Trap or Branch Taken	Trap or Branch Not Taken
Bcc	Byte	**10**(2/0)	**8**(1/0)
	Word	**10**(2/0)	**12**(2/0)
BRA	Byte	**10**(2/0)	—
	Word	**10**(2/0)	—
BSR	Byte	**18**(2/2)	—
	Word	**18**(2/2)	—
DBcc	cc true	—	**12**(2/0)
	cc false	**10**(2/0)	**14**(3/0)
CHK	—	**43**(5/3)+*	**8**(1/0)+
TRAP	—	**34**(4/3)	—
TRAPV	—	**34**(5/3)	**4**(1/0)

+ Add effective address calculation time.
* Indicates maximum value.

Table B-10. JMP, JSR, LEA, PEA, and MOVEM Instruction Clock Periods

Instr	Size	An@	An@+	An@−	An@(d)	An@(d, ix)*	xxx.W	xxx.L	PC@(d)	PC@(d, ix)*
JMP	–	8(2/0)	–	–	10(2/0)	14(3/0)	10(2/0)	12(3/0)	10(2/0)	14(3/0)
JSR	–	16(2/2)	–	–	18(2/2)	22(2/2)	18(2/2)	20(3/2)	18(2/0)	24(2/2)
LEA	–	4(1/0)	–	–	8(2/0)	12(2/0)	8(2/0)	12(3/0)	8(2/0)	12(2/0)
PEA	–	12(1/2)	–	–	16(2/2)	20(2/2)	16(2/2)	20(3/2)	16(2/2)	20(2/2)
MOVEM M → R	Word	12+4n (3+n/0)	12+4n (3+n/0)	–	16+4n (4+n/0)	18+4n (4+n/0)	16+4n (4+n/0)	20+4n (5+n/0)	16+4n (4+n/0)	18+4n (4+n/0)
MOVEM M → R	Long	12+8n (3+2n/0)	12+8n (3+2n/0)	–	16+8n (4+2n/0)	18+8n (4+2n/0)	16+8n (4+2n/0)	20+8n (5+2n/0)	16+8n (4+2n/0)	18+8n (4+2n/0)
MOVEM R → M	Word	8+5n (2/n)	–	8+5n (2/n)	12+5n (3/n)	14+5n (3/n)	12+5n (3/n)	16+5n (4/n)	–	–
MOVEM R → M	Long	8+10n (2/2n)	–	8+10n (2/2n)	12+10n (3/2n)	14+10n (3/2n)	12+10n (3/2n)	16+10n (4/2n)	–	–

n is the number of registers to move.
* The size of the index register (ix) does not affect the instruction's execution time.

216

Table B-11. Multiprecision Instruction Clock Periods

Instruction	Size	op Dn, Dn	op M, M
ADDX	Byte, Word	4(1/0)	18(3/1)
	Long	8(1/0)	30(5/2)
CMPM	Byte, Word	—	12(3/0)
	Long	—	20(5/0)
SUBX	Byte, Word	4(1/0)	18(3/1)
	Long	8(1/0)	30(5/2)
ABCD	Byte	6(1/0)	18(3/1)
SBCD	Byte	6(1/0)	18(3/1)

Table B-12. Miscellaneous Instruction Clock Periods

Instruction	Size	Register	Memory	Register → Memory	Memory → Register
MOVE from SR	—	6(1/0)	8(1/1)+	—	—
MOVE to CCR	—	12(2/0)	12(2/0)+	—	—
MOVE to SR	—	12(2/0)	12(2/0)+	—	—
MOVEP	Word	—		16(2/2)	16(4/0)
MOVEP	Long	—		24(2/4)	24(6/0)
EXG	—	6(1/0)	—	—	—
EXT	Word	4(1/0)	—	—	—
EXT	Long	4(1/0)	—	—	—
LINK	—	16(2/2)	—	—	—
MOVE from USP	—	4(1/0)	—	—	—
MOVE to USP	—	4(1/0)	—	—	—

Table B-12. (cont)

NOP	—	4(1/0)	—	—	—
RESET	—	132(1/0)	—	—	—
RTE	—	20(5/0)	—	—	—
RTR	—	20(5/0)	—	—	—
RTS	—	16(4/0)	—	—	—
STOP	—	4(0/0)	—	—	—
SWAP	—	4(1/0)	—	—	—
UNLK	—	12(3/0)	—	—	—

+ Add effective address calculation time.

Table B-13. Exception Processing Clock Periods

Exception	Periods
Address Error	**50**(4/7)
Bus Error	**50**(4/7)
Interrupt	**44**(5/3)*
Illegal Instruction	**34**(4/3)
Privileged Instruction	**34**(4/3)
Trace	**34**(4/3)

* The interrupt acknowledge bus cycle is assumed to take four external clock periods.

Hexadecimal/Decimal
Conversion Tables

Table C-1. Hexadecimal and Decimal Conversion

HEXADECIMAL COLUMNS

6		5		4		3		2		1	
HEX	DEC	HEX	DEC	HEX	DEC	HEX	DEC	HEX	DEC	HEX	DEC
0	0	0	0	0	0	0	0	0	0	0	0
1	1,048,576	1	65,536	1	4,096	1	256	1	16	1	1
2	2,097,152	2	131,072	2	8,192	2	512	2	32	2	2
3	3,145,728	3	196,608	3	12,288	3	768	3	48	3	3
4	4,194,304	4	262,144	4	16,384	4	1,024	4	64	4	4
5	5,242,880	5	327,680	5	20,480	5	1,280	5	80	5	5
6	6,291,456	6	393,216	6	24,576	6	1,536	6	96	6	6
7	7,340,032	7	458,752	7	28,672	7	1,792	7	112	7	7
8	8,388,608	8	524,288	8	32,768	8	2,048	8	128	8	8
9	9,437,184	9	589,824	9	36,864	9	2,304	9	144	9	9
A	10,485,760	A	655,360	A	40,960	A	2,560	A	160	A	10
B	11,534,336	B	720,896	B	45,056	B	2,816	B	176	B	11
C	12,582,912	C	786,432	C	49,152	C	3,072	C	192	C	12
D	13,631,488	D	851,968	D	53,248	D	3,328	D	208	D	13
E	14,680,064	E	917,504	E	57,344	E	3,584	E	224	E	14
F	15,728,640	F	983,040	F	61,440	F	3,840	F	240	F	15
7654		3210		7654		3210		7654		3210	
Byte		Byte		Byte		Byte		Byte		Byte	

Table C-2. Powers of 2

2^n	n
256	8
512	9
1 024	10
2 048	11
4 096	12
8 192	13
16 384	14
32 768	15
65 536	16
131 072	17
262 144	18
524 288	19
1 048 576	20
2 097 152	21
4 194 304	22
8 388 608	23
16 777 216	24

$$2^0 = 16^0$$
$$2^4 = 16^1$$
$$2^8 = 16^2$$
$$2^{12} = 16^3$$
$$2^{16} = 16^4$$
$$2^{20} = 16^5$$
$$2^{24} = 16^6$$
$$2^{28} = 16^7$$
$$2^{32} = 16^8$$
$$2^{36} = 16^9$$
$$2^{40} = 16^{10}$$
$$2^{44} = 16^{11}$$
$$2^{48} = 16^{12}$$
$$2^{52} = 16^{13}$$
$$2^{56} = 16^{14}$$
$$2^{60} = 16^{15}$$

Table C-3. Powers of 16

16^n	n
1	0
16	1
256	2
4 096	3
65 536	4
1 048 576	5
16 777 216	6
268 435 456	7
4 294 967 296	8
68 719 476 736	9
1 099 511 627 776	10
17 592 186 044 416	11
281 474 976 710 656	12
4 503 599 627 370 496	13
72 057 594 037 927 936	14
1 152 921 504 606 846 976	15

Summary of The 68000 Instruction Set

This appendix contains three summary tables. *Table D-1, Effective Addressing Mode Categories,* lists the addressing modes of the 68000 and categorizes each as a data, memory, control, or alterable addressing mode. Table D-1 also lists the assembler syntax for each mode. This table appeared in Chapter 3, as Table 3-4, and is reproduced here for quick reference.

Table D-2, 68000 Instruction Set, In Alpabetical Order, is a compilation of the instruction information that was tabulated in Chapter 3, but here the entire instruction set is presented alphabetically, for your convenience. Incidentally, a similar reference table is available as a large wall chart from

MICRO PROGRAMS, INC.
251 Jackson Avenue
Syossett, NY 11791

If you plan to do much assembly-language programming for the 68000, this wall chart is highly recommended.

Table D-3, Conditional Tests, is a summary of the conditions that are testable by the Bcc, DBcc, and Scc instructions. The Bcc instructions cannot test the always true (T) and never true (F) conditions, but all 16 of the conditions are testable by the DBcc and Scc instructions. This table appeared in Chapter 3 as Table 3-15.

Table D-1. Effective Addressing Mode Categories

Addressing Mode	Data	Memory	Control	Alterable	Assembler Syntax
Data register direct.	X			X	Dn
Address register direct.				X	An
Register indirect.	X	X	X	X	(An)
Register indirect with postincrement.	X	X		X	(An)+
Register indirect with predecrement.	X	X		X	-(An)
Register indirect with displacement.	X	X	X	X	d(An)
Register indirect with index.	X	X	X	X	d(An,Ri)
Absolute short.	X	X	X	X	xxxx
Absolute long.	X	X	X	X	xxxxxxxx
PC relative with displacement.	X	X	X		d
PC relative with index.	X	X	X		d(Ri)
Immediate.	X	X			#xxxx

The Data, Memory, Control, and Alterable columns fall under the heading **Addressing Categories**.

Table D-2. 68000 Instruction Set, in Alphabetical Order

Mnemonic	Assembler Syntax	Operand Size	Source	Destination	X	N	Z	V	C
ABCD	ABCD Dy,Dx ABCD -(Ay),-(Ax)	8 8	Dn -(An)	Dn -(An)	* *	U U	* *	U U	* *
ADD	ADD <ea>,Dn ADD Dn,<ea>	8, 16, 32 8, 16, 32	All (1) Dn	Dn Alterable	* *	* *	* *	* *	* *
ADDA	ADD <ea>,An	16, 32	All	An	-	-	-	-	-
ADDI	ADDI #d,<ea>	8, 16, 32	#d	Data Alterable	*	*	*	*	*
ADDQ	ADDQ #d,<ea>	8, 16, 32	#d (2)	Alterable (1)	*	*	*	*	*
ADDX	ADDX Dy,Dx ADDX -(Ay),-(Ax)	8, 16, 32 8, 16, 32	Dn -(An)	Dn -(An)	* *	* *	* *	* *	* *
AND	AND <ea>,Dn AND Dn,<ea>	8, 16, 32 8, 16, 32	Data Dn	Dn Alterable	- -	* *	* *	0 0	0 0
ANDI	ANDI #d,<ea> ANDI #d,SR (3)	8, 16, 32 8, 16	#d #d	Data Alterable SR	- *	* *	* *	0 *	0 *
ASL	ASL Dx,Dy ASL #d,Dn ASL <ea>	8, 16, 32 8, 16, 32 16	Dn (4) #d (5) 	Dn Dn Memory Alterable	* * *	* * *	* * *	* * *	* * *
ASR	ASR Dx,Dy ASR #d,Dn ASR <ea>	8, 16, 32 8, 16, 32 16	Dn (4) #d (5) 	Dn Dn Memory Alterable	* * *	* * *	* * *	* * *	* * *

Table D-2. (cont)

Mnemonic	Assembler Syntax	Operand Size	Allowable Addressing Modes Source	Allowable Addressing Modes Destination	Condition Codes X N Z V C
Bcc	Bcc <label>	8, 16	If cc, then PC + d → PC		– – – – –
BCHG	BCHG Dn,<ea> BCHG #d,<ea>	8, 32 8, 32	Dn #d	Data Alterable Data Alterable	– – * – –
BCLR	BCLR Dn,<ea> BCLR #d,<ea>	8, 32 8, 32	Dn #d	Data Alterable Data Alterable	– – * – –
BRA	BRA <label>	8, 16	PC + d → PC		– – – – –
BSET	BSET Dn,<ea> BSET #d,<ea>	8, 32 8, 32	Dn #d	Data Alterable Data Alterable	– – * – –
BSR	BSR <label>	8, 16	PC → -(SP); PC + d → PC		– – – – –
BTST	BTST Dn,<ea> BTST #d,<ea>	8, 32 8, 32	Dn #d	Data, Except Immediate Data, Except Immediate	– – * – –
CHK	CHK <ea>,Dn	16	If Dn < 0 or Dn > (ea), then TRAP	Data	– * U U U
CLR	CLR <ea>	8, 16, 32	Data Alterable		– 0 1 0 0
CMP	CMP <ea>,Dn	8, 16, 32	All (1)	Dn	– * * * *
CMPA	CMPA <ea>,An	16, 32	All	An	– * * * *
CMPI	CMPI #d,<ea>	8, 16, 32	#d	Data Alterable	– * * * *
CMPM	CMPM (Ay)+,(Ax)+	8, 16, 32	(An)+	(An)+	– * * * *

Table D-2. (cont)

Mnemonic	Assembler Syntax	Operand Size	Allowable Addressing Modes — Source	Allowable Addressing Modes — Destination	Condition Codes X N Z V C
DBcc	BDcc Dn,<label>	16	If cc, then Dn − 1 → Dn; if Dn ≠ − 1, then PC + d → PC		− − − − −
DIVS	DIVS <ea>,Dn	16	Data	Dn	− * * * 0
DIVU	DIVU <ea>,Dn	16	Data	Dn	− * * * 0
EOR	EOR Dn,<ea>	8, 16, 32	Dn	Data Alterable	− * * 0 0
EORI	EORI #d,<ea> EORI #d,SR (3)	8, 16, 32 8, 16	#d #d	Data Alterable SR	− * * 0 0 * * * * *
EXG	EXG Rx,Ry	32	Dn or An	Dn or An	− − − − −
EXT	EXT Dn	16, 32	Dn		− * * 0 0
JMP	JMP <ea>		<ea> → PC	Control	− − − − −
JSR	JSR <ea>		PC → −(SP); <ea> → PC	Control	− − − − −
LEA	LEA <ea>,An	32	Control	An	− − − − −
LINK	LINK An,#d	Unsized	An		− − − − −
LSL	LSL Dx,Dy LSL #d,Dn LSL <ea>	8, 16, 32 8, 16, 32 16	Dn (4) #d (5) 	Dn Dn Memory Alterable	* * * 0 * * * * 0 * * * * 0 *
LSR	LSR Dx,Dy LSR #d,Dn LSR <ea>	8, 16, 32 8, 16, 32 16	Dn (4) #d (5) 	Dn Dn Memory Alterable	* 0 * 0 * * 0 * 0 * * 0 * 0 *

Table D-2. (cont)

Mnemonic	Assembler Syntax	Operand Size	Source	Destination	X N Z V C
MOVE	MOVE <ea>,<ea>	8, 16, 32	All (1)	Data Alterable	- * * 0 0
	MOVE <ea>,CCR	16	Data	CCR	* * * * *
	MOVE <ea>,SR (6)	16	Data	SR	* * * * *
	MOVE SR,<ea>	16	SR	Data Alterable	- - - - -
	MOVE USP,An (6)	32	USP	An	- - - - -
	MOVE An,USP (6)	32	An	USP	- - - - -
MOVEA	MOVEA <ea>,An	16, 32	All	An	- - - - -
MOVEM	MOVEM <list>,<ea>	16, 32		Control Alterable or -(An)	- - - - -
	MOVEM <ea>,<list>	16, 32	Control or (An)+		- - - - -
MOVEP	MOVEP Dx,d(Ay)	16, 32	Dn	d(An)	- - - - -
	MOVEP d(Ay),Dx	16, 32	d(An)	Dn	- - - - -
MOVEQ	MOVEQ #d,Dn	32	#d (7)	Dn	- * * 0 0
MULS	MULS <ea>,Dn	16	Data	Dn	- * * 0 0
MULU	MULU <ea>,Dn	16	Data	Dn	- * * 0 0
NBCD	NBCD <ea>	8		Data Alterable	* U * U *
NEG	NEG <ea>	8, 16, 32	Data Alterable		* * * * *
NEGX	NEGX <ea>	8, 16, 32	Data Alterable		* * * * *
NOP	NOP		PC + 2 → PC		- - - - -
NOT	NOT <ea>	8, 16, 32		Data Alterable	- * * 0 0

Table D-2. (cont)

Mnemonic	Assembler Syntax	Operand Size	Source	Destination	X	N	Z	V	C
OR	OR <ea>, Dn OR Dn,<ea>	8, 16, 32 8, 16, 32	Data Dn	Dn Alterable	- -	* *	* *	0 0	0 0
ORI	ORI #d,<ea> ORI #d,SR (3)	8, 16, 32 8, 16	#d #d	Data Alterable SR	- *	* *	* *	0 *	0 *
PEA	PEA <ea>	32	Control		-	-	-	-	-
RESET (6)	RESET				-	-	-	-	-
ROL	ROL Dx,Dy ROL #d,Dn ROL <ea>	8, 16, 32 8, 16, 32 16	Dn (4) #d (5)	Dn Dn Memory Alterable	- - -	* * *	* * *	0 0 0	* * *
ROR	ROR Dx,Dy ROR #d,Dn ROR <ea>	8, 16, 32 8, 16, 32 16	Dn (4) #d (5)	Dn Dn Memory Alterable	- - -	* * *	* * *	0 0 0	* * *
ROXL	ROXL Dx,Dy ROXL #d,Dn ROXL <ea>	8, 16, 32 8, 16, 32 16	Dn (4) #d (5)	Dn Dn Memory Alterable	* * *	* * *	* * *	0 0 0	* * *
ROXR	ROXR Dx,Dy ROXR #d,Dn ROXR <ea>	8, 16, 32 8, 16, 32 16	Dn (4) #d (5)	Dn Dn Memory Alterable	* * *	* * *	* * *	0 0 0	* * *

Table D-2. (cont)

Mnemonic	Assembler Syntax	Operand Size	Allowable Addressing Modes Source	Destination	Condition Codes X N Z V C
RTE (6)	RTE		(SP) + → SR; (SP) + → PC		* * * * *
RTR	RTR		(SP)+ → CCR; (SP) + → PC		* * * * *
RTS	RTS		(SP) + → PC		– – – – –
SBCD	SBCD Dy,Dx SBCD -(Ay),-(Ax)	8 8	Dn -(An)	Dn -(An)	* U * U * * U * U *
Scc	Scc <ea>	8	If cc, then 1s → (ea); otherwise 0s → (ea)	Data Alterable	– – – – –
STOP (6)	STOP #d	16	#d → SR, then STOP		* * * * *
SUB	SUB <ea>,Dn SUB Dn,<ea>	8, 16, 32 8, 16, 32	All (1) Dn	Dn Alterable	* * * * *
SUBA	SUBA <ea>,An	16, 32	All	An	– – – – –
SUBI	SUBI #d,<ea>	8, 16, 32	#d	Data Alterable	* * * * *
SUBQ	SUBQ #d,<ea>	8, 16, 32	#d (2)	Alterable (1)	* * * * *
SUBX	SUBX Dy,Dx SUBX -(Ay),-(Ax)	8, 16, 32 8, 16, 32	Dn -(An)	Dn -(An)	* * * * *
SWAP	SWAP Dn	16	Dn		– – – – –
TAS	TAS <ea>	8	Data Alterable		– * * 0 0

Table D-2. (cont)

Mnemonic	Assembler Syntax	Operand Size	Allowable Addressing Modes		Condition Codes
			Source	Destination	X N Z V C
TRAP	TRAP #\<vector>		PC → -(SP); SR → -(SP); #\<vector> → PC		- - - - -
TRAPV	TRAPV		If V = 1, then TRAP		- - - - -
TST	TST \<ea>	8, 16, 32	Data Alterable		- * * 0 0
UNLK	UNLK An	Unsized		An	- - - - -

Footnotes:

(1) If the operation size is byte, the address register direct addressing mode is not allowed.
(2) Immediate operand, with a value from 1 to 8.
(3) If the operation size is word, the instruction is privileged.
(4) Source data register contains the shift count. Count = 0 to 63, where 0 produces a count of 64.
(5) The data is the shift count, 1 to 8.
(6) This operation is privileged.
(7) Eight bits of immediate data, which are sign-extended to a 32-bit long operand.

Table D-3. Conditional Tests

Suffix "cc"	Condition	True if
EQ	Equal to.	$Z = 1$
NE	Not equal to.	$Z = 0$
MI	Minus.	$N = 1$
PL	Plus.	$N = 0$
*GT	Greater than.	$Z \wedge (N \veebar V) = 0$
*LT	Less than.	$N \veebar V = 1$
*GE	Greater than or equal to.	$N \veebar V = 0$
*LE	Less than or equal to.	$Z \vee (N \veebar V) = 1$
HI	Higher than.	$C \wedge Z = 0$
LS	Lower than or same as.	$C \vee Z = 1$
CS	Carry set.	$C = 1$
CC	Carry clear.	$C = 0$
*VS	Overflow.	$V = 1$
*VC	No overflow.	$V = 0$
T	Always true.	
F	Always false.	

*Two's-complement arithmetic

Symbols: $\wedge$ = Logical AND
$\vee$ = Logical Inclusive-OR
$\veebar$ = Logical Exclusive-OR

Index